"As a popular survey of Catholic Church history from the French Revolution to the present time, the volume is probably unsurpassed in the English language. Catholics wishing to understand the historical background of the present-day condition of their Church will find that introduction in the readable and interesting pages here offered."

Catholic Review Service

"To encompass a story of these dimensions in so short a book is itself an achievement. To do so with balance and good judgment makes the volume a genuine contribution to a popular understanding of the recent history of the Church."

America

"His book is exciting reading. His explanations of little-understood events and papal policies are rewarding. His conclusions are thoughtful and thought-provoking. His manner of writing history is skillful and scholarly yet never dull or humorless. His book should truly fill a gap in current historical literature . . ."

Atlanta Bulletin

"Mr. Hales succeeds in capturing this teeming, eventful era in an absorbing popular history." *Toronto Catholic Review*

". . . a well-written and interesting study which should be read by every educated American Catholic." *The Sign*

"Hales has a lucid, easy style and he is the master of his subject." *The Register*

"This book belongs . . . in the hands of every Catholic who wants to be fully informed about his Church." *The Monitor*

THE
CATHOLIC CHURCH
IN THE
MODERN WORLD

A SURVEY FROM THE FRENCH
REVOLUTION TO THE PRESENT

By E. E. Y. HALES

IMAGE BOOKS

A Division of Doubleday & Company, Inc.
Garden City, New York

IMAGE BOOKS EDITION 1960
by special arrangement with Hanover House

A selection of the Thomas More Book Club, April, 1958
A selection of the Catholic Book Club, July, 1958

PRINTING HISTORY

Image Books edition published February, 1960
1st printing ....January, 1960
2nd printing .... March, 1961

NIHIL OBSTAT: John A. Goodwine, J.C.D.
                Censor Librorum

IMPRIMATUR: ✠ Francis Cardinal Spellman
             Archbishop of New York
             September 12, 1959

The nihil obstat and imprimatur are official declarations
that a book or pamphlet is free of doctrinal or moral error.
No implication is contained therein that those who have
granted the nihil obstat and imprimatur agree with the con-
tents, opinions or statements expressed.

COVER BY JEANYEE WONG
TYPOGRAPHY BY JOSEPH P. ASCHERL

There is not and there never was on this earth, a work of human policy so well deserving of examination as the Roman Catholic Church . . . She saw the commencement of all the governments and of all the ecclesiastical establishments that now exist in the world; and we feel no assurance that she is not destined to see the end of them all. She was great and respected before the Saxon had set foot on Britain, before the Frank had passed the Rhine, when Grecian eloquence still flourished in Antioch, when idols were still worshipped in the temple of Mecca. And she may still exist in undiminished vigour when some traveller from New Zealand shall, in the midst of a vast solitude, take his stand on a broken arch of London Bridge to sketch the ruins of St. Paul's.

LORD MACAULAY,
reviewing von Ranke's
Political History of the Popes, in 1840

Contents

This book is concerned with a factor in modern history which has been influential, and remains so, but which has received little attention.

In the general modern histories we are only made aware of the Catholic Church on certain occasions and generally, be it confessed, when she has seemed to stand in the way of progress or reform. It is thus that we meet her in the conventional picture of France before the French Revolution, of Italy in the time of Cavour, or of Spain at the time of the Republic of 1931. True, we occasionally meet her as the victim of persecution—in Bismarck's Kulturkampf, or in the days of the "Know-Nothings" in America, or in the events of recent years behind the Iron Curtain. It is seldom that we are shown how positive her influence could be.

What is attempted in this book is to look at the life of the Church, in the last two centuries, as a whole, in order that we may understand what it was she was struggling for, what her influence was, and why she acted in a certain recognisable way in her social and political relations. For there is a continuity in Catholic policy which rests, in the last resort, on Rome's determination to safeguard the spiritual independence of her priests and religious orders and to maintain what, through the centuries, has been her concern in certain aspects of the life of Catholics, such as marriage or education. Her policy has exposed her to many conflicts, and involved her closely in world affairs. Ever since the days of the Roman Empire she has been involved in this way and although, in the Middle Ages, her rivalry with kings and emperors may have dominated the stage more obviously than have her conflicts in the last two centuries, no serious student of recent history supposes that her influence ended with the Reformation, or with the French Revolution. Rather, the rise of the omnicompetent State, which has also been often the secular State, has only emphasised the existence of what the Middle Ages called the "two swords," the sword of the spiritual and the sword of the temporal power.

But the drama which has often attached to these conflicts should not be allowed to conceal the fact that the normal state of affairs has been one of harmony and co-operation and that, as Napoleon and Bismarck, for all their animosity, realised, a healthy Church is a bulwark of tremendous value to the temporal life of a State. Rome, after all, is not primarily concerned with conflicts, even when they reach the proportions they have attained today behind the Iron Curtain. She is primarily concerned with safeguarding the Faith, with matters of spiritual jurisdiction, or with spiritual guidance, concerns which are little publicised, and which mostly fall outside the scope of this book.

Mostly, but not altogether. For to some extent we have to concern ourselves here with religious questions, if only because the spiritual and the temporal are inextricably interwoven in all periods of history. It has been necessary to treat, for instance, of what was called "Americanism," and of "Modernism," because, although the main issue in both cases was a religious one, yet the "public relations" of Catholicism were very much affected. Similarly, a chapter has been devoted to the Vatican Council; it was largely concerned with a question of spiritual authority within the Church, but that question was of the greatest interest—or so they supposed—to the governments of the day.

The most difficult problem in a survey of this kind is how to plan it. I set my face against recounting the story exclusively by nations, for the Church is a unity, despite all the national differences. On the other hand her development is not to be measured exclusively by the pontificates of her Popes. I think that, broadly speaking, there is a European story, an American story, and a doctrinal story, though they all react upon each other. For the most part I have isolated them, but I have tried not to do so too closely. Thus American affairs are mostly treated in Chapters 12, 13, 14, and 21; but it seemed to me essential to contrast American experience with European experience in Chapter 6, when discussing Lamennais and the argument about freedom in the days of Gregory XVI, and the New World also has its place in the chapter on *Rerum Novarum* and in the first and last chapters. Similarly, Chapters 10, 11, 15, 16, and 17 are largely concerned with matters doctrinal, but the political bearing, in Europe and America, of the Syllabus of Errors, Papal Infallibility, and Modernism will be obvious to all, and is not ignored in other chapters. The historian who is compelled by his theme to enter into problems theological needs some professional guidance, and this I have been very fortunate to obtain from Father Charles

Davis, of the theological college of St. Edmunds, Ware, in the archdiocese of Westminster, a college to which I am also indebted for the use of its excellent library. Neither Father Davis, however, nor Mr. J. Hampden Jackson and Mr. David Hopkinson, who read the later chapters for me, and to whom I am grateful for some useful criticisms, is to be held responsible for what I have said. Finally I would thank Mr. T. Charles Edwards, of Ampleforth College, York, and the Right Reverend John Tracy Ellis, Professor of Church History at the Catholic University of America, for helpful suggestions, in the preparation of this new edition, and my mother-in-law, Mrs. Joseph S. Porter of New Haven, Connecticut, for seeing that I was supplied with recent American comment, critical as well as appreciative of the Church.

EDWARD HALES

Rye Court
Bishops Stortford
1958

THE CATHOLIC CHURCH
IN THE MODERN WORLD

CHAPTER ONE

The Ancien Régime (Before 1789)

The greatest English historian of the nineteenth century, Lord Macaulay, writing his celebrated essay on the greatest German historian of all time, von Ranke, has some interesting observations to make concerning the critical juncture in the history of the Catholic Church which had been reached in the eighteenth century. Neither Macaulay nor Ranke was a Catholic, but both were very highly perceptive, and both were fascinated by the mighty theme of the history of the Church of Rome. Although they could not grasp what it was that had enabled that Church perpetually to rejuvenate herself while remaining outwardly unchanged, they could and did see, and marvel at, the spectacle of her survival and growth amidst apparent disaster. Provided that we bear in mind what limited their sight, we can with profit reflect upon what, with their immense intelligence, they observed.

"Four times," Macaulay tells us, "since the authority of the Church of Rome was established in Western Christendom, has the human intellect risen up against her yoke. Twice that Church remained completely victorious. Twice she came forth from the conflict bearing the marks of cruel wounds, but with the principle of life still strong within her. When we reflect on the tremendous assaults which she has survived we find it difficult to conceive in what way she is to perish."

The first of the onslaughts described by Macaulay was the Albigensian heresy in the twelfth century; in reaction against it had arisen the Dominican and Franciscan Friars. The second was the Avignon Schism, of the fourteenth century, together with the heresies of Wycliffe and Hus. The third was the "Reformation," more lasting in its consequences, in its "grievous wounds," yet demonstrating the extraordinary vitality of Rome, in as much as the movement was not merely halted, but a part of what had been lost (notably in France, Belgium, Germany, Austria, Hungary, and Poland) was recovered. And the fourth onslaught was the age of the "Enlightenment," the eighteenth century.

In his own inimitable way Macaulay describes the onslaught of the Enlightenment:

"Orthodoxy soon became a synonym for ignorance and stupidity. It was as necessary to the character of an accomplished man that he should despise the religion of his country as that he should know his letters. The new doctrines spread rapidly through Christendom. Paris was the capital of the whole continent. French was a mirror of the language of polite circles . . . the teachers of France were the teachers of Europe."

"The Church of Rome was still, in outward show, as stately and splendid as ever; but her foundation was undermined. No state had quitted her communion or confiscated her revenue; but the reverence of the people was everywhere departing from her.

"The first great warning stroke was the fall of that society [the Jesuits] which, in the conflict with Protestantism, had saved the Catholic Church from destruction . . .

"The movement went on with increasing speed . . . the doctrines of Voltaire were inherited and exaggerated by successors . . . down went the old Church of France with all its pomp and wealth . . . the churches were closed; the bells were silent; the shrines were plundered; the silver crucifixes were melted down. Buffoons, dressed in copes and surplices, came dancing the *carmagnole* even to the bar of the Convention. The bust of Marat was substituted for the statues of the martyrs of Christianity. A prostitute, seated on a chair of state in the chancel of Notre Dame, received the adoration of thousands . . .

"Nor were the calamities of the Church confined to France. The revolutionary spirit, attacked by all Europe, beat all Europe back, became conqueror in its turn, and, not satisfied with the Belgian cities and the rich domains of the spiritual electors, went raging over the Rhine and through the passes of the Alps."

Such is Macaulay's account of the fourth great onslaught suffered in the Church's history. He was writing in the year 1840. Already, as he wrote, he was aware of her recovery after the storm:

"Again doomed to death, the milk-white hind was still fated not to die. Even before the funeral rites had been performed over the ashes of Pius VI a great reaction had commenced which, after a lapse of more than 40 years, appears to be still in progress.

"Some future historian, as able and temperate as Professor Ranke, will, we hope, trace the progress of the Catholic revival of the nineteenth century. We feel that we are drawing too near our own time, and that, if we go on, we shall be in danger of saying much which would be supposed to indicate, and which will certainly excite, angry feelings. . . ."

In the hope that it may be possible to avoid exciting "angry feelings," but without the hope of emulating the ability of Ranke, the attempt is made in this book to recount, first, what Macaulay calls the "fourth great onslaught" upon the Church; next, her recovery; and last, the many storms she has surmounted in her progress during the century since Macaulay died.

To all appearances the barque of Peter sailed, in the eighteenth century, upon calm and gentle seas. It was an era of appeasement. The terrible wars of religion, which had disfigured the seventeenth century, had burned themselves out, and nobody was much inclined to light them afresh. In 1648 the Treaty of Westphalia had ended the Thirty Years' War in Germany, leaving the Catholics in control of the Austrian Empire, most of southern Germany, and much of the Rhineland, but leaving the Lutherans in control of Prussia, Saxony, and most of the north, as well as Scandinavia. The Calvinists were dominant in Holland, but the Catholics were secure in neighbouring Belgium (at that time part of the Spanish Hapsburg domains). In France a bitter struggle had gone against the Protestants, though they had secured, for the time being, some measure of toleration.

But, if armed conflict was over, few were satisfied with the settlement. Thus in France, in 1685, King Louis XIV revoked that Edict of Nantes by which his wiser predecessor, Henry IV, had granted their liberties to the Protestants, or "Huguenots." Louis's rash assertion of the royal power, prompted by his passion for national uniformity, was viewed with much misgiving by Rome, where the true and wider interests of the Church were better appreciated than they were at Paris. One of the immediate consequences of his act was that the ruling classes in England (who thought that there would soon be *dragonnades* against the Protestants in that country too) took such alarm that the cause of Catholic freedom in Britain was set back for a hundred and fifty years. Indeed, Louis XIV's behaviour provided the principal stimulus in England to the expulsion of the Catholic King James II, the French King's friend, in 1688, and to the invitation to Calvinist William from Holland to fill the vacancy, events which led to the insertion, in the British Bill of Rights, of the proviso that the English throne could at no time be occupied by a Catholic.

Northern Europe, however, though still deeply divided on religious issues, was no longer, in the eighteenth century, at war about them; the soldiers had had their say and the result had been a stalemate. Church wars were over. The military attempt to expel Rome from Germany, powerfully reinforced as it had been by Gustavus Adolphus of Sweden, was not to be repeated. But similarly no counter military effort was to be made to dislodge Lutheranism from her strongholds on the Baltic and North seas, while the powerful Lutheran princes of Germany, such as the King of Prussia and the Elector of Saxony, now felt secure.

But where the soldiers had failed, the Catholic missionaries, and notably the Jesuits, had sometimes succeeded. The recovery of Poland had been one of their greatest achievements as had been the reconversion of many elements in the Austrian Empire itself. Calvinism, which had supplanted the Lutheran faith in much of the Rhineland and the Netherlands, and had enjoyed a notable success through John Knox in Scotland (and through Scotland in Northern Ireland and also in New England), had not spread as widely as had at one time seemed likely. Calvin was a Frenchman, and it was in France that his followers had hoped for their greatest results. But the confused French struggle had ended very much in favour of the Catholics, and it was precisely the feeble and scattered character of the Huguenot settlements in France that had tempted Louis XIV to withdraw their remaining liberties. Only in England, amongst the major Western powers of the eighteenth century, was there any serious military attempt to renew the religious wars. The Jacobite invasions of 1715 and 1745 may have been primarily a dynastic attempt to recover for the Stuarts the throne lost by James II, but at times they assumed, on account of the Catholic faith of the Stuart pretenders, "James III" and "Bonnie Prince Charlie," something of the character of religious crusades. Their failure helped to postpone once more for Catholics that religious toleration which was becoming general for other religious groups in the country.

In southern Europe, that is in Spain, Portugal, and Italy,

the Reformation had failed, and religious wars had not plagued the people. The religious wars of the Mediterranean had been directed not against Protestants but against the advancing Mohammedan Turk; and the decisive checkmate to this advance administered at the Spanish naval victory of Lepanto (1571) had seemed, with some reason, to Mediterranean eyes, an event of far greater consequence than the foundering of another Spanish fleet, the famous Armada, off the distant British coasts in 1588. The southern half of Europe had remained so solidly Catholic as to give rise to the notion, in some Protestant minds, that there was something "intrinsically Mediterranean," "Latin," or "Southern," about the Catholic Church; it was an estimate which ignored the fact that the most obviously Catholic countries in Europe in the eighteenth century were all Northern (Ireland, Belgium and Poland), while in the New World the Faith flourished most strongly in the northerly St. Lawrence Valley.

It is a cliché of history that Louis XIV's wars against the Dutch, in the last part of the seventeenth century, were the first "trade wars"; in the previous age wars had been religious in motive. Like all such broad generalisations this is only partly true, but there is enough truth in it to emphasise the point which we are here discussing—namely the changed temper of Western civilisation in the eighteenth century. One has only to compare the professional and dynastic interchanges of arms on the continent of Europe in the age of Louis XV and Frederick the Great with the massacres of the Thirty Years' War, or with the holocaust of Saint Bartholomew, to realise that when we reach the end of the seventeenth century we are in a new age. In the eighteenth century the most important wars in Western civilisation were those between England and France. These wars were primarily trade and colonial wars, and they led first to the expulsion of French rule from America and India and then to the expulsion of British power from its own original settlements in North America. But we should not accept too easily the notion that religion had become somehow separated from politics, from economics, from war. The fate of the Church here on earth can never be entirely divorced from these things, and it was precisely that eighteenth-century trade war between the British and French in North America (which the Americans call the "French and Indian War" and the British the "Seven Years' War") that brought about a reverse to Catholic fortunes in the New World as grave as the revolution of 1688 had caused in England.

For if the thirteen American colonies, on the eastern seaboard, were alarmed by the French soldiers building their forts along the line of the Ohio and Mississippi rivers, and thus surrounding them, those French soldiers were only the successors of the Jesuit missionaries who had first sailed up the St. Lawrence, crossed the Great Lakes, and penetrated down the great rivers, and the defeat of the soldiers meant the disappearance of the missionaries. The Jesuits had been well on the way to converting the Indians, just as the French soldiers had been well on the way to assuming military ascendancy over the British and Dutch colonies. And the same thing was happening in India. But because the heart of the French Empire was rotten, because the political Paris of Louis XV and Madame de Pompadour was even more corrupt and inefficient than was the political London of the Whigs, the French lost the war, and the Church lost North America, surviving only at Quebec, in the North, and in Maryland, Florida, Louisiana, and Mexico in the South.

And again, because the British Navy was more efficient than the French Navy, the trade of the French West Indian islands was ruined in the war, and the Jesuits, heavily involved in that trade, were also ruined, and were compelled to return to Paris to defend themselves. In Paris their archenemies, the lawyers of the *parlement,* saw to it that their ruin was consummated, and the Society of Jesus was expelled from France. And this expulsion, in its turn, led on to the general suppression of the Society by Pope Clement XIV in 1773. Thus did politics, trade, and war determine events of mighty religious magnitude. No doubt it would be folly to suppose that in the long run the barque of Peter depends upon being blown by favourable political or trade winds—she sails under guidance of a very different order. But the historian, concerned with the fortunes of the Church in the transient conditions of this changing world, is at liberty to notice, indeed must notice that, just as the World Peace established by the Roman Emperor Augustus in the first century A.D. proved singularly propitious for the rapid dissemination of the Faith, so the balance of world power in the eighteenth century was tilted against the Church by the victories of Anglo-Saxon arms.

The British policy, whether in North America or in India, was to leave the local inhabitants to their own beliefs and culture. Interested, in America, in protecting the British colonies and, in India, in trade, it was no part of Britain's plan to convert either the Red or the Hindu Indians. So in America the native population was either ignored or exterminated, as policy or security dictated, while in India it was left severely to itself. In either case the Christian Church, whether Catholic or Protestant, made little progress; but this was a matter of small concern to the indifferentist anti-enthusiastic mentality of the English eighteenth century. The fact that the ships of the East India Company refused to take missionaries on board on their voyages to Bombay and Calcutta did not strike that complacent oligarchy as shocking, as it would certainly three generations later have shocked their nineteenth-century grandchildren. Meanwhile, in the words of the great historian of the expansion of Christianity, K. S. Latourette, himself a Protestant, "most of the (Protestant) princes were so intent upon gaining control of the Church in their domains by promoting Protestantism . . . that they could give little attention to missions. . . . Some of the Protestant reformers were frankly not interested in missions to non-Christians."[1]

By contrast, in Central and South America conversion had followed the flag. There was, indeed, something formal, even forceful, about the way in which it was assumed that all those who were the subjects of His Catholic Majesty of Spain must needs become members of the Catholic Church, and the close association in the popular mind between obedience to the political representative of the Catholic King and obedience to the bishop was something which would react severely against the Church in South America in the nineteenth and twentieth centuries. Nevertheless, conversion carried with it not only an outward incorporation, by baptism, into the Body of Christ, but some inward understanding too. If the Jesuit, Dominican, and Franciscan missionaries baptised the "converted" Indians by thousands, they went on to instruct them in the meaning of the sacraments and in the meaning of the Mass. Moreover the Spanish and Portuguese system required that the same should be done even for the Negro slaves, who had been carried overseas to toil in the West Indies or on the American mainland from Florida down to Mexico, Peru, or Buenos Aires. This slavery was a great evil; but it was very

[1] *History of Christianity*, p. 926.

much better within the Catholic fold. In the words of that
coolly impartial and sceptically detached British historian,
the late Mr. H. A. L. Fisher: "The Roman Church honour-
ably endeavoured to improve the lot of the labouring population in the Spanish colonies. The slave was baptised, prepared
for the Mass, retained in his family group, and brought
through his membership of the Church within the system of
Spain. For the British colonies the Church of England made
no comparable effort. While the Spanish Church pressed forward on its missionary enterprise the British planters looked
with active disfavour on the attempt to spread among the
blacks the disturbing ferment of Christian belief."[2]

"The disturbing ferment." That is the key to the riddle.
The British and the Dutch, not only in America but in Africa
and Asia as well, were colonists or traders, who only wanted
to find new lands in which to live according to their own ideas
or else to trade. By comparison the French, Portuguese, and
Spaniards had notions of carrying with them a new civilisation,
of which Catholicism was a very important part. And it should
be noted that although it was the general rule that a Spanish
or Portuguese colony meant a Catholic colony, and a political
claim would normally precede a spiritual claim, this was not
so *on the ground*. Rather, the missionaries were the advance
guard, who often pioneered unaided. Usually the Jesuits,
Dominicans or Franciscans—most generally the Jesuits—had
preceded the soldiers and officers of the State, penetrating,
without military support, far into the native hinterland, carrying with them Christianity and often organising, on their
own, new village communities, living in peace and prosperity,
such as were to be found in California, Texas, and Florida,
as well as in the Gulf of Mexico and the states of South
America. The famous model Jesuit settlements of Paraguay,
which were abandoned in the middle of the eighteenth century because of the jealousy they aroused in the Spanish political power, were only the most celebrated of these Catholic
communities. In India, French and Portuguese missionaries
had done something of the sort, not only in the colonial settlements of Pondicherry and Goa, but far in the interior, away
from European political control. And the successors of Saint

[2] *History of Europe* (Eyre and Spottiswoode, 1935), Vol. III, p.
1029.

Francis Xavier and Matteo Ricci had done the same in Ceylon, the East Indies, and even China and Japan.

In order, then, to understand the world position of the Church in the eighteenth century, we should recognise that already she had extended most marvellously from Peking to Peru, from Montreal to the Philippine Islands; but she had achieved this because the great imperialist powers, the Spaniards, the Portuguese, and the French, had been Catholic powers, ready and willing to support the endeavours of the Catholic missionary orders. In the eighteenth century there came a change because British colonial power superseded French colonial power, the Dutch had gained greatly at the expense of the Portuguese, and already Spain was in decline. The newly imperialist Protestant powers were either, like the British, religiously indifferent, or else, like the Dutch, they were intransigently Calvinist, and determined (as in Ceylon) upon a policy of persecuting the Catholics. In either case it was clear that the world spread of the Faith, so striking in the previous two centuries, was likely to be checked, although the British did not normally interfere with the work of the many mission settlements, and it is very arguable that the complete separation of the Catholic Church from the State in the British dependencies served the true interests of religion better, in the long run, than did the close association of that Church with the Spanish Government in South America. Certainly Rome was very much freer in her relations with the Church in Canada, or in India, than she was with the Church in Latin America, where every Bull or Brief, every appointment, every emissary, was subject to the good will of the Spanish Escurial.

We should not seek to minimise the importance of the decline of the great Catholic empires; but we should also recognise that something subtler and deeper than any shift in world political power was operating against the Church in the eighteenth century. This was the growth of Erastianism (named from the Swiss theologian, Erastus), or, as the French thinkers called it, *Etatism,* the enlarged sense of the omnicompetence of the State to control all aspects of a country's life, including its religion. The Church called this Gallicanism (because it was so evident in France) or Febronianism (after the German theologian "Febronius"), or later Josephism (because the Emperor Joseph II of Austria, in the second half of the eighteenth century, carried the policy to its furthest extremes). It might be expected that Erastianism would be a tendency more peculiar to Protestant countries, especially to those which had an Established Church, than to Catholic; yet it must be admitted that Joseph II of Austria took a political interest in the Church, carrying with it a detailed interference in its affairs, which was even more dangerous to religion than was the indifference of an Anglican George II of England or of a Lutheran Frederick the Great of Prussia.

These eighteenth-century rulers, often called the "enlightened despots," considered it to be their duty to centralise the administration of their states to render them more efficient; in doing so they often suppressed the traditional privileges of Church, aristocracy, city council, or university, together with other "remnants of feudalism." They claimed that in this they served the interests of their people, though they more obviously served the interests of their own thrones. But while it would be out of place here to consider the wider aspects of their work, it is essential to recognise that the exalted and new notion which the eighteenth century entertained of the functions of the State was bound to lead it into conflict with the claims of the Church. If the prince was now to be the "father of his people," if, with Louis XIV, he was to cry *l'Etat, c'est moi!*, then it followed that he would resent much more keenly any interference from Rome (for instance in the appointment of bishops) and that many aspects of life which had hitherto belonged to the spiritual sphere (such as marriage, education, or charity) would come increasingly under state control. Where this process would stop none could determine, and it was disturbing that one of the most powerful princes in Christendom, the Holy Roman Emperor, Joseph II of Austria, should go to the length of deciding the number of candles to be placed upon the altar or of revising the Sacred Liturgy, even though his doing so caused some amusement elsewhere, and especially to his cynically-minded brother monarch Frederick of Prussia.

Rome could not be indifferent to these tendencies, which must lead to the diminution of the influence of religion and were so sadly symptomatic of the growing secularism of the times. But, although that great Pope Innocent XI (1676–89) had withstood Louis XIV at the height of his power on the matter of episcopal appointments in France, no eighteenth-century Pope measured up to Innocent's stature, and the position of the papacy, and with it the vitality and influence of the spiritual power, declined ominously.

Two events, both belonging to the second half of the eighteenth century, illustrate all too clearly the new weakness that had overtaken the papacy. In 1782 Pope Pius VI made the journey to Vienna to try to persuade the Emperor Joseph II to desist from his ecclesiastical policies. Though the Pope was very much a man of his age, in the sense that he was of a tolerant temperament, interested in humanistic scholarship, and a great patron of the Vatican library, he could see clearly enough that the policies of "Josephism" were fatal for the Church and must be countered resolutely. It was not in accordance with precedent for a Pope to journey into Europe in order to plead with a prince; it was the tradition rather for emperors to make the journey to Rome. That Pius made the journey, and that he failed in his mission, were perhaps equally significant; the papacy was now very near its nadir.

But the other event had the more lasting consequences; this was the suppression of the Jesuits throughout the world, by Pope Clement XIV in the year 1773. Founded by Saint Ignatius in 1540 precisely to serve the Popes, in selfless obedience and in the cause of the Church, the Society of Jesus was universally recognised as the papacy's principal source of support. That a Pope, under pressure from various Erastian rulers, should dissolve the Society, was an act so extraordinary and so disastrous in its consequences that it calls for some explanation.

We have noticed already that one of the effects of the Seven Years' War was to ruin the Jesuits engaged in the economic life of the French West Indies—particularly the island of Martinique. These Jesuits had found it necessary to return to Paris to plead their cause; but at Paris their old enemies, the lawyers of the *parlement*, took the opportunity to ruin them, and, with the assistance of other enemies, such as the university and the King's mistress, Madame de Pompadour (whose "repentancies" the Jesuits were unable to take at their face value), they prevailed upon Louis XV to expel the Society from France in the year 1764. At the instance of the Bourbon King Charles III, they were expelled from Spain (1767); under the influence of the "enlightened" minister Pombal they had already been expelled from Portugal. The Bourbons of Naples took the same course, so that by the time that Clement XIV issued his Brief of Suppression the Society had, in fact, already been expelled from a large part of the globe.

Why had there been so widespread a reaction against the Jesuits? Essentially because the temper of politics in the eighteenth century was anti-clerical and the temper of society was secular. The Jesuits represented just those things against which the century had reacted—maintenance of clerical control in matters like marriage or education (which had always been recognised as belonging to the spiritual sphere) and maintenance of the authority of Rome, in all Catholic countries, in Church affairs. They were the first line of the Church's defence, and they were therefore the first casualty when the Church was obliged to yield ground. Recognising this, the Bourbons and their friends had combined to undo them, and the Pope did little more than give recognition to a *fait accompli*. Nevertheless it was a servile act on the part of the papacy or, as Pius XI termed it later, "a painful page of history." At the conclave of 1769, when Cardinal Ganganelli was elected and became Pope Clement XIV, the Bourbon powers combined to bring pressure to bear to prevent the election of a *zelante* (a pro-Jesuit) and the Spanish ambassador threatened a schism in Spain if the Society were not suppressed. Cardinal Ganganelli had been regarded as an appeaser, and after his election he duly yielded to what he had come to regard as the inevitable. "For the sake of peace," run the words of his Brief *Dominus ac Redemptor Noster*, "and because the Society can no longer attain the aims for which it was founded, and on secret grounds which We enclose in our heart, We suppress the said Society." He does not censure or even blame the Jesuits, though he notes the many accusations of a political nature brought against them. He finds that their enemies have made them powerless for good. And the "secret grounds"? These are generally supposed to have been the threat of a schism in Spain, where His Catholic Majesty had often been anti-papal, but never so strongly so as in those days when King Charles III was reigning.

The fall of the Jesuits was also partly due to the Jansenists. We need not enter here into the long-drawn-out struggle between those strange perfectionists, at Port Royal and at Paris, and the Jesuits, whose "lax moral teaching" they criticised. The Jansenists believed in the utter sinfulness of man and his powerlessness to help himself; this drove them into an attitude towards predestination and a disbelief in free will which were almost Calvinist. They were an Elect; everybody else was damned. They accused the Jesuits of making things easy for the penitent, of inventing excuses and subtle formulas by their famous casuistry. But they failed to understand that the Jesuits were concerned to save *all* God's creatures, to bring as many as possible into His Church, the foolish *with* the wise virgins, the tares *with* the wheat, the sinners *with* the righteous. Not for them to reserve the sacraments for the holy, to deny God's grace to those who needed it most.

This was the essence of their quarrel with the Jansenists, and the cause of the papal condemnation of most of the distinctive tenets of the Jansenist theologians. But although the Jesuit doctrines were victorious at Rome, the Jansenists continued, as communities, to flourish in France and in Holland, in Germany and in northern Italy, and we should not minimise their influence at the end of the eighteenth century, for their teachers powerfully strengthened the hands of those who were seeking to reduce the power of Rome, to limit the influence of the Church in public ("worldly") affairs, and to assert the rights of local and elective councils. The Council of Pistoia (1786) saw them boldly and openly asserting the superiority of General Councils to the Pope; and, when the French Revolution broke out, the effect of their propaganda showed itself in the number of French clergy who saw no harm in adopting the Civil Constitution of the Clergy, by which the French hierarchy became an elective and salaried state service, virtually independent of Rome. Thus did a misguided perfectionism, a "holier-than-thou" attitude, a puritan spirit of sect within the Catholic Church, help to sap the foundations of the whole all-embracing religious structure of the eighteenth century.

It is not easy to define at all exactly the influence of Jansenism, though so great an authority as Lord Acton (who was no friend to Rome) thought it was both paramount and disastrous. Nor will it ever be possible to estimate the influence, in this same century, of the Freemasons, whose opposition not only to Rome but to the whole Faith was more radical, being based upon a new and non-Christian philosophy. Whereas Jansenist error, dogmatically speaking, arose only from an erroneous exaggeration of Saint Augustine's teaching on grace, and the Jansenist communities always protested both their loyalty to the Holy Father and their orthodoxy, Freemasonry was extra-Christian if not always anti-Christian. It was condemned by the Pope in the year 1738, but it continued to grow in France, and on the continent of Europe generally until, by the time of the French Revolution, a high proportion of the "enlightened" nobility and bourgeoisie were Freemasons, and it is said that most of the Third Estate, assembled at Versailles in 1789, belonged to the order. There has been much absurd attribution of devil worship, and other extravagances, to the higher ranks of the masonic hierarchy; we can discount this, whether in the eighteenth or in any other century. Philosophically speaking, the beliefs of the eighteenth-century Freemasons were naturalist; they believed in nature, of which they saw man as exclusively a part, and they based an elaborate system of ritual and of mutual philanthropy upon an ideal of human brotherhood derived from this participation in nature. They were thus either pantheist or materialist, and their cardinal religious error lay in their denial of the supernatural, and thus of supernatural grace.

Leaving on one side the common, though doubtful, opinion that the Freemasons were sworn to the destruction of the Church and were responsible for bringing about the French Revolution, we should note that, by popularising "freethinking," naturalist, materialist, or pantheist notions in their numerous lodges, they helped to create that climate of intellectual opinion which came to characterise the century and is loosely called "enlightened." But there were other streams of "light" contributing to create the attractive, if illusory, colours of the rainbow of enlightenment. There were the contributors to Diderot's *Encyclopédie*. There was the mockery of Voltaire. There was the sentimental romanticism of Rousseau. It was becoming fashionable to think exclusively of man as a reasonable, or as an emotional and affectionate animal, a "child of nature," subject only to "nature's laws," tolerant of all ideas, indulgent towards all behaviour, lord of an attractive universe. These ideas did not always harmonise well with one another, but they had this in common: that they ruled out belief in a supernatural order, or in a rigorous code of right and wrong; they "played down" sin, and with it sanctity; and they threw into an invidious light any priesthood that presumed "to bind or to loose," to purvey God's grace through the sacrament or to withhold it. The unique character of the Church, like the unique occasion of the Redemption, from which she arose, was losing all meaning for the "innocent" child of nature or of reason.

We should not exaggerate the numbers affected by the eighteenth-century Enlightenment. Such thoughts were for the few, and especially for the *salons* of Paris and for the readers of Voltaire or Rousseau. France had not lost her faith, if only because France neither frequented the *salons* nor heard about the current fashionable literature.

But many of the clergy read the new books and had been educated in the universities, where the ideas of the Enlightenment were current. What was the effect of this fashionable culture upon the higher clergy of France and Germany, of Italy and Austria?

There is plenty of evidence that it was considerable. Bishop Gregory, the head of the Constitutional Church in France which was set up by the French Revolution, has put it on record in his *Mémoires*, that his youth was tormented by the doubts engendered in his mind at the university, where the exponents of the traditional Faith made a feeble impression compared with that made by the fashionable philosophers who were then all the rage. Many of those priests who were sensitive to the new currents of thought reflected the new philosophy, in their religious teaching and preaching, by "minimising" the personal and particular aspects of Christianity in favour of general phrases which harmonised with contemporary modes of thinking. Thus the First Person of the Trinity could be referred to without embarrassment, for even the philosophers, though tending now to talk about a "Supreme Being," were often still talking about God. But with the Second Person, and His Incarnation, the more intimately Christian aspects of the Faith were revealed, and of these even some of the priests were beginning to be ashamed. They were beginning, as the French historian Jean Leflon has excellently said, to "blush for the doctrine." "Silence sometimes amounted to capitulation; often, indeed, it amounted to a new affirmation . . . the philosophy upon which priests, monks, and even bishops were being nourished penetrated their theology; religion was 'naturalising' itself, as was morality; becoming timid, faith was declining and disappearing; the Enlightenment, triumphing in their minds, was withering what were called the 'ancient prejudices.'"[3]

With the cult of rationalism should be coupled that of ro-

[3] *Histoire de l'Eglise* (Paris, 1951), Vol. 20, *La crise révolutionnaire*, p. 29.

manticism, whose parent was Rousseau. Abandoning the intolerable intellectual struggle to harmonise the new philosophy with the Faith, many were seduced into following a veritable "flight from reason" which led them to the attractive realms of "pure sensibility." But romanticism, though it could be harmonised, as Chateaubriand harmonised it, with Christianity, was really as dangerous to the Faith as was rationalism. For the root of it, as taught by Rousseau and developed later by the romantic poets, was the supremacy of *feeling*, the absolute goodness of uninhibited sentiment. Again the parent-God was nature, for feeling is natural. But the idea that men might safely rely upon these natural feelings as their guide to conduct, though it might serve to draw attention to the valuable sentiments of pity or affection, was, in itself, perhaps the most dangerous of all the ideas to which the eighteenth century gave birth, and the one which has persisted most obstinately to the present day. For feeling may of course be good or evil, controlled or uncontrolled, and those who, in the French Revolution, indulged in an orgy of emotion in the debating halls of the National Assembly, or in the "worship of reason" in Notre Dame, were just as likely to be found following the tumbrils through the streets of Paris or shouting their execrations in the face of the victims of the guillotine on the Place de Grève. For all their worship of her, nature was sometimes rather raw.

No doubt these philosophical influences which were seeping invisibly into Catholic Christianity in the eighteenth century were the most important underlying cause of the grave attacks upon the very foundations of the Faith, not only in France but elsewhere in Europe, which appeared as a consequence of the French Revolution. Without appreciating the penetration of men's minds effected by the Enlightenment and romanticism it is impossible to account for the assaults upon the dogmas of the Church as such—the prohibition of the Mass, and of the sacraments, the closure or secularisation of the churches, which occurred between 1791 and 1799.

On the other hand anti-clericalism, as distinct from anti-Catholicism, was fostered by the outward conditions of the Church's life in the eighteenth century as much as by any weakening of faith. It is necessary to remember that the Church constituted the First Estate of the Realm in France, as elsewhere, with her own courts (not only for clerics but for all men in certain causes, e. g. marriage), her own police, and her own prisons. Her independence as an Estate was in nothing more remarkable than in finance, for not only did she possess vast lands of her own, but she levied a "tenth" upon other landholders, and she was exempt from herself paying taxes to the Crown. This exemption she enjoyed in common with the Second Estate, the nobility; but it rendered her subject to the same jealousy, and we find that it is a recurrent feature of all the new settlements between Church and State, which were made after the French Revolution, that the State always insists upon a financial nexus which shall prevent the Church from ever again becoming a separate Estate, from becoming free, that is, from the economic control of the government. At the same time it is fair to remember what is far too often overlooked, namely that, with her considerable landed establishment, the Church carried the burden not merely of maintaining her own clergy but of providing schools, hospitals, and other social services. The huge hospitals, or *hôtels-Dieu*, which the visitor may see in Italy or France today, though often now put to other purposes, serve as a reminder that this great work of charity was a reality.

The real weakness of the Church on the economic side was the vast disparity between the poverty of many of the parish priests and the wealth of some of the bishops. Some of the episcopal sees in France were worth more than one hundred thousand francs per annum; a parish curé could expect only seven hundred francs. One cannot be surprised that so many of the curés sided with the Third Estate at the time of the Revolution, or that they entered so many requests for a readjustment of rewards. The gulf between their own lot and that of their bishops was too great; it could not fail to reinforce the teaching of those who were arguing that the curé derived his spiritual authority directly from God and not through the mediation of the bishops; such curés insisted that, if the bishops were the descendants of the twelve Apostles, the curés were descended from the seventy-two whom Our Lord sent out to preach His word. Nor can we be surprised that when the French Revolution introduced state salaries for all priests in the Civil Constitution of the Clergy the arrangement seemed to many of the curés to have its advantages.

If, in these Catholic countries, there was too often some jealousy on the part of the lesser clergy towards their superiors, there was also some resentment on the part of the secular clergy as a whole against the regulars. Resentment of this kind is of course in some measure a perennial feature of the life of the Church. But in France, at least in the later eighteenth century, it was becoming very vocal, and when the French Revolution broke out it showed itself to be dangerous. It was accentuated partly by the fact that some of the great abbeys were even more wealthy than the episcopal sees, partly by the fact that the religious houses, though by no means generally corrupt, were suffering from the weakened spirituality of the period and had very often declined seriously in their membership. As often happens when this is the case (and most notably at the time of the suppression of the English monasteries by King Henry VIII), the decline in numbers was accompanied by some relaxation of discipline, and by more pointed comparisons from outside between the extent of the monastic estates and the extent of the numbers they maintained. The most reliable figures show a decline in numbers at the great French religious houses for men, during the generation preceding the French Revolution, of more than 30 per cent. The decline affected all the orders except the *Grande Trappe*. At the same time it is right to notice that there is no evidence of the existence of widespread immorality or laxity, such as had existed, for example, at the time of the Renaissance, and also that the decline, so apparent in the men's congregations, was not accompanied by any comparable decline in those of the women.

Less subject to the dangers of laxity than were the regulars, the secular clergy of the *ancien régime* were more subject to the dangers of worldliness. We have noticed that they often yielded somewhat to the rationalist and romantic philosophy of the century. They also yielded at times to its passionate preoccupation with practical projects of a utilitarian character. This was an age of great economic development, with the consequent construction of canals, increase of shipping, and scientific improvement of agriculture. It was a standing temptation to the bishops to become, as the saying went, "administrators of provinces rather than of the sacraments." The great estates of the Church, whose economic life, based upon the immemorial effort of the shepherd, the ploughman, or the labourer in the vineyard, had gone on little changed from one generation to the next, were now in a period of agricultural revolution, which called for a new preoccupation on the part of their pastors with planning and organisation, a preoccupation, unfortunately, which was liable to be also a distraction.

We have then, on the eve of the French Revolution, to en-
visage a Church in Europe outwardly majestic but sometimes
inwardly weakened by worldliness, by loss of faith, and by an
insufficient sense of the significance of her unity and of her
world-wide mission. And in the years that followed the great
upheaval we shall see her striving to sift the wheat from the
chaff amongst the new ideas, striving to adjust herself to that
Liberty, Equality, and Fraternity which the revolutionaries so
often betrayed.

CHAPTER TWO

The French Revolution (1789–1799)

It is remarkable, and eloquent of the state of opinion on Church matters in the year 1789, that the clergy of France did not look to their own religious authority, that is to the Pope, to cleanse and renew their lives; they looked first where everybody else was looking, to the French monarchy. In the *cahiers* (petitions for reform) which the clergy, like the other Estates, drew up before the meeting of the French Estates-General in 1789, the French hierarchy, from the bishops down to the humblest curés, were agreed in asking the King to make provision for Church reform.

Admittedly, some of the matters they raised concerned the relations between Church and State, in which the King was an interested party. Thus they all wanted the Catholic Church to remain the Established Church of France, with exclusive privileges, and some were critical of the moves which the monarchy had recently made in favour of the French Protestants, Jews, and agnostics. They also had a number of suggestions for strengthening the Church's influence in the moral and cultural life of the country, including stricter censorship of the press. But even supposing these to be matters pertaining to the monarchy, as well as to Rome, what are we to make of the suggestion, contained in the majority of these ecclesiastical *cahiers,* that the monasteries be "reformed," the monks being made to do "useful work" and not allowed to devote themselves to prayer and contemplation? Such suggestions, made to the King, make it very evident that the Gallican theory had penetrated the clergy as a whole, so that even the various religious rules, the rules of Saint Benedict, Cluny, Citeaux, and the rest, originally approved by Rome, were regarded as reformable, indeed as needing reform by the Bourbon monarchy. No doubt this attack, made by the secular priests upon the religious orders, should be viewed as one more manifestation of the age-long conflict between the secular and the regular; but it is significant that in 1789 the seculars, in their desire to reform the regulars, were invoking the power of the State.

The higher clergy assumed that, when the Estates-General met at Versailles, their own Estate, which was the "First Estate," the "Estate of the Church," would deliberate and vote separately, and would submit its proposals to the King for his approval. But, through the influence of the curés, matters turned out very differently. When the Estates of the clergy, and the nobility, and the "Third Estate" assembled, it was found that out of 296 deputies representing the Estate of the clergy no less than 208 were curés; and these curés proceeded to show their readiness to vote with the Third Estate, and many of them even insisted upon taking their seats with that Estate. They thus compelled the Crown to give way and abandon its original plan, by which the three Estates were to have deliberated and voted separately, in favour of one single Assembly in which each individual member had one vote. And by doing so they secured the triumph of the Third Estate, which was as numerous as the other two Estates put together. The ultimate victory of the Revolution was thus assured; the higher clergy and the nobility had been defeated by the parish priests of France. Unwittingly they had made the French Revolution.

But it was a victory of which many of the curés were soon to repent. For rapid, indeed, was the progress of the avalanche of destruction which followed upon their surrender of the Church in France to the whim of a popular constituent assembly. They had not realised that, once the new revolutionary authority had been allowed to assail the Church in her discipline and in her property, it would soon invade the sphere of faith and morals.

As is common in anti-clerical campaigns, the first demands made upon the Church were for her money. The Revolutionary Government was short of funds; what need had the Church of her extensive lands?—let her surrender them to serve as security for the new paper currency, the *assignats*. It was not enough that the clergy had voluntarily surrendered their tithes; the property of the Church must be handed over *in toto* to the State. The plea was made that the Church should retain sufficient property to provide at least a living for her priests, but this plea was dismissed. If the Church retained any property, would she not remain a distinct order within the State? Let her priests rather receive a stipend from the government. Such was the reform decreed by the Constituent Assembly, by 510 votes against 346, on November 2, 1789.

Then, if there were to be no Church property, how could there be religious orders? It was an easy step to their dissolution, for not even the curés were interested in saving them. The nuns, though shorn of much of their property, were allowed to remain in their convents; but the monks, unless they were teaching, or running orphanages, or the like, must leave. They might regroup themselves in certain designated houses, but they were encouraged, rather, to abandon their vows.

And since the State was now to salary a civil service of priests, it was natural that she should reorganise their distribution to her liking. Let there be one bishop for each political Department—this would reduce the episcopacy by more than a third. Let there be fewer curés. Let the bishops be elected by the Departments, the curés by the electoral bodies of their districts. Ten metropolitans would invest the bishops, and the Pope need only be notified of elections; his approval need no longer be obtained in advance. Such, in brief, was the Civil Constitution of the Clergy, voted by the Assembly on July 12, 1790.

Even these drastic innovations in the nationalisation of the Church received the support of a large number of the curés and many of the bishops. So long as the King did not disapprove, it seemed to many of the clergy, nurtured as they were in the Gallican tradition, that all was well. The curés, in particular, were glad enough not to depend upon the bishops for their nomination. A Church weakened by more than a century of dependence on the State, personified by the King, saw little harm, religiously speaking, in becoming dependent upon the State, now personified by a democratic Assembly. But there was this vital difference that in the *ancien régime* the Gallican Church had subsisted upon its own properties; it had not been salaried by the monarchy. Too soon it was now to become apparent how quickly the holder of the purse strings could interfere in the entire sphere of Church discipline and even doctrine. And there was also this further difference, in the long run even more important: Louis XIV and Louis XV might often have recked little of Rome, and the Popes might have made feeble protests as those monarchs encroached upon their traditional prerogatives, but Rome had not hitherto been confronted, without prior consultation, with anything like this entire reorganisation of the French Church, this turning of the hierarchy of her authority upside down, this spoliation presented as a *fait accompli*. It was more than even Pius VI, an elderly and conciliatory pontiff, whose reign came at the conclusion of a long period of decline in the power and prestige of Rome, was prepared to accept. On July 10, 1790, he wrote to Louis XVI telling him he should not approve the new laws. But the Pope's letter arrived on July 23, and the King had approved the Civil Constitution on the previous day.

At this juncture the French bishop-deputies rose to the occasion and presented an united front, insisting upon the incompetence of the temporal power in matters spiritual. The only reply of the Assembly was to subject bishops themselves to investiture by order of the temporal tribunals of the Departments, if the metropolitans should refuse to invest the "Elect of the People." Thus was a gulf dug between the Assembly and the French episcopacy too wide to be crossed, and many of the lower clergy, too, recognised the impasse. It became necessary for the Assembly to try to impose upon the clerical deputies an oath of loyalty to this new Civil Constitution of the Clergy. But only Talleyrand, Bishop of Autun (the same who would adjust his viewpoint to enable him to serve every French régime during the coming two generations) was ready, followed by one or two others, to take this oath. About a hundred of the lower clergy took it, but many retracted, so that in the end only about a third of the clerical deputies accepted the Civil Constitution of the Clergy.

In France as a whole the picture was somewhat similar. Out of 135 beneficed bishops, only four took the oath; amongst the clergy as a whole rather less than half took it. The fidelity of the bishops was creditable and sometimes heroic. It compares very favourably with the behaviour of the bishops in England under King Henry VIII. But, if their conduct seems to throw into an invidious light the behaviour of many of the lesser clergy, it has to be remembered that they were freer than were their humbler brethren to go into exile and await a better day—which, in fact, was what most of them did. The top class of European society was still largely cosmopolitan, and the *émigré* bishop might hope to find congenial company in Vienna, Rome, or even London. There would be financial difficulties, but not so grave as those confronting the lesser clergy who emigrated.

For the curés emigration was hazardous indeed. Moreover many of them still sympathised with the Revolution, and felt that it was the duty of the Gallican Church to harmonise herself with it, in order to "baptise" it, that to leave their presbyteries would be to desert their flocks; and some of them had not been altogether sorry to see the humbling of the local bishop or abbot. It would be wrong to judge too harshly many of those who took the new oath of allegiance. Rome, although her disapproval was known, had delayed in pronouncing herself openly on the subject of the Civil Constitution; she only did that in March 1791. And the King had approved it. The habit of obedience to the State must have seemed to many the natural habit to follow.

The Civil Constitution had divided the Assembly, and now it divided the Church in France for, alongside those priests who accepted it, there were many "refractory" clergy—the name given to those who refused the new oath of obedience which would make them civil servants. Sometimes they said Mass secretly, sometimes, where the police were indulgent, openly. Families would be divided, a brother supporting the "patriot-curé," his sister the "good-curé." But the Constitutional Church held the advantage over the Refractory Church that it was the State Church, and the only legal one; marriages, baptisms, burials could only be legally performed by the Constitutional Clergy, even though, after May 7, 1791, it became legal for the "Romanists" to say Mass, but not to give communion. Rioting, which often involved sacrilege, was rife; and free fights occurred between supporters of the two parties.

Much, however, would depend upon local circumstance. Legally, those priests who refused to take the oath were deprived of their presbyteries, but where these "refractories" were strong, as in the Pas de Calais, in the North, or in Maine, Brittany, and the Vendée, they would often be unmolested; where the Constitutionalists were strong, as in the Ile de France, or in Provence, those priests who refused the new oath would often be driven right out of the village, or imprisoned. In the towns, and especially in Paris, where the seminarists of Saint-Sulpice set a magnificent example, the better-instructed clergy generally retained their traditional religious allegiance and contrived to find places where they could say Mass in safety. But matters were made very much worse for the opponents of the Civil Constitution by the flight of King Louis XVI to Varennes in June 1791 and his denunciation of the work of the Assembly; this break of the monarchy with the Revolution, it was well known, was prompted at least in part by the Pope's condemnation, in March 1791, of the Civil Constitution of the Clergy. It now appeared to some patriotic Frenchmen that the "Refractory" or "Roman" clergy were the allies of the foreign powers, to which the King had intended to flee, that they were in alliance with the avowed enemies of the new France, namely the King of Prussia and the Emperor of Austria, who, by the summer of 1791, had made clear their intention of restoring Louis XVI to his rightful position.

The National Assembly, which in two years had abolished the *ancien régime* and given a new constitution to France, was often heretical and schismatic in its outlook and action, but it was Christian. Indeed a large proportion of its members were clergy. Although it had intended to turn the Church into a Department of State, it had nevertheless intended to maintain her in existence, and it had hoped and expected to keep her in communion with Rome. But it had only succeeded in producing a desperate schism, and it was unfortunate for France that, having given her a new constitution, and being about to dissolve, it decreed, in August 1791, that the Civil Constitution of the Clergy should be regarded as an integral part of the new French constitution, and thus be irreformable by any new government. New revolutions brought new constitutions and the Civil Constitution did not last long, but it lasted long enough to establish its new clergy, so that, for the troubled revolutionary decade which the country suffered until Napoleon restored the rights of Rome by the Concordat of 1801, the Constitutional Church survived, and remnants of it lasted longer. At first it seemed as though it must grow in influence and that the Romanists would be exterminated. For the new Legislative Assembly, unlike its predecessor, reflected the *bourgeoisie*, which was anti-clerical and even anti-Christian, in a sense that the National Assembly had not been. Moreover, the new government became involved, in April 1792, in war with Austria, and the priests who had refused the oath were regarded as a potential fifth column. A new oath, more uncompromising than the last, required them, in September 1792, to swear to be faithful to the nation and to maintain, to the utmost of their power, liberty and equality, and to die, if need be, for the new laws. Already non-jurors were to be sent to French Guiana in South America if they had not left France by August 26; the word of "six active citizens" was sufficient to secure the deportation of suspects. These last brutal provisions were the work of the Paris Com-

mune which, by the month of August 1792, had seized power
The prisons were now filled with those priests who were too
old or too ill to be deported. And for many imprisonment
was followed by death, for it was considered necessary, as a
precaution in case of foreign invasion, to massacre those in the
prisons.

By the end of the year 1792 a situation had developed in
which exile, deportation, or death, had reduced very seriously
the numbers of those clergy who were obedient to Rome and
to the Catholic tradition.

Yet the lot of the Constitutional Church became, before
long, little better than that of the Roman Church. And for
these Constitutionalists life was the more depressing since
they lacked the consolation of having never yielded, of suffering for loyalty to truth, or of that secret respect which often
came the way of the "good-curés" in prison or in hiding. It
seemed hard, indeed, that the support of the State, for which
so much—in some cases even honour—had been sacrificed,
should now be withdrawn; yet this was the bitter disillusionment which the Constitutionalists had to suffer under the
"Convention" (a new constitution-making body) and the
"Committee of Public Safety" (the real seat of power) during
1793-94. At bottom, the reason why the State thus turned
against its own offspring must be sought in the radical conflict
of outlook between Christianity and the spirit of the Revolution. The more *avancé* of the revolutionaries, who by now had
won power, were convinced that they were regenerating society
and bringing about the Kingdom of Heaven upon earth; it
was therefore impossible that they should believe that divine
grace, or the sacraments, or a special order—the priesthood—
set apart by ordination, training, celibacy, and the rest, was
any longer necessary. Since the new apostles of Liberty,
Equality, and Fraternity were regenerating France, what need
had she of priestly absolution? Considerations of this kind
led, at an early stage in the campaign of "de-Christianisation,"
to a step which was to place the Constitutional clergy in a
cruel quandary: marriage was made a civil contract (September 20, 1792); the law ceased to recognise it as a sacrament. From this it soon followed that the marriage of priests,
of members of religious orders, or of divorced persons, was
legitimate. The restraints previously laid upon them were of
a kind unrecognised by the new state faith. To their honour,
many of the Constitutional bishops refused to recognise the

new laws. But the bishop of the Department of Eure had himself duly married in the mayor's parlour and subsequently went through the permitted ceremony of "nuptial benediction." By July 1793 it was necessary for the whole clergy to decide where it stood in this cardinal doctrinal matter, for the Convention then decreed that any cleric who showed any opposition to the divorce law, and any bishop who condemned the marriage of priests, was to be deported. Meanwhile the marriage of priests was actively encouraged; even the Romanists were told they would be left free if they would only show their faith in the Revolution by marrying. Gradually the persecution which they were coming to share in common began to blur the distinction between "Constitutionalist" and "Roman." In September 1793 the Constitutionalists ceased to be a salaried clergy; all they were left with was a pitiful pension.

The merciless pressure put upon the Constitutional clergy to make them as like laymen as possible was part of a campaign which had grown in intensity during the years 1792 and 1793. This campaign was clearly related to the crisis France was passing through at home and abroad after the summer of 1792. Marie Antoinette, Louis XVI's Queen, was the aunt of the Hapsburg Austrian ruler, Francis II, who conceived it to be his duty to make war on her behalf against the French revolutionaries. Frederick William II of Prussia, threatened, like Francis, by the attack on the principle of monarchy in France, and unwilling to let his cousin at Vienna assume, alone, the leadership of the German princes, saw his duty in a similar fashion. The Legislative Assembly in Paris tried to forestall the danger by taking the initiative in the spring of 1792 and invading Belgium (a Hapsburg province) but met with ill success. In July the Duke of Brunswick, commander of the Prussian Army, issued his notorious manifesto threatening vengeance upon the people of France for their treatment of their King. It was in these circumstances that Louis XVI and Marie Antoinette found their palace of the Tuileries invaded by a mob, and the King was compelled to put on the red cap of the revolutionaries; and it was in reply to the Duke of Brunswick that, on August 10, 1792, the Insurrectionary Commune of Paris, assisted by the men from Marseilles (who had marched north singing the "Marseillaise"), dethroned and imprisoned the King, while the Legislative Assembly declared the monarchy abolished. The King's execution followed in January 1793, and that of Marie Antoinette in the following October. Meanwhile the Convention had issued the "Propagandist Decrees," which called upon people everywhere to throw off their chains, rise in revolution, and join their French brethren in amity and peace; but this had only helped to bring Britain in on the side of the opponents of the Revolution, and by the summer of 1793 France was being invaded from the north, the east, and the south, whilst a civil war at home had been provoked by the refusal of the men of the west (Brittany and the Vendée) to accept conscription, and by a federalist movement against the autocracy now exercised by the Insurrectionary Commune of Paris.

It is important to remember this state of affairs, which gave to France almost a "siege mentality." In some ways it was a state of affairs analogous to that which had obtained in England in the time of Queen Elizabeth I. Then, the danger from Philip II of Spain, which was only finally removed by the defeat of the Spanish Armada in 1588, had intensified the religious persecution. Pope Pius V had excommunicated the Queen and was known to be hopeful that the Catholic powers of Europe would help to restore the traditional religion to England. Similarly, in the days of the French Revolution, Pius VI, though slow to move, had at last made clear his hostility to the new régime and was giving encouragement to the Emperor of Austria. The *émigré* bishops were denouncing the Revolution and all its works and were exhorting those lesser clergy still in France to resist. Like the other *émigrés*, these bishops were openly expressing the hope that the invading monarchical armies would be victorious, and that their own restoration to their traditional positions would follow.

But while these considerations go far to account for the attitudes of the revolutionary governments towards the Refractory or Roman clergy, they do not account for the amazing anti-Christian campaign let loose in 1792 and 1793 against the Constitutional clergy, and the entire "cult" of Christianity. That Church had accepted subjection to the new State by accepting the Civil Constitution of the Clergy; its loyalty to the revolutionary régime was unquestionable because it owed its very existence to it. This fact was well appreciated in the Convention, and in the Insurrectionary Commune of Paris. Both of these bodies, whatever the opinions of their members, had to have some realistic regard for French traditions and sentiments. The campaign of violent de-Christianisation did not spring from them but from individual fanatics, acting upon a semi-educated *bourgeoisie*, who had picked up a superficial smattering of eighteenth-century rationalist and romantic philosophy. These men were to be found generally in the local Jacobin clubs, and their enthusiasm to be rid of "superstition" was fanned by the speed with which events were moving, and by the notion that a new age of equality and brotherhood, in which men would be guided only by reason and feeling, was about to dawn. Most prominent among them were the notorious Fouché, one of the *députés-en-mission* sent out by the Convention to raise armies for the war, and Hébert, one of the most abusive journalists ever to lend his genius to a propagandist campaign.

Fouché opened his campaign at Nevers where, seated on the bishop's throne in the cathedral, he systematically denounced the maxims of the Faith. He followed this up by obliging all the clergy of the city to marry, or at least to adopt a child or other dependent. At Moulins he dressed up his Jacobin friends in ecclesiastical vestments, a sport which was followed by a general destruction of the vestments and of all crucifixes and holy images. The Constitutional bishop was persuaded to unfrock himself. An order was made secularising funerals; over the gate of the cemetery were inscribed the words: "Death is an eternal sleep." Similar antics were indulged at Rheims, Amiens, Bourges, and other great seats of the French episcopacy. But it was when the movement reached Paris that it attained to its symbolic climax. The metropolitan bishop (Constitutional) of Paris was Gobel, a feeble figure who had been one of the few pre-revolutionary bishops of France to follow Talleyrand, in the National Assembly, in taking the oath to accept the Civil Constitution of the Clergy. On November 6, 1793, he was dragged from his bed and required to abdicate. His advisory council having recommended that he do so, he proceeded to hand over his letters of office, his pectoral cross and his ring, and to put on the red cap. Since many of the cathedral clergy followed suit it was decided to follow up these events by holding in Notre Dame, on November 10, a feast in honour of reason. On the top of a scaffolding, placed in front of the choir, was erected a temple dedicated to philosophy, and to crown all was installed, in place of "inanimate images," an actress from the Opéra, chosen for her beauty, as a "masterpiece of nature," but entitled, without very evident cause, the "Goddess of Reason." This curious event was the prelude to similar ceremonies in other French cathedrals and churches. But it was also the beginning of a spate of profane charades, with ecclesiastical dress turned into fancy dress, of processions of donkeys wearing mitres on their heads, of the smashing of images; and finally, by the order of Fouché's friend, the *député-en-mission* Chaumette, all churches and chapels in Paris of any Christian cult whatsoever were to be closed, and if anybody demanded that they should be opened he should be arrested forthwith as a suspect.

While Fouché, Chaumette, and their friends were fanning the flames of religious persecution, Hébert was providing fuel with his remarkable paper, *Le Père Duchesne*. What Voltaire and Rousseau had done in an earlier generation for the enlightened classes Hébert did during the Revolution for those whose principal claim to education was only that they could read. His writing was gross and coarse, but it was also lucid and direct; it made its appeal to the lower townspeople. Directed against monarchy and aristocracy, it delighted chiefly in undermining the Church, which it depicted as the anointer of kings and the betrayer of *Le bon sans-culotte, Jésus, modèle de tous les Jacobins*. In the opinion of Robespierre, Hébert, through his paper, was the principal cause of the anti-Christian campaign.

It should not, of course, be supposed that, even at the height of the intoxication, there were not counteracting influences at work. If some of the principal leaders, and notably Marat, were urging on the men of violence and depicting even the Constitutional priests as "mortal enemies" of France, the more responsible revolutionary statesmen, amongst whom we should include both Robespierre and Danton, saw that, in fact, the campaign was a great disservice to the Republic. It gave a new animus to the European war in the year 1793, because it enabled not only the continental powers but even William Pitt and Protestant England to pose before the world as crusaders concerned to save Christianity. It kept alive the great counter-revolution in the Vendée, for if the revolt had begun as a protest against conscription, the heart of that desperate resistance of western France, which was never quelled, was the devotion of the people to their priests and to the Faith. Probably the majority of the members of the Convention doubted the wisdom of the persecution and, although the Commune of Paris and the other communes were more inclined to collaborate with the iconoclasts, one has to remember that they often stood to gain directly from the plundering of the churches. Sometimes they would justify their work of sacrilegious destruction by employing unimpeachable revolutionary arguments. When the Commune of Paris, on a notable occasion, decided to take possession of the magnificent clocks on the towers of the churches, it justified its action by pointing out that these clocks, from their eminence, breathed a spirit of domination over the other buildings, so that it was necessary, in the interests of Equality, that they should be lowered!

The Convention, aware of the dangers at home and abroad, and concerned to preserve the unity of the nation, showed some measure of common sense. Thus, although its members were sentimentally attached to the new revolutionary calendar, with its months descriptively named after the moods of the universal mother, Nature (*Nivôse* and *Pluviôse* for December and January, *Floréal* and *Prairial* for April and May), it was ready to sacrifice the ten-day week when it found that the workers were unfavourably impressed by a decimal system giving them a holiday every tenth instead of every seventh day. Soon it allowed, in addition to the tenth day, the seventh and even the great traditional feast days of the Church to be kept as holidays, although any open manifestation of religion was still dangerous, and the churches were normally kept locked. In December 1793 it went so far as to pass a law against interference with religious liberty; but this seems to have been quite ineffective. What mattered, in practice, was the attitude of the different communes, or of the local Jacobin clubs, or of the *députés-en-mission*. Persecution was the rule, even though there were exceptions. In the provinces, and very generally elsewhere, the churches remained closed, and the flickering flame of the Faith was kept alive only in secret.

With a sound instinct, those who thus sought to destroy the Church concentrated their attention upon the priests. In general the alternatives which the clergy found open to them were either to abdicate their office as priests, or to marry; otherwise they would be likely to suffer imprisonment, exile, or execution, on the vague grounds that they were "counter-revolutionary." Of the eighty-five bishops of the Constitutional Church, twenty-four abdicated their office, while a further twenty-three specifically apostatised, renouncing their Faith. Of these latter, nine took to themselves wives. If more than half the episcopacy thus bowed to the storm, the proportion of the lower clergy who did so was probably even larger. Of those, however, who preferred the alternative of marriage while continuing in office, there is evidence that many went through a merely legal form of contract, their "spouses" sometimes being their own elderly housekeepers.

With the spring of the year 1794 there came some hope of relief. The ascendancy of Robespierre in the Committee of Public Safety had become supreme, and he sent Hébert and his friends to the guillotine. Naturally religious, even puritan, Robespierre detested the irreligion of the Jacobins. He was, himself, profoundly un-Catholic; but he regarded the anti-Christian campaign as a folly. With the fall of Hébert, Fouché and the other leaders of the campaign felt the need to trim their sails to the new wind, the wind of Robespierre's new religion. This orthodoxy, elaborated by the high priest of the Revolution himself, the "sea-green Incorruptible," Robespierre, involved no longer the worship of reason, symbolised by an actress, but the worship of an abstraction, a Supreme Being, and belief in the immortality of the soul. The Convention, overawed by the cold passion of the ascetic little dictator, or merely indifferent, was prepared, by its vote, to endorse Robespierre's opinion that there was, indeed, a Supreme Being, and also to amend the notion, popularised by the *députés-en-mission*, that death was an eternal sleep; it was necessary now to believe in personal immortality again. On June 8, 1794, Robespierre conducted, before a huge gathering on the Champ-de-Mars, a ceremony in honour of the Supreme Being, the dictator himself officiating as high priest, and the painter David acting as master of ceremonies. Similar ceremonies followed in other parts of the country, but the hope of Catholics that the official recognition of a Supreme Being, and of immortality, would lead to a general return to the "Christian Cult" was not realised; indeed, with the fall and execution of the high priest himself, in July 1794, and the seizure of power by his enemies the Thermidorians (amongst whom were Fouché, and the fanatically anti-Christian Tallien) the lot of the priests often became worse. Whereas the lay suspects who had been imprisoned during Robespierre's reign of terror were often released during the following summer the priests generally continued to languish in gaol; and the new rulers were not men who were inclined to put a curb upon the zealots who were harassing the clergy.

In law, however, if not in fact, there was now an appearance of improvement. The tremendous resistance of the Vendée ended at last, in February 1795, with the Treaty of La Jaunaye, which specifically granted religious toleration in the affected regions—a concession which the government found it absolutely necessary to make if the civil war were to be brought to a close. This treaty was followed by a general Edict of Toleration for France as a whole; but the bare bones only of toleration were thrown to the Catholics. They could not use the churches, which were reserved for "Tenth Day" ceremonies and official acts. They could not even advertise, so much as by a notice on a door, a building in which it was intended that Mass should be said. They could raise no money, form no associations, ring no bells, hold no processions. Such remained their status until Napoleon concluded his Concordat with Pope Pius VII in the year 1801. Nevertheless, it was toleration of a kind, and queues formed outside the little rooms where Mass was being said.

With the Constitutional and the Roman priests now on an equal footing (all payments to the former had been withdrawn in the year 1794) both kinds of clergy benefited from the new state of affairs; there was, indeed, in the eyes of the State, no longer any distinction between the two, since the Civil Constitution of the Clergy existed no more. But, inevitably, the Romans, who had suffered so much more severely, enjoyed a greater popular prestige; indeed the position of the Constitutionalists was a little ludicrous now that the State had washed its hands of the Church. Not unnaturally their recruitment was pitiful, and in order to increase numbers they were obliged to allow their priests only a perfunctory training. Despite the indomitable energy and courage of their "Pope," Bishop Gregory of Loir-et-Cher, the future seemed to lie with the Romans, when new blows fell and once more divided and dispersed them.

In May 1795 permission had been given for the partial use by the Roman priests of some of the churches, provided that they made a full act of submission to the laws of the Republic. But this act many of them refused to make, being encouraged by King Louis XVIII from abroad to resist. The bishops themselves were divided on the issue. A clear directive from Rome was much needed, and, indeed, was prepared in Pius VI's Brief of June 1796, *Pastoralis Sollicitudo*, in which he exhorted the clergy of France: "Apply all your strength to demonstrating your submission to those who rule over you. Thereby you will render to God the homage of obedience which is due to Him and you will convince your rulers that true religion is in no wise calculated to upset the civil laws." But this Brief was unfortunately never published, for the leading Constitutional bishop, Gregory, persuaded the government to require from the Pope a revocation of all his writings and pronouncements on the subject of France since the year 1789, which Rome was not prepared to supply. So Pius' Brief, intended to be part of a general settlement between Rome and the new régime in France (known as the Directory), remained unopened in the bag of the papal envoy.

And another opportunity for reconciliation was lost in the following year when the Directory's general in Italy, Bonaparte, who had despoiled the Pope of the northern part of his states, recommended to his government that they should reopen the churches of France to Catholicism (Roman and Apostolic) and thereby ensure that the Roman priests would enjoin upon the faithful the duty of supporting the new régime. Such advice was in advance of its time, and Bonaparte had to wait until he was himself First Consul to see it carried out. In 1797 he was still only a general in the service of the Directory; it was, in fact, the year of the *coup d'état* of Fructidor, by which he prolonged the life of that régime for a further two years. The position of the Romans was made even more difficult in the summer of 1797 by a government decree which required priests not merely to make a formal act of submission to the laws of the Republic but to swear an "Oath of Hatred" of the monarchy—a very much more difficult oath, since it compelled the priests to invoke God Himself against His anointed. Only the Constitutional clergy could take such an oath with any comfort. The Roman priests refusing these new oaths became subject once more to the extreme penalties obtaining in 1792 and 1793. By 1797, however, the guillotine was out of fashion; deportation to Guiana was the normal fate of those who failed to arrange for their own emigration, and who were caught. The British Navy, engaged at that time in blockading the French coast, might save some of these unfortunates, as it saved the 108 priests on board the ship *La Vaillante*. Other ships might be compelled by the blockade to turn back into port with their cargoes. But 258 priests reached the ill-famed territory and 118 of them died there.

The less stupid of the revolutionary leaders appreciated that the assault upon Christianity would remain no more than a temporary manifestation of the grosser instincts of human nature, and would be transient in its effects, unless a positive faith were supplied to replace the old one. The Feast of Reason had been no faith but a folly; its successor, the Feast of the Supreme Being, had introduced at best a nebulous pantheism, and had lost its prestige with the execution of Robespierre, its high priest. Efforts were made, from time to time, to inject a little life into the appalling tedium of the ceremonies of the cult of the Tenth Day, the cult which for long had enjoyed a monopoly of the use of the great cathedrals of France. But although the municipal officials dressed in colourful costumes to read from the pulpits the new laws, or the announcements of births, marriages, and deaths; and although patriotic songs and the legalisation of marriages introduced variety, Paris was bored. Nor did the reading of instructive information about machinery or agriculture, or the recounting of stories of civic virtue, by means of which the authorities sought to enliven these occasions, achieve the desired effect. A new religion, theophilanthropy, was invented in 1796 and supported enthusiastically, though unofficially, by one of the Directors; by 1798 it was enjoying some vogue even in Saint-Sulpice and Notre Dame. The officiator wore white and blue vestments, and hymns to Nature were alternated with readings from the ancient philosophers as well as from the Koran and the Gospels. The theophilanthropists restored belief in a Supreme Being and in immortality, which had been frowned upon since the collapse of the Robespierre régime. But somehow the new cult failed to satisfy, and by the year 1798 access to the churches was becoming generally permissible, again, to all cults, and a priest saying his Mass was liable to provide a powerful counter-attraction to the readings from Seneca or Livy. If, however, the priest exceeded his time limit, he might find himself hailed before the tribunal for interfering with the "liberty of cults." Times were bad for priests who said Mass slowly!

Theophilanthropy went the way of the other religious innovations. The real successor to organised Christianity in France proved to be no rival faith but a licence and a profligacy which showed only its least harmful side in the suggestive fashions popularised by Thérèse Tallien and in the delirium of dancing in the churches, or the convents, or on the

Place de Grève, where the guillotine had stood. Of the various deities invoked by the ideologues of the French Revolution the Goddess Nature would seem to have been the one most in harmony with the spirit of the times, and of the different exhibits held up for popular veneration, no doubt the actress installed in Notre Dame was, after all, the most appropriate, though not even the classical temple upon which she was perched seems to justify the title of "Feast of Reason" for the performance over which she presided.

Yet amidst the persecution, the profligacy, and the prating of pompous official platitudes, the Faith still lay silent in the breasts of brave priests crowded into prisons or into boats, or hidden in the cellars or the cupboards of hospitable houses; in the hearts of those of heroic virtue who disguised themselves in order to pass amongst the condemned, following the very tumbrils with their words of comfort; in the bearing of some of those in exile who made a profound impression upon their hosts in Protestant countries; in the communities of nuns who adhered, throughout, amidst every hardship, to their devotions; amongst the faithful who contrived to find out the secret places where they could kneel behind the priest who was saying Mass. If some of the Romanists were more preoccupied, in their exile, with the fate of the monarchy than with the fate of the Church, if some of their bishops were blind adherents of the *ancien régime,* and if many of the Constitutional clergy dishonoured their calling, it is right that the sacrifice of the devoted, during a period of extreme trial, should be remembered, for without it the remarkable revival of the Church in France, in the following century, is unintelligible.

CHAPTER THREE

Napoleon (1799–1815)

From the time when the French Revolution decided, in the year 1789, to confiscate the property of the Church in France and to turn her priests into elected and salaried officials, conflict with Rome was inevitable. But what gave peculiar poignancy to the conflict was the genuine uncertainty in the minds of some even of the best French clergy as to where their duty lay. The schism between Constitutional and Roman priests, and a little later, the schism between the two groups of Romans themselves, those who followed Louis XVIII and continued (generally from abroad) to anathematise the Revolution, and those who stayed at home and accepted the new government, but not the Civil Constitution of the Clergy, weakened the united witness of Catholicism and disturbed the consciences of the faithful. If we are to try to find the source of this second schism we shall be likely to find it at Rome, and if we are inclined to apportion blame we shall be tempted to place much of it upon the shoulders of the papacy, since it would appear to have been for the papacy to make clear where the duty of the French clergy lay.

We should, however, be chary of placing too much of it on the shoulders of Pope Pius VI personally; for we have seen how his missive, recommending the Romanists to submit to the government, was suppressed in France. It is true that earlier he had delayed for several months before denouncing the Civil Constitution of the Clergy. It is also true that his known sympathies with Louis XVI, and with the counter-revolutionary moves of the *émigrés*, lent support to the views of the more extreme *émigré* Romanists, and helped to make more difficult the work of those who stayed behind to try to go on ministering, often in secrecy, to their flocks. But although one may criticise the elderly Pope (he was seventy-one years old in 1789) for failing to give a sufficiently prompt and clear lead, at any stage in the quarrel, we must remember that the policies of the successive French governments were always shifting, and Rome would not despair of accommodation. The greatest evil lay in that habit of mind which a century and more of Gallicanism had given to the French Church, the

habit of looking to the State and not to Rome in times of
crisis and difficulty. It had been this fact which had made the
lesser clergy, as we saw earlier, seek religious reform, in their
cahiers, from the Estates-General; and it was the same habit
which later caused some of them to look to the King, and
others to look to the revolutionary government when, in reality,
they should both have looked to Rome. And, if Rome was
to blame, this was less because Pius VI was infirm of purpose
than because in the eighteenth century the authority, throughout Europe, of the Holy See had sunk lower than at any time
since the confused years before the advent of Hildebrand
in the eleventh century.

All the same, Rome did not count for nothing in the eyes
of the new French rulers. The more perspicacious of them
knew very well, and none better than the young General
Bonaparte (occupied in 1796 with the French campaign in
northern Italy against the Austrians) that, if a clear directive
could be obtained from the Pope to the effect that it was the
duty of French Catholics to support their new government
and to pray for its success, the effect would be enormous. But,
as we saw in the last chapter, there were forces in the Constitutional Church, as well as in the government, which militated against an arrangement with Rome. And, indeed, it
cannot be said that Napoleon himself, when campaigning in
Italy in 1796 and 1797, was much interested in furthering
religious peace. He knew very well that an understanding with
Rome would make for stability in France and security for
the new régime; but then, the régime in Paris was not to
his taste, and already he intended to supersede it by placing
himself in power. So his policy was to let the religious
settlement with Rome wait until he himself was in a position
to make it along lines of his own choosing; he would not make
a present of it to those whom he regarded as his rivals.

So we find the young general, in the summer of 1796, spar-
ing three weeks to overrun rapidly the northern provinces of
the Papal States (Ravenna, Ferrara, and Bologna—often called
the Legations) and in the following winter running down as
far as Ancona, on the Adriatic, and dictating his terms to the
Pope at Tolentino. But he would not take the time or run
the risk of occupying Rome in force nor would he, as his
government in Paris was demanding, turn out the papal government and replace it by a French government—a step which
some of the Directors, in Paris, conceived would help to bring

the Church in France to heel. He contented himself with depriving the Pope of the Legations—to be incorporated soon in his Cisalpine Republic—of Ancona, and of Avignon (the papal enclave in France), together with a large sum of money, a selection of works of art, and the treasures which the faithful had bestowed upon the famous shrine of Our Lady at Loretto. He wanted to be back at Milan and pursuing his campaign against the Austrians; an occupation of Rome held no military advantages for him.

Nevertheless a French military occupation of Rome soon followed. The revolutionary ideas, fostered by the French minister, Napoleon's brother Joseph, were making headway amongst the Roman populace during 1797, and at the end of December there was a rising in the Trastevere quarter. As a sequel to this the French General Berthier occupied the city in January, and in February 1798 he carried off the aged Pontiff (now eighty years old) first to Siena, then to Florence. In the following year, with Napoleon away in Egypt, the Austrians again invaded Lombardy, and made a bid to release the head of the Church, who was then in course of being conveyed to Parma; so the French Government gave orders that the "citizen Pope" should be moved into France. Across the Alps, from Turin to Briançon, on roads still snow- and icebound, the aged invalid, paralysed in both legs, was painfully dragged; further yet he had to go, as the Austro-Russian armies closed on the French frontiers; but from Valence, where he was shut in the fortress, he could go no further and there, in August, with a prayer for the forgiveness of his enemies, he died.

Even Napoleon, who was to treat his successor as roughly, was moved when, on his return from his Egyptian campaign, he passed through Valence and was told the story. *"C'est trop fort!"* he exclaimed.

On account of the impossibility of assembling the cardinals in Rome, now occupied by Neapolitan troops, the conclave to select a successor to Pius VI was held at Venice. Only with the greatest difficulty, and after an interval of three months, did thirty-five penniless members of the Sacred College manage to reach the island of San Giorgio, facing the Piazzetta, where the Hapsburg Holy Roman Emperor, Francis II, placed the monastery at their disposal, together with some ducats for their expenses. In return, the Emperor hoped for the election of a congenial Pope; indeed he went so far as to indicate to a friendly cardinal his unwillingness to see the election of the candidate who seemed most likely to succeed, Bellisomi, Bishop of Cesena. He thus delayed the election of a new Pope by some weeks.

The state of affairs in Italy had changed very much during the past eighteen months. While Bonaparte had been away in Egypt, the Russian and Austrian armies had overrun the northern part of the peninsula, and the Russians had since retired, leaving the Austrians in control. The Emperor Francis II was willing enough that the new Pope should occupy Rome, together with much of his original states; but he was determined himself to hold on to the Legations Napoleon had seized from the Pope because, with Milan and Venice, they would give him the means of effectively controlling the peninsula.

By March 14, 1800, a compromise candidate, the Benedictine, Chiaramonti, Bishop of Imola, was at last elected, and he assumed the name of Pius VII. Francis was affronted, and refused his permission for the coronation to take place in the great Venetian cathedral of St. Mark's. The new Pope, equally spirited, refused to recognise the Emperor's right to the Legations. Francis II thereupon declined to allow the Pope to pass through the Legations en route to Rome, and embarked him instead, in an ill-manned ship, on a slow voyage down the coast to Pesaro. It was only on July 3, 1800, almost a year after the death of his predecessor, that Pius VII finally entered the Eternal City.

The new Pope's refusal, at the outset of his reign, to be patronised by "His Catholic Majesty," the Hapsburg Emperor, was early evidence not only of his determination to preserve his independence, to which he would always adhere, even against Napoleon at the height of his power, but was also a hint (since the Emperor represented the *ancien régime*) that he was not entirely hostile to the new revolutionary ideas which had now spread from France into Italy. As Bishop of Imola he had found himself, for a short time, a citizen of Bonaparte's Cisalpine Republic; to the surprise of many, and to the pleasure of Bonaparte, he had pronounced that there was nothing incompatible between democracy and the Gospel and had given the advice: "Be good Christians and you will be good Democrats." And now that he had reached

Rome he inaugurated his pontificate with a series of reforms. In the view of the conservatives he was a dangerous radical; moreover it was held against him that he was so young. Was it, they asked, wise, in these turbulent times to choose as Supreme Pontiff a youth of fifty-eight?

To Napoleon, however, the political open-mindedness of the new Pope was a point of some importance in his favour. Four months before Pius VII's election at Venice the young general had carried out (November 10, 1799) the *coup d'état* by which he established himself as First Consul of France; in the following June he won the victory of Marengo over the Austrians, which re-established the French hegemony in Italy. In January 1800 he had secured the pacification of the still-restive region of the Vendée by the simple but necessary expedient of allowing complete liberty to the Roman priests to restore the practice of the Catholic faith there. If the peace and the loyalty of the Vendée could thus be gained by granting what, at heart, the people most desired, why, he considered, could not the other disaffected regions, indeed the whole of France, be won by a similar gesture to the support of his new régime?

To Napoleon, with his realistic mind, it seemed the sensible course. The mass of the French people, he knew very well, was genuinely Catholic; the protracted quarrel with Rome and the persecution of the priests were therefore merely a source of weakness to the State. How much more sensible to make up the quarrel and so convert the Church in France from a brake upon the nation's strength into a driving force in her support, and in particular in support of his own régime! How much better to have contented and obedient congregations offering up prayers, after Mass, in the historic cathedrals and churches, in unison with their priests, for the safety and success of French arms and for the welfare of the First Consul and of his family!

How hypocritical was he?

Not altogether. His reconciliation with Rome did not involve him in so direct a change of religious front as it had involved Henry IV when that astute monarch had ended the French wars of religion by submitting to the Church. His early childhood memories were interwoven with the symbols of the Faith, he had a very strong belief in the value of a strict Catholic education for the young—especially for girls. Nothing, perhaps, in his whole remarkable life, was more re-

markable than that, the very day after the critical Battle of
Friedland, in Poland in May 1807, when the whole issue between his empire and that of the Tsars was at stake, he
settled down to dictate a long letter about the education of
the girls at the boarding school of Ecouen. "What are the girls
brought up at Ecouen going to be taught? You must begin
with religion in all its strictness. Don't allow any compromise
on this point. Religion is an all-important matter in a public
school for girls. It is the mother's surest safeguard, and the
husband's. What we ask of education is not that girls should
think, but that they should believe . . . in the Lycées I only
prescribed the necessary minimum. At Ecouen things must
be entirely different. Nearly all the exact knowledge taught
there must be that of the Gospels. I want the place to produce not women of charm, but women of virtue: they must
be attractive because they have high principles and warm
hearts, not because they are witty or amusing . . . every day
the pupils must have regular prayers, hear Mass, and learn
the Catechism." And the secondary education of boys (aimed
chiefly at producing soldiers and administrators) was likewise
to rest upon a Catholic foundation. The boy of twelve, as
Napoleon's best English biographer, J. M. Thompson, tells
us, was to be "marched from classroom to chapel and counter-
marched from chapel to classroom."

Nevertheless, if Napoleon believed in the value of a
Catholic education and if, despite himself, there lingered
within him, subconsciously, Catholic attitudes and propensi-
ties which belonged to his own upbringing, he was *non-
pratiquant*, save as reasons of state later made it advisable for
him to attend Mass. His active belief was in his own star
rather than in the Star of Bethlehem. And the natural inclina-
tions of his mind lay with the vaguely deistic notions of the
savants of the Institute, with whom he surrounded himself
during his Egyptian campaign. But his personal tastes mattered very little; his vocation was to govern, his destiny to control Europe, perhaps even the whole of civilisation. What mattered to him was to take account of all the relevant factors
and, in respect of France, and of most of Europe, the relevant
religious factor seemed to him to be that the people were
Catholics. And since they were Catholics it seemed to him
that the wise, and indeed the liberal thing to do was to re-
establish the Catholic Church where the Revolution, with
all its talk about Liberty, Equality and Fraternity, had, in

fact, tried to destroy it. "My political method is to govern men as the majority of them want to be governed. That, I think, is the way to recognise the sovereignty of the people. It was by making myself a Catholic that I won the war in the Vendée, by making myself a Moslem that I established myself in Egypt, by making myself an Ultramontane that I gained men's souls in Italy. If I were governing a people of the Jewish race I would rebuild the Temple of Solomon."

Though Napoleon's attitude towards the Church was opportunist, what matters to the historian of Catholicism is to notice that the tough resistance of the priesthood and the faithful in France, and in the territories the French armies occupied, during the ten years of the Revolution, had convinced the realistic man who, for the next fifteen years would be master of France and her dependencies, that he must base his power upon their alliance. That fact is of cardinal importance. It has been argued by some historians of the French Revolution, and most notably by one of the greatest, A. Aulard, that Napoleon, by making a concordat with Rome, suppressed a flourishing and fruitful diversity of cults, all enjoying toleration, because he wanted a unified political system which he could control in his own interests. But, in as much as the "Tenth Day" celebrations, together with the rituals of the theophilanthropists, had the backing of the Revolutionary State, while the Constitutional clergy enjoyed its grudging toleration, and the Roman clergy its active hostility, it is hardly a just view of the matter to regard the revolutionary religious régime which preceded Napoleon as one of "toleration"; and it is extremely significant that when Napoleon was looking for the widest measure of support he could find for his régime he looked to those who were obedient to the Roman priests, rather than to the Constitutionalists or to the supporters of the new religions, although the latter all depended upon the State, and so might be supposed to be the natural props of his new consular régime. The fact was that he chose the religion which he knew to be most deeply embedded in the French and western European conscience, although it was the only one which, spiritually speaking, owed a foreign allegiance, and the only one likely to make pretensions which might clash with his own political power. There has seldom been a more convincing tribute to the underlying strength of the Church than that it was recognised and accepted by this arch-realist, who could ill endure a rival authority.

Napoleon's approach to the new Pope was by way of some convincing demonstrations in northern Italy of his good will. On June 5, 1800, he told the anti-clerical patriots of the Cisalpine Republic, at Milan: "Leave your priests free to say their Mass; the People is sovereign; if it wants its religion, respect its will." And, already building up his position as the new Saint Louis, the new Charlemagne, the Protector of Western Christendom, he went on: "the French are the natural friends of Italy. What can you hope for from Protestants [the British], Greeks [the Russians of the Greek Orthodox Church], or Mohammedans [the Turks]?" (In the previous year the French had been fighting all three in the Mediterranean.) "The French, on the other hand, belong to the same religion as you. We may have had our quarrels, but those are all being settled now." Within ten days he had fought the Battle of Marengo, after which he attended a solemn *Te Deum* in the cathedral of Milan, being carried up to the choir on a dais.

While these impressive displays were going on in the north of Italy, the new Pope was painfully regaining the Eternal City, in the wretched craft provided by "His Catholic Majesty" of Austria. Scarcely had he arrived when he received, to his surprise and pleasure, Napoleon's first overtures.

After the overtures came the bargaining. It soon became apparent that the First Consul was a difficult man with whom to reach agreement. He expected a quick settlement, having understood that Pius was a saintly man, sympathetically inclined, and likely to be only too thankful to see the Church restored on any terms that might be offered. But the Pope, though ready enough to yield where the material possessions of the Church were concerned (he made no difficulty about writing off the loss of the Church's property in France) proved unyielding on matters concerning her spiritual rights and independence. For a whole year the battle was fought out in Paris, and the final result, though it favoured the State, was yet a tremendous achievement on the part of the patient and resourceful papal Secretary of State, Consalvi, who was matched against no less a figure than the ex-Constitutional Bishop of Autun, Talleyrand, now Napoleon's foreign minister. On July 15, 1801, the Concordat was at last signed, and since it lasted long and served as model for many later agreements, it is worth while to notice its principal provisions.

The Concordat was a treaty between "His Holiness Pius VII and the French Government." Though not recognised as the official religion of France, the "Catholic and Roman" religion was recognised in the Preamble as the religion "of the great majority of the French people." It was to be exercised freely and openly, but subject to such police regulations as the government might judge necessary for maintaining public order—this was the proviso invoked on many later occasions as an excuse for renewed governmental interference. All bishops, Constitutional or Roman, were to hand in their resignations, so that new ones might be nominated by the First Consul and invested by the Pope, who also acquired the power to depose them. The lesser clergy were to be nominated by the bishops and approved by the government. The cathedrals and churches were to be handed back to the clergy, and bishops and beneficed clergy were to be paid a suitable salary. There was, however, no provision for seminaries or for cathedral chapters.

Well might Consalvi congratulate himself. There was much that both he and the Pope would greatly have preferred to see agreed differently: for example, they would have preferred an endowment rather than state salaries for the clergy, and some provision for the vital matter of seminaries. But the gains were tremendous, the greatest being the disappearance of the Constitutional Church, and of the various new religions patronised by the Revolution. In one very important matter it was a real advance upon the old state of affairs under the *ancien régime*, for, in those heydays of Gallicanism, it had not been within the power of the Pope to depose a French bishop. But the overriding consideration, for the Pope, was to secure the reopening of the French churches, and the free ministration of the sacraments to the faithful by a clergy whom he could approve, and who were obedient to the laws of the Church. And Napoleon, anxious, if only for his own ends, to see a revitalised Church, was generally at pains to choose bishops of integrity, whom the Pope was able to invest. The majority were chosen from the sometime Romans, but a substantial minority were chosen from the ex-Constitutionalists. The way back into the fold was made easy for the latter, neither Consul nor Pope wishing to pursue a vendetta. Yet not all bitterness could be removed at the stroke of a pen and, in particular, the *émigré* clergy showed their resentment at what the Pope had done. Out of ninety-six *émigré* bishops (this number included some from Belgium and the Rhineland, now united to France), no less than forty-five refused the Pope's demand that they should place their sees at his disposal. They took the line that they had been appointed by the King, and without the consent of Louis XVIII they could not resign their sees. In this attitude those in England were encouraged by the British Government, while all alike were encouraged by Louis XVIII who, though a freethinker and a libertine, was determined to use any weapon which might lie to hand in his desire to restore his dynasty to the throne of France. We are bound to recognise that many of these priests were honest and courageous men, convinced of the rectitude of the course they were taking. But, by their determination, they only helped to create what came to be called the *Petite Eglise,* a schism which continued after the restoration of the Bourbons in 1815, and which even today is not quite extinct in France. The view of these men was that the Revolution was anti-Christ, and that to treat with it was to treat with the Devil himself. Pius VI, they pointed out, had not done so, and if, in consequence, he had lost his states and had died in exile, the successor of Saint Peter should expect to suffer martyrdom if need be. Pius VII, they freely said, by negotiating with the Revolution, incarnate in Napoleon, had betrayed the Church to save his states—a singularly unjust accusation since, in fact, the new Pope had forborne, during the negotiations over the Concordat, from raising the matter of the Legations, which were the most valuable part of his states, and they remained a part of the revolutionary Cisalpine Republic. Certainly the time would come when he would show the same readiness as his predecessor to suffer all things for the Church.

It is important to remember how desperate was the position from which the Concordat with Napoleon saved the Catholic Church; it may be that it was one more ominous than any to which she had been driven throughout the centuries of her history, since the time of the persecutions under the Roman Empire. Harassed in the land of France, traditionally her "eldest daughter," it was the same story in Belgium (now annexed to France), in the Rhineland (also annexed), in Italy, controlled by anti-clericals dependent upon France, in England and Ireland, where the movement for Catholic emancipation had been rejected by King George III, in Poland, partitioned by non-Catholic powers. Even in Austria, where "Josephism" survived, the Church was far from free, while the governments in Portugal and Spain were anti-clerical. The Concordat which Pius VII signed with Napoleon, followed as it was by another in Italy, and by provisional arrangements in Germany, not only served the immediate and vital purpose of enabling the life of the Church to be lived in relative security over much of Europe; it also reminded the world that the Church was not dependent upon any particular kind of political régime, certainly not upon the *ancien régime* of monarchy and aristocracy with which, to its detriment, it had come to be so closely identified. It could rest itself upon the protection of any established political power, always provided that it was granted the necessary liberties to enable it to live its own life, as a "perfect society," and to minister to its members.

However, the price of the Church's liberty has always been eternal vigilance, especially vigilance on the part of Rome, and Napoleon was soon to show how much Rome would need this quality when she was dealing with himself. For in publishing the Concordat, in April 1802, the First Consul published alongside it, without any previous consultation with Rome, what were called the "Organic Articles," designed to regulate the administration of the Church in France. His excuse was that he was only publishing the police regulations which the Concordat had allowed him to make for the maintenance of public order, but a glance at the articles in question shows only too clearly that he was, in fact, concerned to subject the Church, even in matters evidently spiritual, to the control of the State. Thus, no communications of any kind from Rome, or even from a General Council of the Church, were to be published in France without the *placet* of the government, nor were any provincial councils to be held, nor any papal representatives admitted, without similar approval. Still more distressing, no seminary was to be established without the First Consul's consent, and he must approve its regulations; no professor might teach in such a seminary unless he adhered to the Gallican decrees of 1682 (which curtailed the powers of the Church in France, and the powers of the Pope within that Church, and declared the superiority of General Councils to the Pope); and finally, there was to be one catechism and one liturgy for France, there were to be no feast days other than Sundays, and the civil contract must precede the religious ceremony in marriage. It was a bitter pill that the Pope had to swallow in accepting all this, which went so far to nullify the gains secured by the Concordat. And something similar was to follow in Italy, for, although in September 1803 a concordat was signed with the Italian Republic (the new name for the Cisalpine Republic), in the following January the vice-president, Melzi (Napoleon was himself President), published decrees concerning the administration of the Church which resurrected onerous forms of state control, such as had characterised the rule of the Austrians at Milan.

But it should not be supposed that the civil power asserted by Napoleon, and by his satellites in Italy and Germany, in opposition to Rome, necessarily always operated against Rome's interests or against those of the Church. It was a matter of how they were interpreted, and Napoleon, although he conceived of the Church as an institution to be used to inculcate the idea of obedience to his own régime, was concerned, if only for that very reason, to try to see that she was efficient. Thus he noted that the numbers of the clergy had been drastically reduced as a result of the virtual cessation of the training and ordination of priests under the Revolution, and he made no difficulty about the establishment of seminaries and was prepared to pay for six of them from state funds. He also took a firm line with the ex-Constitutional clergy. These priests, he found, were little inclined to make any formal act of submission to Rome because, in obeying the State, they conceived that they had only done their duty. Paradoxically, it was Napoleon himself who compelled them to make their submission to Rome, which was something they were quite prepared to do provided he told them to do it.

One result of lasting consequence to the Church in Europe, and ultimately to the whole world, which flowed from the reorganisation involved in the Concordat, was the appearance of a new centralisation within the Church itself. No longer were the lesser clergy nominated by private patrons, they were nominated by the bishops, and any promotion they gained they would owe to those same bishops. Likewise the cathedral chapters lost their significance; even the administration of vacant dioceses, granted to them by the Council of Trent, was now allotted to the metropolitan bishop. This strictly hierarchical organisation, which is characteristic of the Church today, is doubtless now a source of strength; but it is interesting and perhaps significant to notice that, in its modern form, it dates from the Napoleonic Concordat with Pius VII, and that it owes something, at least, to Napoleon's determination not to allow too much independence to the local curés. For he knew very well that the curés, in 1789, had launched the Revolution. The lesser clergy, after the Concordat, were strictly controlled—and shockingly paid.

In May 1804 a grateful Senate decreed that Napoleon was now Emperor of the French (already this meant of the Belgians, the Dutch, the Rhinelanders, and the North Italians as well) and that his position was hereditary; a plebiscite was held on this latter point, and it endorsed, overwhelmingly, the Senate vote. He was Emperor "by the grace of God and the Constitutions of the Republic"; it was a new title, and not one which was likely to make a profound impression upon the Tsar of Russia, the King of Prussia, the Austrian Emperor, or even King George III of England; but it would certainly appear much more impressive if the Pope were to give it his blessing by coming in person to Paris and crowning him. So, with this end in view, Napoleon invited Pius VII to his capital.

It was not easy for the Pope to accept the invitation. There was no precedent, over more than a thousand years, for a Pope travelling into France to crown a King. And, were he to do so now, the affront to His Christian Majesty, King Louis XVIII, to the bishops still in exile, and above all to the Hapsburg Emperor of Austria, must be cruel. And, in any case, was this a moment to bestow a special favour and honour upon France, the country which had launched the modern persecution of the Church, and some of whose bishops had still not made their submission to Rome since their acceptance of the Civil Constitution of the Clergy? For three months he hesitated; but Consalvi believed the advantages would outweigh the disadvantages, so, after some hard bargaining about the form of ceremony to be adopted, he agreed to make the long journey, accompanied by six cardinals, ten bishops, and a company comprising altogether more than a hundred persons, and conveyed in more than twenty coaches. Thus did the simple Benedictine monk, who personally preferred to make his own bed and mend his own clothes, travel in state over the Mont Cenis pass, in a convoy drawn by a hundred horses, and just ahead of the winter snows.

In the forest of Fontainebleau, while out hunting, Napoleon met the papal procession; it was a calculated "accident," which saved him from having to give a public and deferential greeting, in front of the Parisians, to his distinguished guest. But he lodged him handsomely enough, in the Tuileries, and already the preparations were well in hand: a new annex, in Gothic style, to the west front of Notre Dame, demolition of the choir screen and two altars, to make more room inside, and a roundup of such regalia from St. Denis as had escaped the Revolution. Unfortunately the crown and sword supposed to have been used for the coronation of Charlemagne were now in the keeping of the Hapsburg Emperor, and it was awkward, after defeating his army at Marengo, for Napoleon to approach him for the loan of them.

There were some thorny matters to be settled at the last moment between Emperor and Pope. Thus the Empress Josephine, Pius found to his astonishment, had only been through a form of civil marriage to her husband. Napoleon had kept this dark, but Josephine, only too well aware that the day might come when the Emperor would want to put her away in favour of a more distinguished spouse, let the truth be known so that she might gain the added security of a religious marriage. Napoleon was compelled to give way, and the marriage rite was performed on the very afternoon before the coronation. Then there was difficulty about the crowning itself; here Napoleon had his way and it was agreed, at the last moment, that, since he refused to receive the crown from the hands of the Pope, he should place it on his own head, receiving only the anointing from Pius; the story about his "snatching" the crown from the Pope is untrue. And finally he would neither go to confession beforehand, nor receive communion at the ceremony.

Despite the critics, at Rome and elsewhere, the visit of Pius VII to Paris, for the coronation, was immensely successful—perhaps, indeed, more fruitful in its results for the Pope than for the Emperor. The welcome given to the Head of the Church in the streets of Paris and in the churches which he visited there, the many men who pressed forward to make their communion or to receive rosaries, the women who crowded to have their wedding rings blessed, these were sights surprising, indeed, to an Italian whose ears had been filled only with tales of sacrilege and blasphemy in Paris. It had been worth the risk he took in coming, worth the offence to the Hapsburgs and to the *émigrés*. As the convoy rumbled back to Rome it passed, in the Pope's words, between a people on their knees; he knew now that the Faith had not been rooted out of France, that it was springing up to new life. By his visit he had helped to turn the sentiments of the rising generation of Catholics Romewards, to kindle in their hearts what to many was almost a new affection, an affection for the Holy See which would grow during the coming century until it supplanted the old Gallican loyalty and blossomed into a fanatical fervour in the later years of Pius IX and under his successors of the modern papacy. There were many more quarrels in store between the Popes and the spirit of the French Revolution, as it developed in Europe, but the gesture of reconciliation had been made, the Pope had gone to Paris, nursery of Europe's revolutionaries, he had shown he was not tied to the *ancien régime*, that there was always a home within the Church for men of good will, of any régime, who did not deny the Faith or persecute the faithful.

Such were the long-term consequences which made both the Concordat and the coronation worth while. But immediately, the honeymoon of the temporal and spiritual powers was brief, indeed, for Napoleon, partly because he had so little idea of what was vital to the spiritual life of the Church, quickly multiplied causes for offence. Thus it seemed natural enough to the Emperor that he should honour both himself and the obscure saint, of doubtful authenticity, after whom his mother had named him, by instituting a Feast of Saint Napoleon on August 16, thereby displacing Saint Roch, whose feast fell on that day, and instituting a feast with which he himself would be personally associated, on the day following the great Feast of the Assumption, with which the Bourbons were associated. He could not see that this creation of feast days was an intolerable interference on his part in the spiritual sphere, and one bound to cause serious concern at Rome.

Nor could he see any objection to his rewriting of the catechism so that the commentary following the Fourth Commandment was made to include instructions of value to the Emperor: "Christians owe to the Princes who govern them, and we, in particular, owe to our Emperor Napoleon, love, respect, obedience, loyalty, military service and the taxes ordered for the preservation and defence of the Emperor and his throne: we also owe him fervent prayers for his safety . . ." This reply is followed by: "*Question*: Are there special reasons why we should be more deeply devoted to Napoleon I, our Emperor? *Answer*: Yes there are: for it is he whom God raised up in difficult circumstances to re-establish the public worship of the Holy Religion of our ancestors, and to be its Protector . . . he has become the Lord's Anointed by the consecration he received from the Sovereign Pontiff, the Head of the Universal Church . . . *Question:* What ought one to think of those who fail in their duty towards our Emperor? *Answer:* According to the Apostle St. Paul they would be resisting the order established by God Himself, and rendering themselves worthy of eternal damnation . . ." This was not a catechism which ever had the approval of Rome, but it did have the approval of the French bishops.

It was, however, Napoleon's Italian policy which led to the final rupture of relations with the Pope, outwardly so cordial in Paris. The Emperor had followed up the ceremony in Notre Dame by having himself anointed King of Italy in the Duomo of Milan (the Italian republic was now a kingdom) and placing the historic crown of Lombardy upon his own head. In spite of the Pope's protests he had maintained the secularist legislation in Italy and, in particular, the civil-marriage laws which so shocked traditional Italian opinion. But it was his war policy which brought matters to a head. In February 1806 Napoleon turned the Bourbons out of Naples and put his brother Joseph on the throne. The Papal States were now shut in, from north and south; they had lost the Legations in the north, and the ports of Ancona on the east and Civitavecchia on the west coast, which Napoleon had seized to prevent them from falling to the British Navy; but they remained, nevertheless, the one part of Italy not under French control. Meanwhile, it had become the Emperor's policy to compel Britain, his most persistent enemy, to sue for peace, by closing the entire continental coast line to her shipping; almost the whole of this coast line was by now under his control, but the coasts of the Papal States were an exception. He therefore ordered the Pope to enter into his system and to exclude the British. Was not Britain a Protestant power? Was he not the new Charlemagne? Wherein could there lie any difficulty?

Yet Pius VII, entirely at the Emperor's mercy, obstinately refused and quietly asked for the return of the Legations, of Ancona, and of Civitavecchia. He explained that his sacred office made it quite impossible for him to enter into any general military alliance against England, a power that had not offended him. Napoleon, declaring that the court of Rome was the most unreasonable power in the world, reminded the Pope that the Emperor Charles V had imprisoned Pope Clement VII, and Philip the Fair had arrested Boniface; if Pius did not comply with his wishes, he would cancel the

Donation of Charlemagne and eliminate the Papal States altogether. Still Pius refused; so in January 1808 Napoleon sent General Miollis to occupy the castle of Sant' Angelo in order to overawe the Vatican. If the Pope would impose the blockade against British commerce he should retain his states, if not he should lose them. Pius maintained his refusal. He had already sacrificed his great Secretary of State, Consalvi, in 1806, to placate Napoleon, but it had been of no use, for Napoleon now ordered the expulsion from Rome of all the cardinals who were subjects of the Emperor or of his satellites; even the new Secretary of State, Doria, had to go. Pius replaced him by Gabrielli, but Gabrielli was duly arrested and sent away to Sinigaglia. Pius thereupon appointed Cardinal Pacca and retained him in his own apartments to prevent his arrest. In May 1809 Napoleon formally incorporated the whole of the Papal States into his empire; on June 10, General Miollis raised the French flag upon the Sant' Angelo, and Pius barricaded himself into the Quirinal and issued a Bull excommunicating those, however eminent, who attacked the Holy See. Napoleon's reply to this was that a priest who preached discord when he should preach peace was abusing his office and ought to be arrested. Thereupon General Miollis (acting, perhaps, prematurely—rather in the spirit of those knights who rushed off to Canterbury Cathedral when they heard King Henry II of England cry "who will rid me of this turbulent priest?") sent a subordinate, General Radet, with a party of troops with scaling ladders, forced an entry into the Quirinal, and arrested the Pope, who was rushed off, at a half hour's notice, with no change of clothes and no money, on an improvised journey, shut up in a locked coach, in the heat of July, along with his Secretary of State, Cardinal Pacca.

For forty-two days they travelled, stopping at wayside inns, right up the peninsula to the Alps, to Avignon, and finally down to Savona on the Italian coast west of Genoa; on the journey the Pope developed dysentery. Napoleon pretended afterwards that he had never intended the outrage; he said he would have preferred to supervise more closely "an operation of such importance." But he made no attempt to restore the Pope to Rome, and he prepared for him the archbishop's palace in Paris, which he had decided would be a more convenient location in future for the Head of the Church.

At Savona, though lodged comfortably at the bishop's palace, Pius preferred once more to become the "poor monk

Chiaramonti," washing his own clothes, sewing on his own buttons, reading, praying. His Secretary of State was removed from him and was held a close prisoner in the fortress of Fenestrelle. Deprived of his councillors, and even of his secretaries, the Pope tried, at first, to continue to conduct, through his valet, the most essential business of his office, but when Napoleon discovered that he had written to Cardinal Maury, deploring his acceptance of the See of Paris, he ordered the removal of his writing paper, pen, ink, and "all means of writing." To this the Pope could only reply by passive resistance, but it was effective resistance because, if he could not write, he could not invest with their sees the bishops newly created by Napoleon, and this proved to be extremely awkward for the Emperor, since the bishops, Gallican though many of them were, did not regard themselves as canonically invested without the Pope's approval.

Throughout the years 1810 and 1811, when Napoleon was at the height of his power, master of the whole continent save Russia, and with even the Tsar his ally, Pius held out, while the Emperor raged against the "imbecile old man." Every effort (including, as would seem likely, on one occasion, an extra dose of a sedative, administered to him by his doctor, Portal) was used to try to secure his compliance with the various demands brought to him by Napoleon's envoys; but they never secured his signature. He continued to demand that he be enabled to return to Rome, that he be free in all respects to play his part as Pope, that his states be restored to him. He continued to decline to invest the bishops, and even managed to smuggle out a letter to Cardinal Maury to reprimand him for assuming the archbishopric of Paris and to inform him that all his acts and decrees would be regarded as null and void. Napoleon tried to meet the situation by summoning to Paris first an ecclesiastical committee, and then an imperial council comprising six cardinals, eight archbishops, and twenty-one bishops; but from neither of these bodies did he obtain full satisfaction. It is true that he gained ecclesiastical approval for the annulment of his marriage to poor Josephine (whose church ceremony had thus failed to save her) and a Notre Dame marriage to Princess Marie Louise of Austria, although half the cardinals dared his displeasure (and suffered severely) by refusing to attend this royal wedding. It is true, also, that the French bishops told Napoleon that the papal excommunication, since it did not name him personally, and since it concerned a temporal matter (the seizure of the Papal States), need not be held to cut him off from the Church. But the investiture difficulty was not solved, the Pope would not consider coming to Paris, and increasingly some of the French bishops, and some of the younger clergy, began to show resistance, being greatly encouraged in this by the magnificent example of M. Emery, superior at the seminary of Saint-Sulpice, who had often bravely stood his ground during the Revolution and who now withstood Napoleon, in full council, for two hours of argument. This last effort literally killed him; he died within a month of making it. But his example was effective with those who were beginning to lead France forward into ultramontanism.

By the fateful year 1812 Napoleon had decided that he must settle matters personally with the Pope. He was preparing his great invasion of Russia, with the Grande Armée, to punish the Tsar Alexander for lifting the continental blockade against England. He intended this to be his decisive campaign, the prelude to a general peace on his own terms. On his return to Paris, master of the world, he meant to settle the religious question once and for all, and for this he would need to have the Pope closer to hand. So he arranged to have him removed to Fontainebleau, where he must await the return of the conqueror.

Accordingly, at midnight on June 9, 1812, the Pope was carried secretly to a waiting coach. Its lights were shaded, the rims of its wheels were bound around with cloth, its mules had had their iron shoes removed, and their white bodies were blackened. Silently the Pope was conveyed away from the episcopal palace, in which, to aid in the deception, the lights were kept on in his room, food was carried to and fro, and a ceremonial visit was paid each day, for fifteen days, by the prefect.

But the Pope's escort, Lagorce, though he had had his prisoner dressed humbly in black, though he kept the windows curtained, though he had prepared relays of horses and organised everything for a rapid and secret journey, found himself confronted, as the coach mounted the Mont Cenis pass, with an unexpected hazard, for the Pope became acutely ill. When they took him to the hospital at the top of the pass the doctor said he could not travel further without endangering his life. Desperate, Lagorce appealed for instructions; he was told that the journey must continue. So the Pope was given the last sacraments, a litter was provided so that he could lie down in the coach, and Lagorce jostled on. Pius reached Fontainebleau alive, on June 19, after ten days of agony; but he took many weeks to recover.

There had, after all, been no hurry. Napoleon had expected to be back from Russia in August, but it was not until December 18 that he returned, with one companion, and dictated his bulletin announcing the dissolution of the Grande Armée, and leaving a quarter of a million dead, frozen, or starving men in the Russian snows. The circumstances were not quite those in which he had hoped to have his conversations with the Pope at Fontainebleau; moreover it was necessary to raise a new army as quickly as possible and go into battle again, in Germany, against the menacing Prussian and Russian armies. All the same, a settlement with the Church was more important than ever, and the day after he reached Paris he wrote personally to Pius (his first letter to him for six years), assuring him of his "continued friendship" and his determination "to put an end to the differences separating Church from State." He sent in advance cardinals and bishops favourable to his designs; their visits to Fontainebleau were without effect, but they were received patiently and courteously—all, that is, except the disobedient Cardinal Maury, whose uncanonical occupation of the archbishopric of Paris Pius could in no wise endure, and to whom it was made very clear that his visits to Fontainebleau were unwelcome. Then followed the Emperor himself, bursting into the palace and embracing the august prisoner, with whom he now spent six days absolutely alone.

What passed between them?

Nobody knows, but many have tried to guess. Whether Napoleon smashed a set of Sèvres china or pulled the Pope's hair, or whether Pius, as Alfred de Vigny has it, ridiculed his infuriated gaoler, the issue of the *tête-à-tête* was a scrap of paper, signed by Pius, in which it was agreed, as the basis of a new understanding, that the Pope should exercise his powers in France and Italy as heretofore, be compensated for his territorial losses, and have his administrative staff, his diplomatic representation, and the papal archives returned to him "wherever he should reside." Thus the issue whether the Holy See should be in Paris or in Rome was left in abeyance for the time being. But Napoleon's most immediate need, that the Pope should either invest the new French bishops or should agree that after a period of six months the metropolitan might do so, was conceded by the Pope.

As soon as he was back in Paris the Emperor published these purely provisional and confidential "Heads of Proposals" as a new concordat called the "Concordat of Fontainebleau," and ordered *Te Deums* in honour of the reconciliation of Church and State; when Pius sent him a formal retraction he suppressed it. "He has betrayed me," said the Pope, and, in his bitter indignation, and in his self-reproach, he fasted, and spoke of himself as "defiled." Whereupon Napoleon reduced him once more to a captivity as close as he had suffered at Savona; this time he was allowed no visitor at all, not even to serve his Mass.

Who would have supposed, in the spring of the year 1813, when Napoleon rode forth with his new army to do battle in Germany and the Pope was an ailing and solitary prisoner at Fontainebleau, that within a year the Pope would be driving forth from the palace gates, to return, openly and in triumph, to Rome, while the Emperor, at the same palace, would have signed his own unconditional abdication, and would have been hurried, in custody and secrecy—as he had compelled the Pope to travel—along the southern road to the Mediterranean, and to exile at Elba? Yet such was the will of the god of battles in whom the Emperor had trusted. ("Does he imagine," Napoleon had asked about the Pope, a few years earlier, "that his excommunication will make the weapons fall from the hands of my soldiers . . . ?")

A little later, when he heard the rather exaggerated reports of Napoleon's sufferings on the island of St. Helena, Pius ordered Consalvi to write to London, to the Prince Regent, to ask him to lighten the lot of the exile. ". . . to Napoleon more than to anyone, save God alone, is due the restoration of our holy religion in the great Kingdom of France. The pious and courageous initiative of 1801 has long ago effaced the memory of later wrongs. Savona and Fontainebleau were only mistakes due to temper, or the errors of an ambitious man: the Concordat was the saving act of a Christian and a hero."

This, surely, was an expression of forgiveness saintlike in its quality.

CHAPTER FOUR

The Restoration of 1815

When in May 1814 Pius VII returned after his long exile to the Quirinal palace, in Rome, he found on the walls paintings of naked classical goddesses—the fashion of the times, and a decoration intended to be enjoyed by Napoleon, who had been expected to take up his residence there from time to time. "We will give them a little more to wear," remarked the Pope, "and so make them into Madonnas."

So Rome would strive to "baptise the past" as, centuries before, she had baptised the pagan Temple of Vesta, or the ancient Roman Pantheon, turning them into places of Christian worship. But would she succeed in "baptising the principles of 1789," in Christianising the Revolution? That was the real challenge. To many the French and European revolutions seemed incapable of conversion, they had been intrinsically evil, a work of the devil—such was the teaching of the powerful philosopher, Count Joseph de Maistre, as well as the rather natural opinion of the restored Bourbons and *émigrés*. On the other hand a new generation had grown up in the Church since 1789, a generation which looked differently at the whole political problem, which saw no antithesis between Catholicism and liberty, and which found expression in the words of Dupanloup, the later Bishop of Orleans, when he cried: "we accept, we invoke the principles and the liberties proclaimed in '89 . . . you made the Revolution of 1789 without us, and against us, but for us, God wishing it so in spite of you."

"There was yet some good in them," said Pius IX, later, of the Principles of 1789, "for instance, equality of all before the Law." And the work of Napoleon, intolerable in its attempt to subject the Church to the service of the State, had yet destroyed an archaic system of privilege in Italy and Germany which had nothing to commend it from a spiritual point of view. If the Church had suffered, alongside the society in which she had been rooted, it had been at least partly because she had reflected, on the material side, a privileged social, judicial, and political régime, which was no longer felt to be tolerable. The new passion for liberty and equality was a passion compounded of good and evil. If, on the one hand, it was violent and often degenerated into mere blind envy and iconoclasm, on the other hand, at its best, and especially amongst some of the clergy who supported the Revolution, it enshrined a truly Christian hankering after a more just society. Moreover, looking at the problem, as Rome was bound to look at it, from the point of view of the freedom enjoyed by the Church in pursuing her own spiritual purposes, a return to the conditions of the *ancien régime* seemed to have little to commend it. For the *ancien régime*, as we have already noticed, was the heyday of State-controlled Churches, when the See of Peter was reduced to a position in which it was almost ineffectual, and when the intellectual life of Europe was becoming ever more estranged from all religion.

Historians have very generally blamed Rome for her failure, in the period between 1815 and 1870, to understand and to harmonise her policies with the new spirit of liberalism. Whether that criticism is justified is probably the most difficult as well as the most important problem relating to Church history in the nineteenth century; to it is related the equally serious criticism that she failed, until the pontificate of Leo XIII (1878–1903), to make a serious attempt to meet the social problem of the new industrial proletariat, allowing the workers to drift away from Christianity. But whatever the justice of these criticisms, to which we must return later, the immediate problem in the year 1815 was the restoration of the organised life of the Church, all over the continent, which had been completely dislocated by Napoleon's moves and countermoves and by the occupation of Rome and the imprisonment of the Pope.

During the five years of his imprisonment Pius VII had withheld his approval from the appointments to episcopal sees made by Napoleon and by his satellite governments. For this reason a large number of sees throughout Europe were unoccupied in 1814; others were occupied by "bishops" whose tenure was uncanonical. Moreover the *Curia* had been prevented from exercising even the ordinary magistracy of the Church by the fact that the very archives had been removed from Rome and lodged in Paris. The confusion had become further complicated by the territorial readjustments which took place in Europe, not only in Napoleon's time, but after his exile. Thus the Rhineland, traditionally Catholic, and of which extensive regions had been ruled over by ecclesiastics like the Archbishops of Cologne, Mainz, and Trier, who were also temporal princes, had become merged in Napoleon's French Empire or in his Confederation of the Rhine. After the fall of the Emperor these old states were not restored and the Germanic Confederation which appeared in their place was founded upon the Napoleonic reorganisation. But, since the conquerors of Napoleon must have their reward, very substantial gains in the Rhineland were made in 1815 by Protestant Prussia, whose King, Frederick William III, thus became the ruler of a large Catholic population.

Poland presented another problem. Napoleon had created an independent Grand Duchy of Warsaw, thus reconstituting a great Catholic state which had been destroyed by the partitions of the eighteenth century—not the least of the services to the Church for which Pius VII was grateful to him. But in 1815 Protestant Prussia regained the Polish territory of Posen (which she had earlier seized in the second partition of Poland in 1793) while Orthodox Russia acquired a general suzerainty over what remained, which was euphemistically called the "Kingdom of Poland." Moreover the territorial position in the peninsula of Italy, on the doorstep of Rome herself, was highly confused. Napoleon had made one of his generals, Murat, King of Naples; at the crisis of the Emperor's fortunes he had turned traitor, had joined the allies, and was trying, in 1814, to create a united and independent Italian kingdom of his own, an enterprise which involved him in occupying Rome and the Papal States while Austria, watchful to forestall him, had occupied the northern part of those states—the Legations of Ravenna, Ferrara, and Bologna.

Pius VII had thus returned to Rome, in the summer of 1814, to find himself no longer in effective possession of his own states, and to find Europe in so grave a political confusion that he could hardly tell with whom to attempt to negotiate the re-establishment of her Churches. Confronted, on his doorstep, with Murat, anxious to relieve him of his principality; in Germany with a rationalist Bishop of Constance—Wessenberg—who was heading a movement directed towards forming a schismatic German National Church; in South America with revolutions which were throwing out the Catholic hierarchy along with the Spanish temporal power; it is not surprising that the Pope, though by no means by nature a

blind conservative, felt driven towards the view that Rome
should, for the sake of order, lend her support to the re-
establishment of the traditional monarchies. Her first consideration had necessarily to be to restore and to foster the life
of the Church, and for this it was vital to provide for the
vacant sees, to secure the obedience, or sometimes the removal, of those uncanonically invested, and to enable the life
of the religious orders to be renewed where it had been violently disrupted by the closure of monasteries and convents.
One necessary step was to restore that Society of Jesus whose
suppression by Clement XIV in 1773 had been the prelude
to two generations of disaster. An equally essential need was
to make provision for seminaries for the training of priests.
The widespread closure of the seminaries, the hostility displayed by many of the revolutionary governments towards the
pursuit of vocations, and the involvement of most of the young
manhood of Europe in war had created by the year 1815 a
general shortage of priests, especially acute in France, and had
also had a most deleterious effect upon the quality of theological study.

If, in these conditions, Rome had to strive as best she might
for the renewal of the life of the Church in all her different
members, the only way in which she could accomplish this,
after the year 1815, was to make concordats with the different
governments, mostly monarchical, which were restored as a result of the Congress of Vienna. It is a mistake, though one
which is often made, to suppose that because the general settlement of Europe in 1815 was achieved by the restoration of
monarchies, mostly absolute in character, and because Rome
entered into understandings with these monarchies, mostly by
means of concordats, she thereby gave the sanction of her
special blessing to the monarchical form of government, or to
what was called the "principle of legitimacy." Two examples
are sufficient to show that this was not the case: when Napoleon escaped from Elba and embarked upon the adventure of
the "Hundred Days," which led to his defeat at Waterloo, the
allied powers, in their concern to defeat him, sought from the
Pope that he should excommunicate the "usurper" and should
call upon Catholics to resist him. But, true to his principle of
political and military neutrality—which had previously operated in favour of England—Pius refused to do this, in spite of
the fact that the advance of Murat from Naples, in support
of Napoleon, compelled him to withdraw yet again from

Rome, though for a few weeks only, and go to Genoa. He took the line that, if the French wanted Napoleon, he was not prepared to use spiritual sanctions to persuade them to embrace the Bourbons. And again, a little later, when the Tsar Alexander sought to secure a spiritual blessing for his "Holy Alliance" of legitimate monarchs, the Pope, well aware that the settlement of 1815 was a very imperfect one, and of the greedy ambitions and intentions which governed the minds of many of the restored rulers, turned a deaf ear to the Tsar's suggestions.

Pius VII, in fact, remained throughout his life faithful to the principle he had laid down in his utterance before he became Pope, when he was Bishop of Imola (a diocese in Napoleon's "Cisalpine Republic"), the principle that there was nothing to prevent good Catholics from being good republicans. Rome, as she had often shown in the past, could have very happy relations with republics. But one thing was absolutely necessary to the Church, and therefore to Rome, in Pius VII's stormy days, as in all days, namely that there should be established government and order in all countries, and that the ruling powers, of whatever kind they might be, should allow to the Church her rights and liberties. The position in Europe in the year 1815 was that, after a generation of upheaval and war, it seemed to most responsible people that the ordering of society had been better achieved by the traditional hereditary monarchies, and that it would be wise to return to them. It was on this tide of opinion that the Bourbons were restored to France, to Spain, and to Naples, and to it the various lesser princes of the German and Italian states owed their return. Confronted, therefore, with governments of this kind, Pius VII, guided by his brilliant Secretary of State, Cardinal Consalvi, struck such bargains as he was able with a view to providing for the life of the Church.

They were often not easy to strike. The restored rulers might execrate the name of Napoleon, but they very generally shared with him a desire to subject the Church to the State, and the least they were expecting was to be restored to a relationship with Rome of the Gallican kind, which had provided the general pattern under the *ancien régime*. Thus King Louis XVIII of France, a Voltairean sceptic in his youth, though persuaded by the tumultuous events of the years 1789 to 1814 that Catholicism had much to commend it, as an ally

of law and order, proved little inclined to offer greater freedom
to the Church in France than had been granted by Napoleon.
Consalvi found it best, after years of patient negotiation,
simply to renew the Napoleonic Concordat of the year 1801.
With certain modifications—notably an increase in the number
of bishoprics to be endowed—that Concordat was, in fact, renewed in the year 1819. Even the Organic Articles, by which
the Church had remained at the mercy of the Napoleonic
State, remained the law of France, although it was hoped
and expected that only when relations between the King and
Rome were very bad would the former insist upon censoring
communications from Rome, or upon excluding any papal
envoy, as those articles permitted him to do.

The French Concordat of 1801 served likewise as a model
for agreements signed between Rome and other powers, with
modifications according to place and circumstance. Thus in
the Kingdom of Naples the Church secured more exclusive
rights, for instance in the field of education; in Prussia and
in the Kingdom of the Netherlands (the present Holland and
Belgium), which were ruled over by Protestant kings, she had
to be content with less, although she successfully maintained
her principle that in such countries the King could not nominate the bishops, as Catholic kings were permitted to do.

In short, if it is true that Rome hailed with a profound
relief the general restoration of monarchical governments in
1815, this was rather because she anticipated a general return
of law and order and peace than because she secured from
those governments any special privileges. Peace, thanks chiefly
to the guiding genius of the Austrian chancellor, Prince Metternich, was very generally maintained until the year 1848,
and during that period a real renewal of the life of the Church
became very evident. Yet the historian today can perceive very
clearly that the renewed vigour of the Church in the nineteenth century, which contrasts so favourably with her quies-
cence in the eighteenth, owes more to the Napoleonic Concordat of 1801 than it does to the restoration settlements of
1815 and the years immediately following. For it was in 1801
that Rome secured the vital principle that she could refuse
to invest the bishops chosen by the ruler or could, if necessary,
remove those whom she had already invested. In the long run
these rights, so necessary to the independence of the Church,
were to prove a mortal blow to the old-fashioned Gallicanism,
with its doctrine of the supremacy of the State, and were to

open the way to the ultramontanism that developed so fast in the pontificate of Pius IX (1846–78), and which has become an important characteristic of the Church today.

In the restoration settlements of 1815 Rome made no attempt to recover the extensive lands and properties which had been alienated from the Church, all over Europe, during the time of troubles. And the ecclesiastical principalities, which had been a feature of eighteenth-century Europe, and notably of the Rhineland, were never restored. Yet, paradoxically, Cardinal Consalvi fought a prolonged battle with consummate skill, both before and during the Congress of Vienna, for the restoration of the whole of the temporal domains of the papacy. He was not entirely successful, because he lost the papal city of Avignon to France, and he lost the Principality of Benevento to Naples, although for this latter he obtained some compensation. But the Papal States proper, extending from the mouth of the river Po down as far south as Ancona, on the Adriatic coast of Italy, and down to more than sixty miles south of Rome, on Italy's western shore, he recovered *in toto*.

Without question Cardinal Consalvi was the greatest statesman whom Rome produced in the modern age. As the negotiator of the Concordat with Napoleon, and the man who persuaded Pius VII to go to Paris to crown the Emperor, the Church owes to him her restoration in France on tolerable terms after the French Revolution. Moreover, after 1815, it was he who, in the teeth of the opposition of the conservative cardinals, the *Zelanti*, insisted upon retaining the more beneficial of the changes introduced into the Papal States by Napoleon's administration, and it was he who prevented harsh reprisals against those who had served the Corsican conqueror. But he combined a sense of what was practicable and prudent with an equally strong sense of the points upon which the Church could not yield; and it was Napoleon's keen realisation of this latter quality in Pius VII's Secretary of State that had led him to compel the Pope to sacrifice the cardinal in 1806, an event which prefaced the later lamentable impasse between Emperor and Pope.

With his firm grasp both of principle and practice, Consalvi combined an excellent judgement of those with whom he was dealing and skill in the technique of negotiation. It is an open question whether the palm should be given to him or to Talleyrand amongst the diplomats of the Congress of Vienna; in the opinion of the British representative, Lord Castlereagh—

no mean judge—Consalvi "surpassed them all," and it was Talleyrand himself who proposed that the papal Secretary of State should be invited to join the inner ring of representatives of the principal powers, which controlled the Congress, and indeed that he should be given the presidency. Consalvi declined both suggestions. He saw that if he accepted he would inevitably involve Rome in taking sides in the bargaining between the powers. It seemed better for her to stand outside the conflict, while reiterating her demand for her traditional rights—a course of action, it should be added, toward which his own and his court's poverty helped to drive him, since he was unable to maintain an entourage or to provide parties on the scale which the Russian and Austrian plenipotentiaries deemed indispensable.

Consalvi, of course, like the plenipotentiary of defeated France, was in no position to "negotiate from strength." So far as material resources were concerned he represented a sovereign who was obliged to leave his capital on the approach of even a Neapolitan army. But he had one very powerful card to play, namely the universal respect felt for Pius VII. The mutual jealousies of the powers were such that it was intolerable to all of them that any one of their number (and particularly Austria, the most powerful) should gain a preponderant position in Italy. There were numerous plans to give the northern part of the Papal States (the Legations) to one ruler or another—for instance to Napoleon's widow, the Hapsburg Marie Louise, who was a favourite candidate and seemed to deserve some compensation for her ill fortune. Again, while Murat was still King of Naples (he was captured and executed for his support of Napoleon during the Hundred Days) he made a strong bid to retain the Marches (the district north of Ancona), which he had occupied. But the integrity of Pius VII, and the policy of strict neutrality which his interpretation of his sacred office had led him to pursue, were strong arguments for restoring to him the whole of the traditional territories of the Papal States in central Italy, arguments which appealed particularly to the British Government (Consalvi called upon the Prince Regent in London) and to Talleyrand, both of whom disliked equally the notion of an Austrian-dominated Italy or of a "Jacobin" or "Carbonari" Italy, united by revolutionary means, which was supposed to be Murat's objective. It is strange, in the light of all that was to follow during the nineteenth century, to remember that

British and French diplomacy united at Vienna to safeguard the restoration of the Papal States.

But it is also in the light of what was to follow that an historian of the Church must question whether it was really in her true interests that she should achieve this political success. The Papal States, the oldest sovereignty in Europe, had originated in the gift of the Carolingian kings of the eighth century, whose very proper intention had been that the Holy See should possess sufficient temporal substance to prevent her from being at the mercy of every turbulent faction in central Italy. In the Middle Ages this temporal power had very largely achieved the purpose for which it was intended, and, even as late as the sixteenth century, though insufficient to protect the Pope from an invading Holy Roman Emperor, or from a King of France, it was sufficient to give the Bishop of Rome independence from the domination of a Medici at Florence or a Sforza at Milan. But already, in that century, it was becoming a serious danger to the spiritual functions of the papacy, because it involved the Popes in entering into the field of Italian state politics, which were becoming highly competitive, and into pursuing policies which may have been necessary when Italian princes, educated by Machiavelli, were becoming more formidable, but which could not fail to push the papacy into an undue preoccupation with Italian political issues. However, in the strenuous days of the Catholic Reformation, during the second half of the sixteenth and throughout the seventeenth century, the Popes rose far above their parochial Italian problems and took a European and a world view of their mission; while in the eighteenth century the Italian peninsula was not a major theatre of active conflict. In the nineteenth century, with the rising tide of the new nationalism, and with new Italian ambitions for the political reorganisation of the peninsula, the extensive Papal States necessarily became a major preoccupation for the Pope, while their usefulness as a source of protection and independence was much less in an age when the great powers had taken over the virtual control of Europe.

Today the political independence of the Vatican State (which corresponds closely, in area, with the Leonine State of the fifth century, before the Carolingian accretions) rests upon its international guarantee. The Papal States of 1815, restored to their fullest extent by the exertions of Consalvi, also rested upon international guarantee, which was their real safeguard. But whereas today no foreign political power is likely to have economic or political reasons for seeking to encroach upon the Vatican City, a papal principality which cut right across the centre of the Italian peninsula, and which counted three million subjects, was an economic and political reality and not merely a convenient legal token. Moreover, the part which Consalvi fought so hard to win, namely the Legations of Bologna, Ferrara, and Ravenna, was the part which, economically and politically speaking, was least like Rome and least enamoured of her. The Legations (sometimes called the Romagna) had a long tradition of hostility to Rome, from which they were separated by more than two hundred miles and by the Apennine mountains; economically speaking they belonged in the Po valley, and looked towards Milan, to which, indeed, they had been joined in Napoleon's Cisalpine Republic and in his Kingdom of Italy. It was from this region that the later revolutionary hostility to the Papal States, during the revolution of the Italian Risorgimento, would come, and it may well seem that it would have been the better part of wisdom for Consalvi to abandon the papal claim to them, which had indeed been renounced by Pius VI in the Treaty of Tolentino in 1797.

But as against this judgement, which is easier to pronounce in the twentieth century than it was in 1815, two important considerations, which weighed with Consalvi, have to be borne in mind. One is that the Legations were, economically speaking, much the most valuable part of the Papal States; indeed, as was found later, Umbria, the Marches, and the Patrimony of Saint Peter were hardly economically viable without them. And the other is that the great power which was seeking to establish itself at Bologna was Austria, already in possession of Venice and Milan, and also, through members of her ruling Hapsburg family, a controlling influence in the Italian Duchies of Modena, Parma, and Tuscany. The influence exercised after 1815 by Prince Metternich, the Austrian chancellor, in Italy was immense; if the Austrian Empire were to be allowed to extend across the Po to Bologna, all independence for the Papal States (which might still be achieved by playing off France against Austria) would be at an end. Pius VII had not evaded the clutches of His Christian Majesty, the Emperor of France, merely to fall into those of His Catholic Majesty, the Emperor of Austria. When Consalvi returned from Vienna to a royal welcome in Rome it was confidently supposed that he had saved the independence of the Papal States and had thereby secured the independence of the Church.

CHAPTER FIVE

Rome versus Revolution (1815–1832)

Despite the liberalism of his early days, and despite his sympathy with Napoleon, it was only natural that Pius VII, for the reasons we have just discussed, should share the contemporary preference, after 1815, for hereditary monarchy. Neither republics nor revolutionary dictatorships had proved good allies of the Church; and, although the Pope was well aware that the monarchies of the *ancien régime* had also often been far from friendly to Catholic independence, they had hardly been so dangerous as the revolutionaries. Moreover the Pope was now in his seventies; the blessings of order and peace, after all that he and the Church had suffered, seemed very great blessings. If the restored monarchs were ready to make reasonable concordats with Rome, and if they seemed likely to maintain themselves in power, then it appeared to be a clear duty to support them.

Events in Spain and Portugal, and in their South American colonies, were a further cause of the hardening of the Pope's attitude in favour of monarchies. It is true that in both countries of the Iberian Peninsula the kings showed the traditional royal hostility to Roman "interference." It is also true that in Spain, in particular, the restored Bourbon, Ferdinand VII, was a constant anxiety to Rome, on account of the indiscreet extremism of his policies, which aimed at crushing all elements of liberalism by abrogating the Spanish Constitution of 1812, by resurrecting the Spanish Inquisition, and by dispossessing all those who had acquired land under the rule of Napoleon's brother Joseph. But when the revolutionaries rose against Ferdinand in 1820 they proved—not unnaturally—to be as violently anti-clerical as they were anti-royalist, and it was inevitable that the Pope, confronted by the arrest of priests, the closure of monasteries and convents, and the expulsion of the Jesuits, should rally to the defence of the Church, and should lend moral support to the French intervention on the King's behalf, in 1823, which was decided upon by the powers at the Congress of Verona. It was also natural that she looked askance, for some years, upon the various revolutionary gov-

ernments which emerged in the Spanish South American
colonies. For the South American revolutionaries, in whose
view Church and State were identified in the persons of the
bishops nominated by Ferdinand VII, were as rough in their
handling of ecclesiastical authority as were their Spanish
confrères. It was, of course, grievous to Rome to see the Church
suffering through the follies of royal absolutism, but she could
not desert the clergy when they became the victims of the
blind and sometimes selfish policies of their political superiors.
She was bound to show her disapproval of the anti-clerical and
persecuting republican régimes which replaced the Spanish
authority; even after the Spanish colonies had achieved their
independence she continued, for a time, to invest the bishops
nominated by King Ferdinand with their Latin-American sees.

But gradually, supported by the attitude of President Mon-
roe of the United States, with his doctrine of "America for
the Americans," and by the policy of the British Foreign Secretary, Castlereagh, and his successor Canning, who threatened
to use the British Navy to prevent royalist reinforcements from
reaching South America, the revolutionary régimes were able
to stabilise themselves after a period of much instability, and
the new rulers began to see the need to reach an understanding
with Rome in order to satisfy the innate Catholic loyalties
of their populations. So, in the 1820s the time seemed ripe
to Rome to make new arrangements in Latin America, in
accordance with the new state of political affairs, and before
Pius VII died in 1823 some important steps had already been
taken. A mission had been sent to Chile, which included
the young Mastai-Ferretti, the future Pius IX, and negotiations had been undertaken by Consalvi with the governments
of Colombia and of the United Provinces of Rio de la
Plata (the future Argentine Republic). The immediate need,
in the absence of any bishops or archbishops, was to conse-
crate new priests, to provide seminaries, and to appoint vicars
apostolic for the different territories. In Mexico, separated
from Spain in 1821, the political instability prevented Consalvi
from concluding an agreement; but in Brazil, separated from
Portugal in 1822, the political stability of the independent
empire enabled the continuance of a full Catholic hierarchy
without revolutionary change.

The alliance of the Church with "legitimacy," that is, with
established governments, generally monarchical, also charac-

terised the negotiations undertaken by Consalvi with the
British Government. The emancipation from their grievous
disabilities of the Catholics in Ireland, where they constituted
the overwhelming majority of the population, and of those in
England, where they constituted only a small minority of less
than two hundred thousand souls, had been promised by the
British Government in the year 1800, at the time of the Act
of Union between the two islands, which abolished the Parliament of Dublin and provided for Irish members at Westminster. But King George III had insisted upon maintaining the
exclusive political privileges of the Church of which he was
Supreme Head, and his Prime Minister, William Pitt, who
had promised the relief, felt obliged, in consequence, to resign. With the better relations which developed between
London and Rome as a result of Pius VII's stand against
Napoleon, Consalvi was able to reopen the matter; but for
long nothing was accomplished because London envisaged a
concordat which would free the Catholics only on condition
that the British Government was given the right to veto clerical appointments, to exact an oath of allegiance, and to censor
all communications with Rome. The British Catholics were
ready to accept these conditions, but the Irish, led by Daniel
O'Connell, most emphatically were not; understandably, it
seemed to them intolerable that their Church should be so
subject to the Protestant government of a country which had
oppressed them for so long. Through his Catholic Association,
O'Connell conducted a remarkably successful campaign of
non-violent agitation; he also secured his own election to Westminster by an overwhelming majority, despite his ineligibility,
as a Catholic, for a seat in the British Parliament. The British
government gave way, and in 1829 almost all the disabilities
which, for more than a hundred and fifty years, had prevented
Catholics from playing any part in public life, were removed
throughout the British Empire, and no more was heard of
the means by which that government had proposed to control
the Church. It was a resounding victory, one of the greatest
political victories ever won by the Church, and it was won
without bloodshed.

Ireland was not the only country where the cause of revolution and the cause of the Church were marching hand in
hand. It had been one of the less imaginative provisions of the
Congress of Vienna to unite Holland and Belgium into one

Kingdom of the Netherlands, since the former country was an ancient bulwark of Protestantism and the latter was devotedly Catholic. It was hardly likely that an arrangement which placed the Belgians under the suzerainty of Dutch King William of the House of Orange would prove amicable; and, when the King proceeded to favour his minority of Dutch subjects at the expense of the Belgians, he united against himself both the clerical party in Belgium and the liberals, who were normally at odds with the clericals. The result was the Belgian revolution of 1830, which eventually led to the separation and independence of Belgium. Pope Leo XII, who, in 1823, had succeeded Pius VII, did not favour this movement; in 1827 he had negotiated a concordat with King William, and he preferred to stand by this rather than see the risk of a revolution which might lead to the upset of the whole European order. But King William was a monarch of the kind known as "enlightened"; he believed that it was for him to correct and control the Church, and, even after signing the Concordat, he had still interfered at every turn, demanding to be consulted before the nomination of bishops, and subjecting letters from the Holy See to his *placet* before they could be received. The Church only achieved her liberty through the revolution, and thus in conflict with the advice of Leo, and of his successor Pius VIII (1829), whose Secretary of State, Cardinal Albani, described the alliance of the Church in Belgium with the liberals as "monstrous." There would be many conflicts, in the years to come, between the Belgium Church and the anti-clerical liberals; indeed, those conflicts are still in evidence. But, at this crisis in the country's affairs, the alliance between the Church and the liberals benefited both, and by making that alliance the Church gained advantages far larger and more lasting than the concessions for which Rome had bargained, often in vain, with the King.

The Belgian revolution of 1830, like the revolutions which followed in the German and Italian states, and the desperate revolt of the Poles against the Russians, had been occasioned by the July revolution of that year in Paris, which drove out the restored Bourbons and established the House of Orleans, in the person of Louis Philippe. This Paris revolution was the victory of the French *bourgeoisie* over the remnants of the restored aristocracy, and it set up a constitution broadly similar to that of England, though one which enfranchised the upper middle classes some two years sooner than the Great

Reform Bill achieved the same objective across the English Channel. Louis Philippe, personally, was a sceptic, of the then fashionable outlook of Voltaire, and the class which his revolution brought to power was very generally similar in its point of view. It is therefore, at first sight, rather surprising that, in this single instance of the July revolution of 1830 in Paris, Rome adopted a different attitude from the one which by now had become customary with her in her dealings with liberal agitations. After a mere two months, and far in advance of the great powers of Europe, Pius VIII recognised the new King and insisted—to the delight of the surprised sceptic—upon styling him, as his predecessors had been styled, "His Most Christian Majesty," and added that the French clergy should take the oath of allegiance to him. But Pius VIII knew very well what he was doing. Better informed on the affairs of France than on those of most parts of the world, he was well aware that the last of the Bourbons, Charles X, who had succeeded his brother Louis XVIII in 1824, had been pursuing an impracticable attempt to restore an absolute monarchy; even the Tsar Alexander and Metternich were aware that the King was attempting the impossible, and were counselling moderation in the hope of averting a renewal of revolution. Moreover, the Gallican attitude of Charles X's Archbishop of Paris, Monsignor de Quélen, the constant interferences of that King with Church affairs, and the favour he had shown to the returned *émigré* priests of the *Petite Eglise*, who had put their allegiance to the Bourbons above their allegiance to the Holy See, rankled at Rome. Pius VIII was as much inclined to listen to the strictures upon Charles X's régime of the rebellious Breton priest, Lamennais, as to his own nuncio in Paris, Cardinal Lambruschini, who favoured Charles X and expected him to succeed.

But the governing factor in Rome's attitude towards the French revolution of 1830 was the Pope's realistic conviction that a change of the kind accomplished was inevitable, and that it was best to rally the Church in support of the new régime rather than to risk further and more radical revolution, which might bring with it a return to the conditions of 1793. And in this Pius VIII showed much wisdom, for, as is well known, the revolution, though it had been made in the streets of Paris, resulted in a constitution of a very moderate kind, which fell far short of satisfying the radical revolutionaries of Paris or of Lyons. In short, it is at least doubtful whether the papacy's attitude towards this revolution should rightly be regarded as an exception to its general policy, at this time, of supporting the *status quo*. By extending a welcome to Louis Philippe, at a time when the new King was very anxious to win the approval of the powers, and to be regarded as "respectable," Pius VIII gave a lead which helped, for a spell, to preserve monarchical government in France.

The revolutionary movements of 1830–31 in the German states were of minor consequence only. Those in Italy were more important but, in as much as they expressed themselves in the form of an attempt on the part of the secret society of the Carbonari to create a new republican state, in the centre of the peninsula, at the expense of the Papal States, and of the Duchies of Modena and Parma, it was not to be expected that the newly elected Pope, Gregory XVI (1831), would be inclined to welcome them; indeed, he was so dismayed that he was prepared to swallow the pride which had prompted Pius VII and Consalvi to keep the Austrians north of the river Po, and to invite them to come south and suppress the revolution. This was not a move which was calculated to enhance the new Pope's popularity amongst his subjects at Bologna, but it was at least understandable. What was far harder to understand and, indeed, gave scandal to many men of good will both in Europe and in America, was the new Pope's handling of the great Polish revolt against the oppressive tyranny of the Russian Tsar Nicholas I, successor of Alexander.

The maintenance of Catholicism in Poland had been one of the greatest achievements of the Jesuits in the struggles arising from the Reformation, and when it is remembered that the Polish kingdom of the seventeenth century embraced the vast Slavic territory of Lithuania, to the northeast, and Podolia and Galicia in the south, it will be realised how powerful a bastion of the Church she constituted in the east of Europe, thrusting into the heart of the Muscovite territory of the Orthodox Faith. But the unscrupulous partitions of Poland at the end of the eighteenth century, which divided the flat and ill-protected country between her powerful neighbours Russia, Prussia, and Austria, lent a different aspect to the religious situation. The large majority of Poles were now subject to the Protestant King of Prussia and to the Orthodox Tsar of Russia; and after 1815 the latter became

lord of Warsaw, and so of the heart of the ancient Polish kingdom. He was supposed, by the terms of the constitution agreed
in 1815 at Vienna, to grant full liberty of worship to his
Catholic subjects, and the Tsar Alexander had made some
show at first of doing so; but after Alexander's death in 1825
Nicholas I set silently to work to achieve his personal objective
—one sovereign, one law, and one faith. Baffled by the enormous distance, and by the extreme secretiveness and duplicity
of the Tsar, Rome was badly informed as to what was going
on. The particular objective of the Tsar's animosity was the
Uniate Church in Russia—that part of the Catholic Church
amongst the Slavs which, while in obedience to Rome, was
allowed to preserve its own Greek liturgy. The Uniates
flourished especially in the ex-Polish territories of White
Russia and Lithuania. Without consulting Rome, the Tsar, by
a ukase of April 1828, abolished the existing Uniate dioceses
and chapters and set up a new seminary for the instruction
of Uniate priests in suitable principles congenial to the throne.
Leo XII's protests were ignored. Ten years later, through the
agency of the renegade priest Siemaszko, whom he had made
Metropolitan of Lithuania, covered with honours and riches,
and used as his chief means of persuasion, the Tsar secured
the signature of a large majority of the Uniate priests to an
Act of Schism by which they joined themselves to the Orthodox Church. It was thus that the Uniate Church virtually
disappeared in Russia. But it remained strong in the Balkan
territories, which at this date were mostly still subject to the
Turkish Empire.

The Latin Church, centred upon Warsaw, was unlikely to
prove equally susceptible to a process of absorption into
Orthodoxy, so the new Tsar proceeded, instead, by way of
trying to get it under his control and of separating it from
the direct influence of Rome. The Pope's letters were inter-
cepted; thus a Brief addressed by Leo XII soon after Nicholas'
accession in 1825, urging the Polish bishops to resist new
legislation taking marriage questions out of the Church courts,
never reached those to whom it was addressed. Similarly
Nicholas removed the primate of Poland and replaced him by
an octogenarian puppet of his own, Cieciszewski, whose
faculties were so far decayed that he could barely trace his
own signature. Leo was not even informed of this change for
more than six months; in the end he felt obliged to recognise
the *fait accompli*.

In the face of such great provocation from the Tsar, it seems almost incredible that, when the Polish revolt broke out in September 1830, Rome counselled the Polish clergy to preach to their flocks submission to the Russian overlord. But it is at least explicable, though not necessarily justifiable, if we remember, first, that the Polish revolt started as an aristocratic intrigue at Warsaw and only later developed into a national and popular crusade; and second that, at the time when he had to make up his mind what advice to give to the Polish bishops, the new Pope, Gregory XVI, was confronted with the Carbonari uprising on his own doorstep in the Papal States. Throughout the year 1831 a war was waged by the Poles against the Russians, and at least one signal victory, at Iganie, was won against the Tsar's armies. But without aid from the new bourgeois King of France (who was more interested in obtaining the Tsar's recognition of his own legitimacy) the Poles' chances of final success were very slender, and a case can be made for Gregory XVI's view that more was to be obtained for the Church in Poland by a policy of restraint, which might induce the Tsar, when peace had been restored, to treat the Polish Church with more respect. But such an attitude argued an undue optimism, and a Brief which Gregory XVI sent to the Tsar when all was over, criticising him sharply for his episcopal appointments, for his interference in clerical and monastic discipline, and for his interruption of communications with Rome, remained both unpublished and unheeded. On the other hand his Brief to the Bishops of Poland, *Superiori Anno*, of June 1832, issued after the revolt had been finally crushed, in which he castigated those who "under cover of religion have set themselves against the legitimate power of princes," and warned the bishops that "all their efforts should be directed against impostors and propagators of new ideas," was published and advertised by the Russian Government at the very time when Russian troops were taking their most brutal reprisals against the unfortunate Poles. The effect of Gregory's attitude upon the liberals in western Europe and in North America may easily be imagined; in France the Breton priest Lamennais, and his liberal friends Montalembert and Lacordaire, who had been supporting the Poles in their paper, *L'Avenir*, were equally dismayed and were confirmed in their view that, by throwing her weight into the scale of monarchical absolutism, Rome was prejudicing the whole future of the Church.

CHAPTER SIX

The Argument About Freedom:
Lamennais; America (1831–1846)

Of the writing of books about Lamennais there is no end, so exciting is the subject. The sensitive, frail, passionate, prophetic *abbé*, who could write French as revolutionary as Rousseau's and as romantic as Chateaubriand's, is the most fascinating figure in the religious history of the first half of the nineteenth century. And even today it is not seldom argued, even by the orthodox, that in the political policy he advocated he was right and Gregory XVI was wrong. Lamennais had no doubt that the revolutionary cause in the years 1830–31 in Poland and in Belgium, in Ireland and in Italy, was the cause of truth and justice, and that the Church should lend her full support to democratic movements everywhere. He argued that the People—not the aristocracy, or the episcopacy, or the *bourgeoisie*, but the common people, the peasants and artisans, the class which came to be called the proletariat (and which Lamennais called the Fourth Estate)—was emerging for the first time in history and would control the future. And he believed it was right, religiously speaking, that this should be so, for in the People, and not in any aristocracy or caste was hidden the Word of God.

It might be supposed that such a view would lead the *abbé* to a profound suspicion of Rome and of the papacy—and so, in the end, it did. But in the 1820s, when he was developing his ideas, and in 1831–32, when he was conducting his campaign in *L'Avenir* with the help of Montalembert and Lacordaire, he was as passionately Roman, papal, ultramontane, in his belief as he was full of faith in the People. For he believed it to be the rôle of Rome to discern and express the word hidden inarticulate in the masses and to thwart the evil intentions of kings, nobles, and even bishops, who stood between the People and the Pope, who kept them oppressed, who perverted and thwarted the true life of the Church. For Lamennais had belonged to that ultramontane movement whose teacher was the Count Joseph de Maistre, and whose text was the count's book *Du Pape* (1819). These ultramontanes had witnessed the attempts of the French Revolution

and Napoleon to subject the Church to the service of the
State, and they had read about the policies of Joseph II of
Austria or Louis XIV of France. They had reached the conclusion that only a much closer attachment to the Pope could
save Catholicism from being undermined by subservience to
the State. The weakness of the eighteenth-century Church,
and all the ills she had suffered since the Revolution, they
attributed precisely to this subservience, in short to Gallicanism or Josephism. <u>Lamennais, then, shared with the other
ultramontanes a belief in the necessity of reasserting the papal
supremacy over the temporal ruler in all matters affecting the
Church.</u> But where he and his young friends of *L'Avenir* went
much further was in asserting that the Pope should find protection for the Church no longer in concordats with kings,
however well disposed they might be towards the Holy See,
nor in any "State Establishment," but in breaking the whole
traditional alliance of Church with government and putting
faith instead in the People.

How was this to be done?

By supporting the democratic and revolutionary movement
wherever it showed itself. Where the peoples were in arms
against their rulers let the Pope, Lamennais cried, support
them instead of supporting their masters. And in states where
some liberties already existed, as in the post-1830 France of
Louis Philippe, let the Pope support the more advanced
liberals who demanded universal suffrage, provincial liberties,
absolute freedom of the press, freedom of association, freedom
of speech, freedom of education. The Church, he insisted, had
everything to gain by the overthrow of the traditional political
powers which held her, as they held the People, in thrall. The
natural alliance was that between *Le Pape* and *Le Peuple*;
the unnatural alliance, which had cost the Church so dear and
had perverted her principles, was between *Le Pape* and *Le
Roi*.

Such were the principles Lamennais had been preaching in
the time of the last of the Bourbons, Charles X of France;
and Pius VIII, as we saw, had at least appreciated that the
Breton priest might be right in anticipating the downfall of
the Bourbon monarchy, and with it grave danger for its ally
the Church, whose leadership had become so closely interwoven with the Bourbon cause. But after the revolution of
1830, and the establishment of the bourgeois-liberal Orleanist
régime of Louis Philippe, Lamennais maintained his stric-

tures and went on to launch his vigorous campaign in
L'Avenir. For the more liberal régime of the new King, with
his ostentatious indifference to religion, seemed as dangerous
to the Church as Charles X or Napoleon had been. It might
leave her freer from state interference, but it was offensive that
a king of Louis Philippe's character should have the power to
nominate bishops, to receive or refuse to receive missives or
legates from Rome, or to grant or to refuse permission to the
religious orders to live their lives undisturbed or to educate the
young. True religion could never flourish under such tutelage.
It could only flourish in "a free Church in a free State."

Lamennais' arguments make more convincing reading today
than they did in his own time. True, *L'Avenir* attracted much
attention, receiving contributions from the greatest French
writers, even from Victor Hugo and Lamartine. But this attention came mostly from the freethinking, the intellectuals,
the social revolutionaries; certainly it did not come from the
French hierarchy, who quickly ranged themselves against the
paper and so adversely affected its sales that its editor was
obliged, if only for financial reasons, to try to secure from
Rome a reversal of their verdict.

To the ardent *abbé* it seemed natural that, since his vision
of a new ecclesiastical order embraced a new rôle for the
papacy, and since denunciations both of his theology and of
his politics were being despatched from France to Rome, he
and his friends should lay their case before the Supreme
Pontiff. So, styling themselves the "pilgrims of God and of
liberty," he, Montalembert, and Lacordaire suspended publication of *L'Avenir* and took the path to Rome, announcing
confidently in advance their absolute certainty that they would
win her full approval. It was December 30, 1831, when they
arrived in Rome. The new Pope, Gregory XVI, had just been
engaged in suppressing, with Austrian help, the dangerous
Carbonari revolt in his own dominion. Even had he been a
Pope who, like Pius VII, or like his own successor Pius IX,
was possessed of generous romantic feelings, disposing him towards a certain sympathy with popular movements, it was not
a moment when he was likely to indulge them. But he was
far from being so disposed by temperament. In the monastic
simplicity of his Camaldolite obedience he might be far removed from any affection for the trappings or externals of
sovereignty, but he believed very strongly in hierarchy, order,
and the virtue of obedience. The Catholic precept of "obedi-

ence to the Powers that be," deriving explicitly from the teaching of Saint Paul, and implicitly from Our Lord's command "render unto Caesar . . ." was not a precept likely to be reversed by any Pope as a result of the excited exigencies of what the Romans call an *esaltato*; but least of all was it likely to be reversed by Gregory, who saw in the revolution of 1830 a recrudescence of the dangerous passions of 1789, and who had even been prepared to counsel a Catholic people, the Poles, to obey a schismatic sovereign who was denying them the most elementary Catholic freedoms.

When Lamennais and his friends arrived in Rome they found that none of the ambassadors of the powers was prepared to support their request for an audience with the Pope; they were, indeed, busily engaged in pressing for a condemnation of the programme of *L'Avenir*. But Gregory accepted the memorandum the pilgrims had brought, telling them that he would examine it and pronounce upon it in due course, whilst warning them that this would take time, and hinting that they would no doubt want to be getting home to their duties. A brief and purely formal audience was arranged for them in the presence of their chief French opponent, the Cardinal de Rohan; immediately after this Lacordaire took the hint and started on his journey back; but Lamennais and Montalembert stayed on in Rome, the Breton *abbé* persisting in his determination at any cost to argue his case with the Pope. Since, however, no further invitation was extended to him, he left, at last, in July, returning by way of Munich, where he went to see the philosopher Schelling. It was there that the Pope's verdict upon *L'Avenir* reached him in the shape of the encyclical, *Mirari Vos*. The *abbé* found that, though his good intentions were appreciated, the programme of *L'Avenir* was condemned root and branch. A programme of the kind invoked by the paper was "absurd, and supremely injurious for the Church"; State indifference in matters of religion was a "perverse view"; liberty of conscience (by which Lamennais meant liberty for everybody to pick and choose between religions) was an "absurd or rather ludicrous maxim"; liberty of the press was "execrable"; separation of Church and State was "a dream."

This was the end of *L'Avenir* but not of Lamennais. Stirred by the events in Poland, and by the Polish poet Mickiewicz's passionate poem, the *Book of the Polish Pilgrimage*, the Breton wrote his *Paroles d'un Croyant*, an eloquent religious

protest, in the style of the Old Testament, against all authority. The attitude of this book, which can only be described as
anarchist, was duly condemned by Gregory in *Singulari Nos*
(June 1834) as worthy of eternal reprobation. So Lamennais
lost his faith in Rome and soon after in the Christian revelation itself. Though he was never excommunicated, he ceased
to perform his office as a priest and came to denounce the
very priesthood itself and the basic articles of Christian faith,
finding "the Truth" in "the People" alone. Embittered and
unreconciled, he died in 1852, leaving his friends Lacordaire
and Montalembert, who had not followed him in his revolt, to
win many practical victories for the liberty of the Church in
France.

The *affaire Lamennais*, dramatic in itself, has always occupied a prominent place in the modern history of the Church
because the attitude which Gregory XVI took up towards the
tenets of *L'Avenir* became a precedent of great importance.
On such matters as the relations of Church and State, toleration, or liberty of the press, it went far to mark out the line
taken later by Pius IX when he issued his Syllabus of Errors
in the year 1864. On the more strictly theological side,
Gregory's condemnation, especially in *Singulari Nos*, of
Lamennais' doctrine that the evolution of truth was part of
the progressive evolution of the people (a view which was
later called immanentism) was followed by Pius X in his condemnation of modernism in *Pascendi Gregis* in 1907.

It is not difficult to see that Lamennais, especially in his
later writings, became hopelessly heretical, abandoning the
very idea of divine revelation through Christ, and adopting a
notion of the divinity of humanity which was really panthe-
istic. Yet the practical programme advocated in his *L'Avenir*
has in fact become the usual working pattern, today, over much
of the Western world, and it would be difficult to argue that
the life of the Church in countries where it is still sheltered
by concordats is healthier or more vigorous than it is where
it is unsheltered. It even seems that the pattern of the "free
Church in a free State" is the one towards which the world is
tending to move; and it is a pattern which in many cases
secures the sympathy of Rome. At the same time it would be
unhistorical to argue from this modern development of religious freedom that Gregory XVI should have accepted
Lamennais' programme in the year 1832. Over Europe as a
whole such a step, so soon after the French Revolution, would

certainly have been regarded as a "sell-out to secularism." Whether in Catholic or in Protestant countries, the traditional alliance of State and Church, of throne and altar, was far too strong for the State to abandon the Church without the general inference being drawn that the Church was no longer regarded as of any account. It was only with the utmost reluctance that Pius X, even in the twentieth century, was driven to accept the disestablishment of the Church in France. To say that Gregory XVI should not only have accepted it but should have introduced it in the 1830s as an "experiment," when the vast majority of Catholics were opposed to it, is to say that he, the pastor of all the faithful, should have dismayed his flock and deliberately have exposed them to all the hazards and the hardships they had suffered in the years between 1790 and 1801, those years when the link between Rome and the French Government had been broken.

But if it is unhistorical to criticise Gregory for not following Lamennais in his vision of a free Church in a free State, in the Europe of the 1830s, it is nevertheless necessary to recognise that, even by the standards of his own times, the Pope's encyclicals can only be called reactionary. Thus the terms which he employed: "absurd," "ridiculous," "execrable," "perverse," "worthy of eternal reprobation," though intended in their precise theological signification and not in their popular acceptance, were undoubtedly harsh, and were felt to be such by men of good will in France who were very well disposed towards the Church.

It is worth reflecting that, had the issue raised by Lamennais been raised not by a priest from Brittany, a province of France, "Eldest Daughter of the Church," but by a priest from the diocese of Baltimore in the United States, the reply from Rome might well have been different. For the lively growth of the Church in North America, under conditions which were beginning to look like those invoked by Lamennais, would have made it hard, indeed, for Gregory to speak to the Americans in quite the same terms as he used in *Singulari Nos*. The separation of Church and State was, in that country, already a reality, and indeed almost an article of faith, in as much as the number of competing churches had made any Establishment impossible. And "freedom of conscience," in the sense of the right of all citizens to enrol in the church of their choice, freedom of speech, and freedom of the press, were already very widely (though not universally) defended there. In short, those conditions of free competition which Lamennais and his friends believed would redound to the health and to the ultimate victory of the Catholic Church already, in large measure, existed across the Atlantic, and the results were going far to sustain Lamennais' thesis. Unembarrassed by any interference and supervision on the part of the State, untrammelled by any American equivalent of French Gallicanism or Austrian Josephism, Rome was able to create new dioceses and to invest new bishops without the need of a ruler's *placet*, and to issue her instructions without waiting for a secular *exequatur*. In practice Gregory, like his predecessors, left those on the spot in America very free to deal as they thought best with the rapidly increasing problems created by the expanding territories, the enormous distances, and the immigration of peoples of different languages and traditions. In the last years of his pontificate, that is in the 1840s, this expansion was particularly rapid, bringing the Catholic population to nearly a million, an expansion due in part to the increased immigration from Ireland at the time of the potato famine. In consequence, the Church in the United States had ceased to consist of one province only, with a metropolitan at Baltimore; new metropolitan sees had been created at Oregon City (to supervise the newly settled areas of the Far West) as well as at St. Louis, New York, Cincinnati, and New Orleans.

We shall return to a fuller consideration of America in this period in Chapter 12. Here we are only concerned with the challenge afforded by the New World to the politico-religious theories of Gregory XVI's times. But it is important to remember that the pioneer conditions still obtaining in the United States, and the Protestant origins of most of the people, make it fallacious to draw deductions from the American Church as to what the Pope might have done in the time of Gregory XVI in Europe. On the old continent Rome was trying to save countries which had been Catholic throughout the centuries, indeed a whole Catholic civilisation, from the damaging offensive of secularism and impiety. In the United States, apart from a small aristocratic connection in and around Baltimore, the Catholics consisted for the most part of the poorest classes of immigrants, whom the troubled conditions at home, in Ireland, Poland, Germany, and later Italy, drove to seek a new life across the Atlantic. The dominant parties and culture not only of New England but of the South as well were Protestant and hostile to the Church; only the mutual disagreements and rivalries of the different Protestant Churches created conditions under which toleration became a necessity, so that Catholicism, too, had to be tolerated. The great task of the bishops and clergy in those early days of American Catholicism was, after making provision for the sacraments, and for the maintenance of faith and morals, to create and sustain some sort of cultural standard amongst their flocks; and in this work the rather austere French priests, trained at Saint-Sulpice, who emigrated to America during the troublous years of the French Revolution, performed a heroic work.

To the north, in Canada, the settlement of population in Gregory XVI's time was still confined mainly to Nova Scotia, the St. Lawrence Valley, and the Great Lakes. We are at the period when Lord Durham, of the famous "Report," found "two nations warring in the bosom of a single State"—Upper Canada, English, Protestant, and centred upon Ottawa and Toronto; Lower Canada, French, Catholic, and centred upon Quebec and Montreal. To the liberal wisdom of Lord Durham and to the governor, Lord Elgin, were due, however, changes which gave a wide measure of local autonomy to Lower Canada, and which freed the Catholics from the many legal disabilities to which, like their brethren in Ireland and in England, they had been subjected. Under conditions then similar to those pertaining in the United States (in that the State was officially neutral and indifferent in the matter of religion) and with only personal, racial, and class prejudices to contend with, the Church was making progress in Canada (see below, p. 150) and, at least by implication, was thereby raising a doubt as to the permanent or universal purport, at least across the Atlantic, of the papal denunciation of the programme of *L'Avenir*.

In the Latin-American states the dispassionate observer in the 1840s might readily sympathise with the views of Lamennais; at least he could hardly draw the conclusion that the life of the Church appeared to be benefiting from her status as the official religion. For her fortunes, which had for so long been intimately linked with the crowns of Spain and Portugal, were still at the mercy of the State, although the State, in most cases, was now a "liberal" and anti-clerical dictatorship.

The populations of Mexico and South America were, of course, traditionally Catholic, being the descendants of the Spaniards, or the Portuguese, or of those Indians whom they had converted. The problem was not, as in North America, that of how the Church could be nourished, sustained, and enabled to grow in the midst of a Protestant population. It was the problem of how its own virtue could be sustained and its faith safeguarded against the attacks of secularism and anticlericalism. The general picture of Latin-American Catholicism in the middle of the nineteenth century was one of few vocations, of a lax and even sometimes an immoral clergy insufficient in numbers; and of waves of violent governmental anti-clericalism particularly in the Mexico of Benito Juárez or the Argentine of De Rosas. The aims of the anti-clericals were similar to those of their European counterparts, namely the confiscation and dissolution of monasteries and convents, the secularisation of marriage and of education, and state control over clerical appointments, seminaries, and contacts with Rome. And the problem for Rome was not dissimilar to the problem confronting her in France, or in the Iberian Peninsula, though her hold upon the situation was much weaker and the level of the clergy much lower. Few could doubt the need for an infusion of new life into the churches of Latin America, and the mission sent by Pius VII to Chile was only one of many efforts which Rome made to regularise matters and to infuse new discipline. But there lacked the stimulus of well-trained priests from Europe, who proved so great a source of strength to the growing Church in North America; local suspicion and self-sufficiency proved strong enough to stifle the demand for them. Though officially Catholic, most of the states of Latin America were, in fact, drifting dangerously in their religion. And, if the tutelage of their Catholic Majesties of Spain had not always been an unmixed blessing, the tutelage of the new democracies and dictatorships often only served to provide the least desirable elements of Establishment without providing the advantage of truly Catholic political leadership. It is tempting to argue that here, in Latin America, was to be found the soil where the liberties invoked by Lamennais might have brought most benefit in renewing the life of the Church. Yet it would be very rash to do so, for there were lacking both that devotion to Rome and that spirit of obedience which are indispensable to any Catholic revival; and there appears, too, to have been lacking the zeal, intelligence, and spirit of self-sacrifice which made the French

Liberal Catholics so effective a fighting force. A mere breaking of the connection between Church and State would hardly have been likely to save the situation and might, in Mexico or in the Argentine, merely have served to smother the dimly smouldering sparks of the Faith.

The brightest feature of the pontificate of Gregory XVI was to be found in the mission field. No doubt political and economic expansion had much to do with affording opportunity to the Church, in Africa and Asia, in the '30s and '40s of the nineteenth century; but to the Pope belonged the credit of taking advantage of them. One important factor was the weakening of the Mohammedan Empire of the Ottoman Turks, which induced the Sultan (after the successful revolt of the Greeks which secured their national independence in 1830) to grant wider toleration to the Christians in their remaining East Mediterranean empire. On the mainland of the Balkan Peninsula the chief beneficiaries of the decline of the Turkish power were the members of the Greek Orthodox Church; but the Catholics, especially the Uniates, enjoyed a new lease of life and renewed contacts with Rome, while in Asia Minor, Syria, Palestine, and Egypt (a country which secured its independence from Constantinople by the exertions of Mehemet Ali and the aid of the French) missionary activity, upon a considerable scale, became possible for the first time since the Middle Ages. At the other end of the Mediterranean the French conquest of Algeria opened up a new theatre for religious activity, while in the Far East, China (for the first time since the failure of the great Jesuit attempt to convert her more than two centuries earlier, in the days of Saint Francis Xavier and Matteo Ricci) was opened up to Western influences as an indirect result of a British trade war. There were failures, too, for the Church to record: an unsuccessful attempt to launch a mission in Abyssinia, and poor progress in India, where the Portuguese were jealous of the French missionaries, and the British East India Company often still refused to grant them facilities. But the Westernisation of the world was now well launched. That it carried with it, first in one place and then in another, increased conversion to the Catholic faith, was at least partly due to the interest taken by the Pope in the founding of new missionary orders, and to his zeal in helping to provide houses of study for them.

CHAPTER SEVEN

Pius IX and Mazzini (1846–1850)

The year 1846 witnessed the death of Pope Gregory XVI and the election, at the early age of fifty-four, of Mastai-Ferretti, Bishop of Imola in the Papal States. He took the title of Pius IX in honour of Pius VII, his patron in youth, and a Pope whose liberal outlook had appealed to his own generosity of temperament. Though little was known about him, the new Pope was reputed to have some sympathy with the Italian liberals and to have been looked upon somewhat askance by Gregory XVI and by his Secretary of State, Cardinal Lambruschini. When he began his pontificate by granting an amnesty to about a thousand prisoners and exiles of central Italy who had suffered under his predecessor, and when he went on to hold garden parties in the Quirinal, to light the streets of Rome with gas, and to project railways to link Rome with Civitavecchia and Ostia, it was plain for all to see that a fresh wind was blowing in the capital of the Catholic world. But the question in everybody's mind was whether he would show any sympathy with the democratic and liberal movements now bubbling to the surface once more and commanding the attention of Europe. And, in particular, what would be his attitude towards the growing quarrel between the Italian patriots and the Austrians?

Since 1815 Vienna had ruled the Italian provinces of Lombardy and Venetia, and indirectly she now sustained the rulers of the rest of the peninsula. So it was very relevant to ask what would be the new Pope's attitude towards the rising Italian liberalism and nationalism. At first he seemed to favour the liberals. He set up within a year of his accession a consultative assembly with lay representation, to advise him in his government of the Papal States. And when the Austrian Chancellor Metternich, alarmed at what was happening at Rome, ordered the occupation of the city of Ferrara (the citadel, not the city, had by treaty been assigned to Austrian control) the new Pope demanded and secured an Austrian withdrawal on pain of excommunication of those concerned for violating the property of the Church. The enthusiasm aroused by these events amongst liberals throughout the world knew no bounds, nor was it confined to Catholics. Probably no Pope in modern times has enjoyed so wide a popularity as that enjoyed in those first months by Pius IX, or "Pio Nono"—the Italian name by which he was generally known. Messages of congratulation poured in from across the Atlantic as well as from Protestant England; it was felt that the Pope had aligned the Church with the cause of democracy everywhere, and had set an example of which all ruling princes would have to take note. From the meeting halls of working men in New York to the common rooms of colleges at Oxford were echoed the cries of *viva Pio Nono!* which rang in the piazzas of Italy.

A few there were who, from the first, saw the danger, and notably Metternich at Vienna, the real arbiter of Europe. How, he asked himself, could the Pope control the ferment which was growing in Italy? Yet how could he share his sovereignty with a democratic assembly, or give his blessing to a national movement in the peninsula which, if unchecked, must lead to war? And behind the moderate liberals who were now the Pope's friends lay, the chancellor knew well enough, much more violent revolutionaries, socialist and anti-clerical, who were ready enough, in Paris or in Rome, to brush aside the moderates and to seize power when their opportunity should come.

Pushed partly by the pressure of the democratic clubs of Rome, partly by his own liberal leanings, but probably most by events in Sicily and in Paris (where the early weeks of the Year of Revolutions, 1848, had seen the winning of new constitutions) Pius IX, not altogether willingly, went on to grant such extensive further liberties for his subjects that it looked almost as though he were pursuing the programme advocated by *L'Avenir.* Thus he gave to the city of Rome her own elective municipal government, he gave a wide measure of liberty to the press, and in March 1848 he granted a constitution to the Papal States, which provided for an elective chamber capable of vetoing what the Pope proposed. It was in taking this last step that the Pope was driven to go further than his peculiar position as both a temporal and a spiritual sovereign permitted. For it was unthinkable that his spiritual sovereignty should be in any way limited by an elected assembly of Roman laymen; and yet, in practice, it proved impossible to separate sharply his spiritual from his temporal capacity. Thus, as temporal ruler of the Papal States, he might find himself drawn into an offensive alliance of Italian states to drive the Austrians out of Italy; but clearly, as spiritual ruler of all the faithful, he must seek to prevent a fratricidal war, and one intended to alter the treaty settlement of 1815 approved by Consalvi and Pius VII, a settlement which had maintained the European peace for more than a generation. A war to expel the Austrians from Italy might seem to the liberals to be a "just war," and thus to be deserving of a papal blessing; but in fact it would be a revolutionary war, and also one which would have to be waged against a Catholic people who had for long been the papacy's chief source of support.

It was in fact <u>precisely on this issue of war against Austria</u> <u>that the brief experiment of the liberal papacy broke down.</u> Though as ardently Italian as any of his subjects, and profoundly suspicious, as we have seen, of Austrian intentions in Lombardy, Pius IX refused, as he was bound to refuse, to bless the popular Italian crusade which was developing against the Austrians, or to allow his own small army to be used for more than its legitimate purpose of defending the northern frontier of the Papal States. For this inaction he was roundly accused by the liberals of deserting the Italian movement, and the immense popularity which he had won vanished during the summer of the year 1848.

It had been a disastrous summer for the Italians. In the spring the strongest Italian state, Piedmont, taking advantage of a revolution at Vienna, had declared war upon the Austrians, and the Piedmontese army, led by King Charles Albert, advancing into Lombardy, had been soundly defeated. The King had been ill-supported by volunteers from the rest of Italy, and it was widely felt that if the Pope had lent his support, the issue might have been different.

The disillusionment showed itself in Rome in the form of ever greater demands by the liberals. In vain did Pius IX accept as Premier of Rome one after another of the leaders of the new Chamber of Deputies; none of these laymen was able to bridge the widening gulf between that liberal and nationalist body and the Pope. At last in November 1848 the ablest of them, Pellegrino Rossi, who was the only one who seemed likely to be able to carry on the government of the Papal States in the interests both of Rome and of Italy, was murdered by returned volunteers from the North as he entered the palace of the *Cancelleria*, where the Chamber was sitting. The indifference of the Chamber to this crime, and the disgraceful scenes which followed, when a lewd mob ironically intoned the psalm *Miserere* beneath the windows of the unfortunate victim's widow, marked the final breach between the Pope and the liberal revolutionaries. Besieged night and day in his palace of the Quirinal, he soon became the prisoner there of the mob and, unable to effect anything more for his friends or for his state, he determined to try to escape so that he might be able, in some place of tranquility, to carry out his spiritual duties. It was thus that the plot was hatched that led to his flight by night, dressed as a simple priest, to Gaeta in the Kingdom of Naples. It was an escape efficiently executed, with the help of the French and Bavarian ambassadors, in circumstances rather analogous to those which had proved so disastrous to King Louis XVI on his famous flight to Varennes.

The Pope's flight took place on November 24, 1848. Within a few weeks a provisional junta had organised elections (boycotted by those loyal to the Pope) which returned an extremist assembly. It was this assembly which summoned to the city the leading Italian and European revolutionary, Giuseppe Mazzini, and one of the greatest captains of guerilla warfare the world has ever known, Giuseppe Garibaldi, together with his legion. Mazzini was elected First Triumvir and took up his position in the Quirinal. Since he and Garibaldi were both profoundly anti-clerical, and since the mystical Mazzini invoked "a new religious synthesis," "God and the People," which he hoped would be presented to the world by a "Third Rome" (the Second Rome, that of the Popes, being now apparently moribund), the stage was set for events of far more than local significance. Two religious and political ideologies were, in fact, in conflict around the historic seven hills, as surely as they had been in the Paris of Robespierre, or as they would later be in the Madrid of 1937, when another International Brigade, not much larger than Garibaldi's, would attract the attention of the world.

For the significance of this struggle is misunderstood if it is seen only as a rising of the Roman people. Neither Mazzini nor Garibaldi nor their Minister of War, Avezzana, were Romans, any more than was Garibaldi's fighting force, which came from regions as widely separated as South America and Lombardy. And the Catholic powers, as a matter of high principle and of loyalty, felt the need to rally to the defence of the Pope to restore him to his agelong sovereignty in the See of Saint Peter. Mazzini himself, who had vision, imagination, and even understanding (though his worship was the worship of a strange God), realised what was at stake. Before he reached Rome, and when it still seemed that the revolutionaries would try to compromise with the papacy, he wrote to the provisional government: ". . . you can if you will create a well ordered world. You have in your hands the fate of Italy, and the fate of Italy is that of the world. You do not know, O ye forgetful people, the power exercised by the conjunction of four letters which form the name of your city; you do not know that that which is merely a word elsewhere when coming from Rome is a fact, an imperious decree—*Urbi et Orbi. Perdio!* Do not your monuments, your historical memories, put a single inspiration into the minds of the men who direct your affairs? . . . Providence makes of a Pope a voluntary fugitive—takes every obstacle out of your path, like a mother for her child—and you, in ingratitude, remain doubtful . . ."

The resolution of Mazzini was matched, on the other side, by that of Pio Nono who, from Gaeta, called upon the Catholic world to restore him to his rightful position. Unfortunately the Catholic powers, ready enough to undertake the task, indulged, rather like the crusaders of old, in political suspicions of each other's motives. Moreover France, to whom the honour most naturally belonged, had just acquired a revolutionary republican government of her own, some of whose members had some natural links of sympathy with the republicans of Rome.

Nevertheless, even revolutionary France was so shocked by what had occurred at Rome that the freethinking ex-Carbonari president, Louis Napoleon, nephew of the great Napoleon, anxious to court popularity, and anxious also to forestall an Austrian intervention, sent General Oudinot to restore the Pope. But he underrated the difficulty of the task, misconceiving the resolution of Mazzini, the genius of Garibaldi, and the ideological fervour of the cosmopolitan band of anticlericals who supported them. His first rather casual attack around the walls of the Vatican was beaten off with serious losses, so that he was obliged to withdraw and wait for the arrival of artillery and reinforcements, leaving Garibaldi free, in the meantime, to beat off the rather halfhearted attempt staged by the King of Naples in the interests of his distinguished guest. But when Oudinot renewed his attack in June 1849 the end, despite the gallantry of the defence, was inevitable. The only real hope for the Roman Republic, as

Mazzini perfectly understood, was to gain the sympathy and the friendship of the new French Republic, which had been the outcome of the Paris revolution of March, 1848. He was well versed in history and he could, with some reason, hope that this Second French Republic would be animated towards the Church, and towards the papacy, by the same spirit of hostility as the First French Republic of 1793. But, to the eternal credit of those like Lamennais' friends, Montalembert and Lacordaire, who had striven for the rebirth of the Church in France, the Paris of the Second Republic was animated quite differently in this respect from the Paris of the First. Though there were anti-clericals in the Assembly, the Assembly as a whole was not anti-clerical; in fact Lacordaire, who had restored the Dominican Order to France, and whose sermons in Notre Dame had been a notable feature of the Catholic revival, himself took his seat in the Assembly, and took it amongst the deputies of the Left, as an elected representative of the People. Mazzini never understood that it was possible, as a Catholic, to take one's stand with the People; but the Liberal Catholic movement had in fact made this possible.

Against the will of Mazzini, but in accordance with the advice of Garibaldi, the Roman Republic yielded to General Oudinot at the beginning of July 1849; he was given a popular ovation upon his entry, as was Pio Nono when he returned in the following spring.

Henceforth the Pope ruled without the help of a popular assembly. He was not to be persuaded that there existed in the Papal States a moderate middle class sufficient in numbers and self-discipline to share governmental responsibility. He had watched his constitutional premiers losing control over the situation in Rome until the last and ablest of them had become the victim of the mob. "Your Holiness will remember what they did to Rossi," Cardinal Antonelli would whisper in his ear, when he contemplated an extension of popular liberties, and the warning was sufficient. Cardinal Antonelli himself, faithful and courageous during the revolution, able in his handling of the French intervention and occupation, was confirmed in the full position of Secretary of State, which he retained until his death in 1876, although he was never admitted to the priesthood. The Jesuits were restored to their full liberties, and the Pope personally assisted them to launch that very important paper, the *Civiltà Cattolica*, which would become and would remain an authoritative (though not an official) vehicle of Catholic thought on religious and political matters.

Certainly this papal restoration of 1850 marked an important turning point in the modern history of the papacy, and one which tended to direct it in what may be broadly called an authoritarian rather than a liberal direction. It was natural, after the cataclysmic events of the first three years of Pio Nono's pontificate, that this should be so. But several misconceptions on this matter are still given wide publicity. One is that henceforth the Pope condemned constitutional or democratic governments as such, and in particular tried to secure the abrogation of the constitution of Piedmont, which later became that of the United Kingdom of Italy. This is not the case. Throughout his reign he insisted upon what had been the traditional Catholic position in this matter, namely that the Church is "indifferent" to forms of government, being concerned only to defend the necessary liberties of the Faith. Another commonly expressed view is that it was at this time that the Jesuits acquired an ascendancy at Rome so pronounced that they virtually "ran the papacy," and have done so ever since. It is true that, after its eclipse in 1773, and its rather uncertain position even when restored in 1814 (Pio Nono himself felt compelled to invite the Jesuits to leave Rome in 1848), the Society enjoyed greatly increased influence when the Pope had returned from Gaeta in 1850. But quarrels between the Pope and the editors of the *Civiltà* were numerous, and it was not the Pope who had to give way. Nothing could be further from the mark than to suppose that the Pope was "run" by the Jesuits. Nor, assuredly, was he "run" by Antonelli, who understood perfectly the limits of his position, and within them conducted the foreign relations of the papacy with devotion and considerable skill.

The growing centralisation of the spiritual power in the hands of the Pope, in the later part of Pio Nono's reign, and, on the political side, his checking of the Liberal Catholic movement, were deemed by him to be necessary because of anti-clerical governments, and because of anti-Catholic revolutionaries.

CHAPTER EIGHT

Progress in Protestant Europe (1850–1854)

It is an interesting reflection of the many-sidedness of papal activity in this period that at the very time when Pio Nono was contending with the Italian revolutionaries at Rome, in the year 1848, he was also considering, in some tranquility, with representatives from England, how best to restore the Catholic hierarchy in that country. When it is remembered that in the middle of the nineteenth century Great Britain, commercially speaking, led the world, and that politically she enjoyed an influence as great as that of any other power, it will be appreciated that such a proposal carried with it important implications.

When Queen Elizabeth I, in the year 1559, confirmed the breach with Rome effected by her father, Henry VIII, and proceeded to suppress the Mass and most of the rest of Catholic faith and practice, the government embarked upon a long period of persecution of the Catholics which lasted legally (though there was much variation in its enforcement) until the passing of the <u>Catholic Emancipation Act of 1829</u>. In England itself, by the end of the eighteenth century, the Catholic body had been reduced to a mere handful of some thirty thousand souls, still some of them belonging to the great families of the land, but deprived of political influence.

But around the turn of the century the number of Catholics was rising rapidly, as a result of the immigration of Irish workers into Lancashire and Yorkshire, in response to the demands of the cotton and woollen industry; later there were religious movements, of which the Oxford movement was the most important, leading especially to conversions amongst the intellectuals. By the middle of the century the number of Catholics had risen to around a million, and it seemed to Pio Nono and his advisers that the time had come for the restoration of the normal episcopal ordering of the Church in England, in place of the jurisdiction of the vicars apostolic who had been ministering to her spiritual needs whilst she was still regarded as a missionary country. This was the matter upon which the Pope was conferring in Rome with representatives from England in the year 1848, and there seemed every reason to expect the matter to be arranged amicably. The British Prime Minister, Lord John Russell, was favourable to the idea and indeed anxious, on account of Irish, Canadian, and other imperial problems, to renew diplomatic contact with the Holy See. A Bull of Restoration was accordingly drafted. But before it could be published the revolution had broken out in Rome, the Pope had fled to Gaeta, and nothing more could be done.

Unfortunately, when Pio Nono returned to Rome in 1850 and resumed consideration of the matter the atmosphere had quite changed. The man he had designated for the metropolitan archbishopric to be created at Westminster, Thomas Walsh, was dead, and Nicholas Wiseman, whom he now proposed to install, was a far less conciliatory character. More important, the whole attitude of English people towards the Pope had changed. Whereas in 1848 Pio Nono had been almost a hero in the eyes of Englishmen, now he was disliked and even detested by them as a tyrant; the change had been brought about by the Roman revolution and British sympathy with Mazzini and Garibaldi. Sympathy with revolution, whether in South America, France, Austria, Greece, Poland, Belgium, the German states, or the Italian states, was a constant factor in England in the nineteenth century; the assumption was always that rulers were tyrants and that "the people" were rising to throw off oppression.

In the case of the Roman revolution this rather naïve conviction was strengthened by two factors. One was the heroic stand made by Mazzini and Garibaldi against professional armies. The other was that the dispossessed ruler, though recently popular, was also the Pope, and ever since the sixteenth century hatred of the Pope had been assiduously nurtured in England by those interested in one aspect or another of the Reformation. This was the one matter upon which those interested in the fate of the State Establishment and those interested in promoting any of the sects which that Establishment termed "Nonconformist" were agreed. The "Giant Pope" of John Bunyan's *Pilgrim's Progress* was a myth that served not only those whose appeal was to "free conscience" but also those who sought to maintain the royal supremacy in the matter of religion. It had become axiomatic in England that the Pope was a tyrant, and generally a dissolute one at that—a notion deriving from the time of Alexander VI (1492–1503) but curiously inappropriate when applied to the austere Popes of the Catholic Reformation, or to the personal simplicity of a Pius VII or a Gregory XVI. Pius VII, as we saw, by his calm and courageous attitude towards Napoleon, had reintroduced something of respect for the papacy into the better-informed parts of the British population, whilst the French exiles in England, and especially the *émigré* religious orders, had not been without their beneficial influence. But when, in 1849, the Pope seemed once again to have identified himself with tyranny, the British were ready enough to listen to the tales of the exiles after the collapse of the Roman revolution, and especially to those of the most popular of the exiles, Felice Orsini, an irresponsible man who had already killed his own cook by accident, and who was later unsuccessfully to throw a bomb at the Emperor Napoleon III, killing only the bystanders.

In 1850, then, the British populace was in one of its most pronounced "anti-tyranny" moods; it was the year when the Austrian General Haynau was manhandled by the Southwark draymen. It was the worst possible moment for the publication of Pio Nono's Bull of Restoration of the Catholic hierarchy to England, and a certain flamboyance of language employed by the new cardinal archbishop, Nicholas Wiseman, in his exultant pastoral letter "From out the Flaminian Gate" of Rome, did not help matters. The storm of protest shook the country and was fanned even by the Prime Minister, Lord John Russell, and by the Bench of Bishops of the Established Church. It found expression in riots reminiscent of those incited by Lord George Gordon in the previous century. Pio Nono was burnt in effigy. There was particular resentment that Westminster had been chosen as the seat of the Catholic archbishopric. It was felt that in some way Westminster Abbey was insulted. It was forgotten that that abbey, though it had become something of a national Pantheon, was originally part of a Benedictine monastery owing closest allegiance to Rome. It was felt that the authority of the Archbishop of Canterbury was somehow being attacked. It was forgotten that the authority of the See of Canterbury had been conferred upon it by Rome.

In choosing the new Catholic sees it was necessary to select places which were not already the sees of Anglican bishoprics. It was bitter, indeed, for Catholics to have to forego the great historic names, the cities with the glorious cathedrals: Canterbury and York, Lincoln and Salisbury, Hereford and Worcester, so illustrious in medieval Catholic history, and to take in their place titles such as Northampton or Brentwood, Salford or Portsmouth, which lacked the historic ring; but they had no choice in the matter. By the Catholic Emancipation Act of 1829 the Anglican titles might not be used. More surprising, by a new Ecclesiastical Titles Bill, introduced at the height of the storm, even the new titles were made illegal; and in 1852 Catholic public processions were banned and Catholic priests were not allowed to appear publicly in their ecclesiastical habits. But these acts soon became a dead letter, and in fact Pio Nono did not allow himself to be deterred from proceeding calmly to the appointment of the new bishops. Despite pressure that he should at least withdraw Wiseman from Westminster, he maintained him there—a sensible course because the new archbishop, by his courage and persuasive skill, succeeded in calming the opposition and in maintaining his precarious position. If the progress of the Catholic Church in England has proved slower than the zealots of 1850 hoped, it has proved, nevertheless, to be steady.

A rather similar situation arose soon afterwards in Holland, now separated once again from Catholic Belgium. The Calvinist Dutch who, at the beginning of the eighteenth century, had still been regarded, with some justice, as the Protestant bulwark of Europe, by the middle of the nineteenth century were turning in significant numbers towards Catholicism. It was not merely a matter of the two southern provinces of Limburg and Brabant, traditionally Catholic; it was a matter of progress in the North too, particularly at Amsterdam, and in spite of serious disabilities. But although the proportion of Catholics in Holland, where they formed about a third of the population, was much higher than it was in England, the Pope was very circumspect in the matter of restoring the Dutch hierarchy. He had not forgotten that the Jansenist heresy had been started by a Dutch bishop in the seventeenth century and had developed—or so the Jesuits said—partly as a result of the independent-mindedness of the Dutch episcopacy. There were still in Holland some ten thousand "Old Catholics" of Jansenist origin who were out of communion with the Holy See.

The Pope was inclined to wait and see how the restoration of the hierarchy worked in England. Only when he saw that Cardinal Wiseman, despite the outcry, was going to be able to maintain his position at Westminster did Pio Nono issue the Bull restoring the hierarchy to Holland (March 1853). The immediate effect was very much the same in the one country as in the other. There was a violent outcry, known as the "April Agitation," sufficiently strong to bring about the fall of the government of the Premier Thorbecke, who had been involved in the negotiations. And, just as in England the choice of Westminster for the metropolitan archbishopric had been a particular source of irritation, so in Holland the choice of Utrecht, illustrious in the story of Dutch resistance to Spain, produced a similar annoyance, despite the ancient medieval and Catholic associations of the city. And there was the added difficulty that at Utrecht the new Catholic archbishop found himself living alongside the heretical "Old Catholic" archbishop of Jansenist origin.

Progress, however, in Holland after the restoration of the hierarchy was rapid. And elsewhere, too, the early 1850s, in spite of the storms encountered on both sides of the North Sea, were a time of hope and of forward movement for the Church in Protestant states. Especially was this so in Germany, where one of the results of the revolution of 1848 in Berlin was the removal of religious disabilities in the Kingdom of Prussia. In the Catholic provinces of the Rhineland, which formed part of this kingdom, not only were the civil disabilities of Catholics removed, but the Church itself was freed from the embarrassments of state supervision and enabled to form her associations, to develop schools, to have free contact with Rome, and to be invested by Rome with her bishops, without any requirement of royal *placet* or *exequatur*. In fact, in Protestant Prussia, as in Protestant America, the Church was now freer to fulfil her mission than she was in Catholic but Josephist Austria, where the Hapsburgs maintained their onerous control, or in Catholic but Gallican France, where Napoleon III, by the month of December, 1852, had established the Second Empire.

But if the revolutions of 1848 had not been unhelpful to the Church in some parts of Europe, because they had helped to remove some of the disabilities of Catholics, yet the general failure of those revolutions, and the restoration of governments in some sort traditional in character, had been very generally welcome to the papacy. Rome had not been the only capital where the revolutionaries had shown an anti-clerical temper; and if in Paris the Dominican Lacordaire had felt able to take his seat on the Left of the new republican Assembly he did not feel able to retain it there for long, for Louis Blanc, Ledru-Rollin, and their Socialist friends were too profoundly anti-Christian for such an association to be maintained. And so it was in the rest of Europe. Between the real revolutionaries, such as Kossuth in Hungary or Mazzini and Garibaldi in Italy, and the Church, the conflict at bottom was inescapable, because in the last resort it rested upon differing conceptions of man and of his relation to society. Inevitably the Church was concerned first and foremost with the maintaining of a polity in which she was free to minister to the needs of the individual soul and in which, in her own department, she was sovereign. But the revolutionaries were either, like Louis Blanc, materialist in their philosophy and thus hostile to the whole of the Church's spiritual claim, or else, like Mazzini, had ideas for "regenerating" society which were not Christian and which, from a Christian point of view, were not free.

To Pio Nono the European upheavals of 1848–49 appeared to be a recrudescence of those of the great French Revolution; and, although this was a harsh and rather inaccurate view of what had happened in some parts of Europe, it was not so far from the mark in regard to what had happened at Rome, the place that naturally came most directly under his view. When he was restored to Rome in April 1850 and drove through the Lateran Gate to be welcomed by a cheering crowd, it seemed to the Pope that a nightmare had been lifted and an evil spirit of rebellion exorcised; and he had no doubt that he owed this restoration, and Europe owed her general return to tranquility, to the intercession of the Blessed Virgin, whom, throughout his life, he had held in especial honour, and whose aid he had sought in all times of difficulty. It was therefore natural that after his return he should be increasingly inclined to heed the steadily swelling stream of petitions which he was receiving, particularly from France, demanding a definition of the historic and popular belief in her immaculate conception.

Since before the 1848 revolution, a theological commission appointed by the Pope had been considering all the implications of defining the belief that the Blessed Virgin was miraculously freed, at her conception, from the taint of original sin. It was a belief whose scriptural warrant was contained in the message of the Angel Gabriel, "Hail Mary, full of grace," and which was strengthened by the logical corollaries to be deduced from Mary's divine maternity, defined at the Council of Ephesus in A.D. 431.

From Gaeta, in February 1849, the Pope had issued the encyclical *Ubi Primum*, asking the bishops for their prayers and advice. The replies of the overwhelming majority were favourable to the definition and often enthusiastic. A draft was then prepared which was amended by the bishops summoned to Rome for the formal proclamation of the definition and on December 8, 1854, the Pope marked the traditional feast day of the Immaculate Conception by reading it publicly in Saint Peter's. So began a century in which devotion to Our Lady would be greatly increased throughout the world, a century within which would be seen the complementary definition, made by Pope Pius XII, in 1950, of the analogous dogma of the Assumption of the Blessed Virgin into Heaven. Moreover, by this definition was established the precedent that, for the formal definition of Catholic dogma (an uncommon occurrence) it was sufficient that the Pope should act on his own authority, with only such consultation with the Church as might seem to him proper. This precedent was not without its bearing upon the terms in which the dogma of Papal Infallibility came to be defined sixteen years later at the Council of the Vatican. In fact, if it was one result of consequence, arising from this definition, that devotion to Our Lady was increased, it was another that the authority of the Pope in the Church was signally strengthened.

So the long pontificate of Pope Pius IX, after an exciting but hardly a reassuring beginning, was now sailing, in the 1850s, in calmer waters; by the year 1855 Pio Nono could already point to real achievements, especially in England and Holland.

But really the middle '50s were the lull between two storms, and a greater and more prolonged tempest lay ahead. Before his reign, the longest in papal history, should come to an end in the year 1878, the whole map of central Europe would have changed. Germany and Italy would have emerged as united nations, the Papal States would have disappeared, and the Pope, who had suffered such a buffeting, would have been shorn of his temporal power and set at naught by the rulers of all the great powers. Yet he would have been invested, at the Vatican Council, with a spiritual authority unparalleled by any Pope for the previous three centuries. And the Church, under his guidance, having flatly contradicted the confident sophistries of an age of superficial progress, having condemned its easygoing optimisms and denounced its crude secularism, would have lost the good will of many, but would have saved her own soul, would have renewed her strength, and would have girded herself for the battles of a new age.

CHAPTER NINE

The Loss of the Papal States (1858–1870)

Immediately the battlefield lay in Italy, as previously it had lain in France, and later it would lie in Germany. This was because the movement for Italian unification, known as the Risorgimento, carried with it the destruction, not only of the Papal States, but of the Church's control, throughout the peninsula, of many departments of life. It meant the end of her control of matrimony and of education, which had traditionally been regarded as her concern, and of the monasteries and convents, which the new nationalist movement regarded as "useless" and "medieval."

After the collapse of the revolutions of 1848–49 the eyes of those in Italy who looked to a new order, which should free the peninsula from the Austrians, and from the *ancien régime* of petty principalities, were turned towards Piedmont. At Turin, her capital, the young King Victor Emmanuel II, alone amongst Italian rulers, had preserved a constitution—the one granted by his father, Charles Albert, in 1848. And to him, alone, belonged an army which, though it had shown its inferiority to the Austrians both in 1848 and in 1849, might yet hope some day to challenge them afresh and to liberate Milan and Venice from the rule of Vienna. To an Italian movement of this kind there was no particular reason why the Pope, religiously speaking, should find himself in opposition, always provided that he was not expected to send an army from the Papal States to fight for it. He had shown, both in 1847 and in 1848, that he was ready to consider movements for closer co-operation between the different Italian states, even perhaps their confederation. He had shown in his own state that he was not opposed to giving the people a share in the government. He had appealed to the Austrian Emperor to recognise frankly that Austrian rule was powerless for good in the Italian peninsula, and had urged him voluntarily to withdraw his troops from Lombardy and Venetia. It is therefore incorrect to assert that he was opposed to all the aspirations which went to make the Italian Risorgimento; it would even be true to say that in 1847 he was the Italian ruler who had shown most sympathy with the Italian cause. But in the '50s, on account of his own experiences in 1848–49, and also on account of the new tendencies apparent in the movement, he had become differently disposed. He saw, as he had begun to suspect in 1848, that the Piedmontese government was really interested in expanding its own power in northern Italy, and he saw no reason why he should help to promote what seemed to be merely an upsetting of the traditional balance of power in the peninsula.

More important, from 1850 onwards, the Turin government was pursuing a determinedly secularist policy. Since 1848 the usual pattern of secularist legislation had shown itself in Piedmont. First there was an education law depriving the Church of control over education, then followed abolition of Church courts, of the judicial immunities of the clergy, of sanctuary rights, of feast days; finally all check was withdrawn from press attacks on the Church. More serious, however, was the "Law of the Convents," introduced into the Piedmontese parliament of Turin in 1854, and the special concern of Cavour, who was now King Victor Emmanuel's premier. By this law it was proposed to suppress the Piedmontese monasteries and convents, save for a few which were engaged in teaching and charitable work of a kind which the State would find it awkward to see disappear. The essential point, in the Pope's eyes, was that Victor Emmanuel's government was deciding, unilaterally, what kind of spiritual life should be allowed to the Church and what should not. There was room for negotiation on some of these matters, but Cavour did not want to negotiate. It is true that Joseph II of Austria had introduced "reforms" of this kind, and that the French revolutionary governments had gone much further, and it has sometimes been argued—rather loosely—that Victor Emmanuel was merely bringing his kingdom "up to date." But by the 1850s the religious orders were flourishing again in France, and even in England, while the Austrian Government was negotiating a new concordat with Rome, designed to satisfy the needs of the Church and to remove the offensive features of "Josephism." The Turin government was, in fact, one of the most extreme in its anti-clericalism at this time, and it was a matter of great concern to the Pope that an Italian government should pursue such policies.

If the Pope's misgivings about the Italian Risorgimento had first been aroused by the hostility shown by Garibaldi and Mazzini at Rome, it was now reinforced by Cavour's behaviour towards the Church. Later, it became clear that the unification of Italy must involve the liquidation of the Papal States, so that a further cause for the Pope's hostility was added. But this had by no means been clear at first. The current schemes of 1847 and 1848 were for a federation of the Italian states under the presidency of the Pope, and even as late as 1860 it was a scheme of this kind that Napoleon III and many of the Italian moderates favoured. But those in power at Turin were determined upon something different. They may not have been determined, indeed they were probably not determined to unite the whole of Italy under the House of Savoy; but they were determined that northern Italy, at least, should be under their own control, and this meant at any rate the separation of the Legations from the Papal States.

It has been the common view of historians of the "Whig" or liberal school that the Pope opposed the Risorgimento because he was determined to hold on to his own states, that his states were, in fact, the worst-governed states in Europe, and that his wretched subjects were sighing for liberation by Victor Emmanuel or by Garibaldi. Such a view is now seen to have been very highly coloured. Much has been learnt in the twentieth century about the methods by which governments which seek to incorporate territories not their own go about their business, and plebiscites have lost something of their magic as revelations of the true popular will. When a ruler is hailed first as the most enlightened of his century and then as the most retrograde it is natural today to question whether either view was disinterested or truthful.

Anglo-American opinion was informed by those whose concern it was to paint a black picture of life in the Papal States, and it was a black picture that their audiences wanted. Yet although we must necessarily discount the stories of that life spread by fanatics like the apostate priest Gavazzi, in America, or by the assassin Felice Orsini in England; although we must remember that Cavour made a habit of feeding the more violently anti-Catholic Protestant societies in England, headed by Lord Shaftesbury, with information calculated to inflame opinion against the rule of Rome; and although we should not overlook the system of *agents provocateurs* by which the Turin government stirred up trouble in the Papal States, so as to acquire the right to "restore order," it still remains true that a case rested against the continuance of the temporal power in Italy. No doubt it is absurd to stigmatise it because it was run by priests—as though priests were less likely than laymen to be concerned for justice, truth, or mercy. No doubt it is illogical to protest that the Pope, as Vicar of Christ, should not have maintained an army for his protection, and at the same time to complain that he should have sent an effective force to the Piedmontese to help them in their campaign against the Austrians. No doubt it is unjust to protest against the Pope's dependence upon the intervention of France or Austria when, in fact, the intervention of one of these great powers was always undertaken to prevent the intervention of the other. But it still remains true that, in its administration and in its legal machinery, the papal régime was out of date; it may have been a paternal theocracy, it may have been more merciful than the general run of petty despotisms in Germany or Italy at that time, but politically and economically it was behind the times.

Looking back from the present day, it is hard to avoid the conclusion which was reached earlier in this book that the tremendous diplomatic effort by which Cardinal Consalvi, at the Congress of Vienna, secured the restoration of the Papal States in their entirety was a misplaced effort. The value of those states as a defence for Rome had gone in an age of secularist power politics, and the attempt to administer them caused a division of effort and often much embarrassment to the Pope. Any inefficiency or apparent injustice in his temporal domain easily became a cause of scandal which the Church's enemies were not slow to exploit.

The Pope himself, however, held a paternalistic view of his temporal position. He conceived of his subjects rather as though they were the Levites of the Temple in the days of the Old Testament, a people "set apart" to minister to the special needs of the capital of Christendom. This was their special privilege and duty; it put them into a particularly close relationship with the Church, and incidentally it spared them from many of the trials of membership of a powerful nation state, such as high taxation, conscription, and foreign wars. The states as a whole he regarded as belonging to the Church in the same sense as her religious buildings belonged to her, and as equally inalienable; he was fond of calling them the "robe of Jesus Christ" and of pointing out that, even on Calvary, that robe remained whole. In any case, in his view it was beyond his powers, since he was only a temporary occupant of the throne of Saint Peter, to alienate them.

It will easily be appreciated that, given this attitude on the part of the Pope and given the attitude of either Mazzini and Garibaldi, on the one hand, or Victor Emmanuel and Cavour on the other, compromise was bound to be difficult. But it might not have been impossible had it not been for the advanced anti-clerical position occupied by the Pope's opponents. If he yielded any of his states, either to the Mazzinian republicans, or to the government of Turin, it meant yielding up his subjects to a régime under which the religious orders would be persecuted, and the rest of the secularist programme would be put into force, and this was something which Pio Nono could not contemplate. In every fresh province which the House of Savoy annexed the anti-clerical laws of Turin were introduced, meeting often enough with stiff opposition from the local inhabitants. This fact alone made all attempts at negotiation between Turin and Rome futile.

It was at Plombières, in July 1858, at a secret interview between the Emperor Napoleon III and Cavour, that liquidation of the Papal States first became part of the programme of the highest European circles. The first objective of the Paris-Turin alliance was to drive the Austrians out of northern Italy, but when, by the following July, the alliance had expelled them from Milan and a truce had been concluded (which still left the Austrians in Venice) the question arose as to how the Italian peninsula was to be reorganised. The Pope had no official reason as yet to suppose that he was to be deprived of any of his states; but the effect of the retreat of the Austrians was to cause a revolt in the Legations, where the Austrians had been providing a police force. The insurgents, amongst whom were Piedmontese agents, lost no time in organising a plebiscite which invited Victor Emmanuel to assume suzerainty over the Legations, and this invitation the King was graciously pleased to accept, his patron and ally Napoleon not being willing to prevent him from doing so. It thus became apparent to the Pope that he could no longer count upon either Vienna or Paris to maintain the treaty settlement of 1815, by which his states were guaranteed, and that Turin was actively concerned to disrupt them. It was a sombre outlook, but it was one which, perhaps with more spirit than shrewd sense, he determined to meet by raising his own army. His Secretary of State, Cardinal Antonelli, who understood very clearly that in the last resort the survival of the Papal States must depend upon the good will of France, was opposed to the adventure; but Pio Nono ignored him and entrusted a very much more ardent spirit, the Belgian, Monsignor de Mérode, with the office of Minister of War and the task of raising an international force of volunteers to reinforce his small professional army in the defence of the papacy.

De Mérode (who was a brother-in-law of Montalembert) acted with remarkable energy. First he dashed off to France to secure the services of General Lamoricière, the conqueror of Algiers, who immediately agreed to come. "When a father calls his son to defend him," cried the old general, "there is only one thing to do—to go." Then he launched a recruiting campaign in Ireland (till the British Government stopped it), in Belgium, in France (till Napoleon stopped it), in Austria, in Poland, in Spain, and in Portugal. When he was not sorting out the volunteers, as they arrived, into fighting companies he was improvising equipment in the old coach houses and cellars of the Vatican.

To Antonelli the whole business was abhorrent. In common with many of the cardinals he disliked the eccentricities of de Mérode; but he had the special grievance that the post of War Minister, given by the Pope to the Belgian, curtailed the traditional powers of the Secretary of State, which had embraced the control of military defence. Besides, the whole plan seemed to him chimerical. It was not likely that any scratch army of volunteers would be a match for the Piedmontese regulars. But, even more important, the whole effort was bound to annoy Napoleon III, upon whose good will he rightly saw the maintenance of what remained of the Papal States must depend. For the French troops who had ejected Garibaldi from Rome in 1849 had remained in occupation of the city and, although the French Emperor had allowed Victor Emmanuel to absorb Bologna and the rest of the Legations, he had no intention, as yet, of allowing the rest of his states to be taken from the Pope. Napoleon felt that de Mérode's whole effort implied that the Pope had lost confidence in French protection and this, indeed, was true, though Antonelli thought it was better to disguise the fact. And particularly annoying to the French Emperor was the choice of Lamoricière as commander in chief. For the "conqueror of Algiers" had been Louis Philippe's general, and he had served the Second French Republic of 1848. He was one of those who had opposed the *coup d'état* by which Napoleon had made himself Emperor in 1852, and he was thus altogether out of favour. So were the "legitimist" supporters of the Bourbons who flocked to Rome. When the commander of Napoleon's garrison at Rome, General Goyon, embraced Lamoricière as his brother French soldier-in-arms, he was committing a grave diplomatic error, for which he was duly rebuked. But, in the months that followed, the zeal of the volunteer general and of his following showed up to serious disadvantage the inactivity of Goyon, the official representative of the military might of France.

The purpose of the new army was to defend the Papal States against further revolution or aggression and perhaps, if the diplomatic situation should take a more favourable turn, to recover the Legations from Victor Emmanuel. In the summer of 1860 events moved rapidly. In May Garibaldi arrived with his "Thousand" in Sicily and began his lightning advance through the island and on to Naples. This was enough to decide Napoleon to keep General Goyon's troops at Rome, for he had no more wish than had the Pope to see Rome become a Garibaldian republic. Nor had Cavour; and it was to forestall any such occurrence that he decided to march Piedmontese troops down into the Papal States to check the guerilla leader's advance. The excuse which Cavour gave to the world for invading the papal provinces of Umbria and the Marches was that he had to "restore order" in the face of the revolutionary situation existing there. Actually, however, such small disturbances as there were in those provinces had been created by his own *agents provocateurs* entering from Tuscany. The peaceful peasants of Umbria showed no desire whatever for the Piedmontese, whom they regarded as foreigners. The attack was unprovoked and unexpected; it was launched on September 11, 1860, and Antonelli only received the ultimatum on September 10. Lamoricière's troops were caught scattered at various centres—Terni, Spoleto, Perugia, Orvieto, and Ancona. They had supposed that they might have to deal with local republican movements, or with a move by Garibaldi from the South. They had not reckoned with an ordered invasion by a professional army from the North, because Napoleon had repeatedly given it to be understood that he would never allow the Piedmontese to invade. When they did so, however, it was with the Emperor's tacit consent, even though, as a gesture to

conciliate Catholic opinion in France, he withdrew his ambassador from Turin and reinforced the French garrison at
Rome.

Faced with a desperate situation, Lamoricière did what was
possible. Concentrating his forces as best he could, he pushed
rapidly across towards Ancona, with a view to standing a siege
there. The long Piedmontese lines of communication would
thus have lain between himself on the Adriatic and General
Goyon at Rome. But the well-planned Piedmontese advance
was too rapid for him, and he was cut off near Castelfidardo
before he could reach Ancona. On the evening of September
17 those who could received communion close by at the Holy
House of Loretto; the next day Lamoricière's little force of
six thousand was overwhelmed by the seventeen thousand
commanded by the Piedmontese General Cialdini, and the
gallant Pimodan, chief of staff to the papal commander, was
killed. Lamoricière reached Ancona and attempted to defend
it, but the arrival of several frigates of the Piedmontese navy,
which sailed up the Adriatic and outgunned the mole of the
harbour, killing more than 25 of its 150 defenders, settled the
issue, and the general was compelled to surrender.

So ended, within a year, the almost quixotic attempt of de
Mérode to raise a volunteer Catholic international army to
save the Papal States. And so was the papal power reduced
to a narrow strip of land, along the western coast of Italy,
known as the Patrimony of Saint Peter. It was not yet quite
the end of those states, nor was it quite the end of the papal
army. De Mérode's successor, General Kanzler, was destined
to organise the papal Zouaves, recruited for the most part in
France, and to defeat, in 1867, at Mentana, an attempt by
Garibaldi to seize Rome. But in reality, as Antonelli understood, the defence of the Pope at Rome rested upon the good
will of the French Government, which alone was strong
enough to prevent the Piedmontese army from occupying the
city. It was when France herself was *in extremis* in the
Franco-Prussian War of 1870, and was compelled to withdraw
her last troops from Italy, that the Piedmontese effected their
entry into the city through the Porta Pia, and the oldest temporal sovereignty in Europe disappeared.

CHAPTER TEN

The Syllabus of Errors (1864)

It has been necessary to recount these mainly political and military matters in some detail because it is quite impossible to appreciate the important religious developments of the later half of Pio Nono's long pontificate unless they are understood. For what was done in Italy was done in the name of certain principles and was accompanied by speeches in the Chamber of Deputies at Turin, by articles in the Piedmontese press, and by pamphlets in France, which supplied the ideology of it all. The words most in evidence in this barrage of complacent justification were "progress," "liberalism," and "modern civilisation"; and so it came about that in the year 1864 the Pope published his famous "Syllabus of Errors" in which, in eighty propositions, he condemned a series of current errors and concluded with the statement that it was an error to say that "the Roman Pontiff can and should reconcile himself with, and accommodate himself to progress, liberalism, and modern civilisation."

Everybody in Italy knew what this condemnation meant. But separated from its context, and regarded as a universal reprobation, it seemed, to say the least, disquieting, and it profoundly shocked opinion in France, England, and America, both inside and outside the Church. It has to be remembered that Pio Nono was concerned with the working out of these modern principles in Italy. The condemnation was lifted, like all the condemnations of the Syllabus, from an earlier encyclical, and it is to that encyclical that we must turn in order to see precisely what the general phrases mean. It is called *Jamdudum Cernimus*, and it was issued on March 18, 1861, as a denunciation of the extension of the anti-clerical laws of Piedmont (and particularly the laws dissolving the convents) to the newly united provinces of the rest of Italy. Turin was saying that monasteries, convents, the sacramental view of marriage, and belief in the religious basis of education were out of date, and was giving effect to her attitude in her legislation for the new kingdom as a whole, which now included the Legations, Umbria, and the Marches, recently seized from Rome. She was doing this in the name of progress, liberalism, and modern civilisation, and was adding that the Pope should learn to reconcile himself to these things. The Pope was therefore replying that it was an error to say that he should be reconciled to them. This reply, which he made in the encyclical *Jamdudum Cernimus*, was really the only one which he could properly make. Where the misunderstanding arose, which led to the *furore* throughout the world, was in the *universalising* of this condemnation when it was crystallised into Proposition 80 of the Syllabus of Errors. It was surprising to good English or American liberals, to Mr. Gladstone or to President Lincoln, to learn that the Pope had condemned progress, liberalism, and even modern civilisation! What were they to make of it?

Though the issues involved are still a matter for argument, upon which Catholic historians are not entirely agreed, it would seem that, tactically speaking, the issue of the Syllabus was a move whose wisdom may well be doubted. It was, of course, issued only to the bishops throughout the world, and they were in a better position than was the general public to understand the interpretation which should be put upon the various condemnations, or at any rate to secure from Rome the necessary clarifications. To them, dogmatically speaking, it presented no fundamental difficulties. Trouble arose, however, because a document of this kind, condemning in general terms the errors of the age, had been expected from Rome for some months and was awaited with curiosity by friends, but still more by foes, and was duly seized upon, when it appeared, by governments and by the press, which gave it wide publicity. To the ordinary reader it appeared to condemn not only progress, liberalism, and modern civilisation, but a whole lot of other things which Englishmen and Americans, in particular, had come to hold sacred, such as freedom of speech, freedom of the press, religious toleration, and (in America) the separation of Church and State.

It cannot be said that the Syllabus was happily drafted—Pio Nono himself called it "raw meat needing to be cooked." Each of the propositions was taken from some encyclical or brief issued from Rome during the period since Pius VI. Each proposition was an index reference, referring the reader to some encyclical, in which the proposition in question was discussed more fully. Thus, to take one of the most startling, Proposition 77 reads: "it is an error to say that it is no longer expedient that the Catholic religion should be established to the exclusion of all others." The reader is referred to an allocution in which this theme is developed and explained. If he turns to it he finds that the allocution is concerned with Spain. In other words, the Pope is not concerned with a universal principle, but with the position in a particular state at a particular date. He is expressing his "wonder and distress" (no more) that in a Catholic country (Spain) it should be proposed to disestablish the Church and to place any and every religion upon a precisely equal footing. There is nothing remarkable about such a statement. Disestablishment and toleration were far from the normal practice of the day, whether in Protestant or in Catholic states. And, when the Pope universalises the censure in the phrase quoted as Proposition 77 of the Syllabus of Errors, he is only saying that he refuses to recognise it as a rule of *universal* validity that in *all* countries *every* sort of religion should forthwith be *openly* tolerated, and the Catholic Church should be disestablished.

And so with the other contentious propositions. In relation to freedom of speech the Pope refuses to recognise that it ought to be laid down as a principle of universal validity, at all times, that there should be absolute freedom of speech and absolute freedom of the press. In relation to force, he refuses to accept the view that the Church never has any right to employ force. And in like manner he condemns the assertions that the Church would be better off without the temporal power, that the State alone should have control over education, or that the ultimate authority rests with the totality of the people rather than with God.

A large number of the propositions were concerned with condemnations which any Christian would accept, such as the denunciation of the errors of atheism, communism, pantheism, or the denial of the divinity of Our Lord. But it is surprising to find errors of this kind mixed in with those concerned with the temporal power, or with a free press, which are clearly more contentious. And the cumulative effect of reading the whole Syllabus is naturally very harsh, and to the layman often provoking. The most recent and scholarly historian of the pontificate of Pius IX, Roger Aubert of Louvain, has described its effect by saying that "the majority of Catholics were stupefied."[1] Even many of the bishops, especially in France and in Germany, were somewhat at a loss to know

---

[1] *Le Pontificat de Pie Neuf* (Paris, 1952), p. 255.

how to interpret it. In France the position was aggravated by the refusal of the government to allow the priests to explain the text from the pulpit, although the press was left free to publish and comment as it pleased. It was the great Bishop of Orleans, Dupanloup, who saved the situation by promptly publishing a pamphlet in which he explained the denunciations of the Syllabus in terms of what was called the "thesis" and the "hypothesis." What was denounced, he explained, was the thesis, the general proposition, the notion, for instance, that the *ultimate and universal ideal* was a society with rival religious beliefs, and in which many children were brought up in ignorance of the Faith or in hostility to it. It was impossible that the Church should hold such a state of things to be an *ideal* for society. But to assert, as a consequence of this thesis, the hypothesis that in the present state of society it was necessarily wrong to have a very wide measure of freedom of speech or of the press, or even (it might be) to disestablish the Catholic Church, was quite incorrect. There was no intention of trying to interfere with such liberties, for example, as Napoleon III chose to permit in France, or to criticise those much fuller liberties which pertained in England or in America. Conversely, however, because America had no Established Church, and a secular education only, and enjoyed the "benefits" of divorce laws, it was not correct to say that such things should be introduced universally—for example in the Papal States.

Such was Dupanloup's reasoning on the Syllabus and, though it was accepted a little grudgingly at Rome, it earned for the Bishop of Orleans more than six hundred letters of congratulation from bishops all over the world, who now knew where they stood. Some there were who regarded the distinction between thesis and hypothesis as specious (it was an invention of the *Civiltà Cattolica*). But if the wits of Paris enjoyed saying: "The thesis is when the Church condemns the Jews; the hypothesis is when the papal nuncio dines with the Baron de Rothschild," the argument was none the less perfectly valid, and it remains applicable to a wide range of matters where the Church is concerned with order and discipline, rather than with faith.

It will readily be seen that the stand which the Pope had taken in the Syllabus on the relations of Church and State, on civil liberties, and on toleration, though logical, was very far from that which had been advocated by Lamennais in *L'Avenir*. Lamennais, it is true, had since drifted into apostasy, so that his programme was discountenanced; but his friends Lacordaire and Montalembert had carried on the fight from within the Church. Montalembert, in particular, a passionate liberal but also a passionate Catholic, in his paper the *Correspondant*, had carried on the Liberal Catholic struggle, and had gathered round him an able group of collaborators such as the Comte de Falloux, who secured in 1850 the right of the Church once more to run schools in France, and Frédéric Ozanam, who promoted the charitable societies of Saint Vincent de Paul. Montalembert, though he had bowed to Gregory XVI's condemnation of the programme of *L'Avenir*, was working for the reconciliation of the "Principles of 1789" with Catholicism. He was an outspoken opponent of Napoleon III, he was a member of the French Academy, and he was regarded as the greatest orator in France. He was a warm admirer of British freedom (though not of British policy in Ireland or in India) and he was convinced that the practical alliance of the Church in Ireland and in Belgium with the cause of national freedom had been right and just. Despite Gregory's denunciation of the idea of a "free Church in a free State" he continued to employ the phrase and to advocate the idea, condemning it only as it was used by Cavour, whose perversion of it he called "a despoiled Church in a spoliative State," and a mere cloak for secularism. The one exception which he made in his general advocacy of democratic institutions was the case of the Papal States, where he thought that a theocratic government was necessary and was the real guarantee of liberty everywhere else.

The Pope, as a result of his experiences in Italy, was not much enamoured of Montalembert or of the programme of his *Correspondant*; he much preferred the French journalist Louis Veuillot, whose paper, *L'Univers*, carried on an incessant warfare with the *Correspondant* and enjoyed a far wider circulation than its rival. Veuillot preached on authoritarian politics and was anti-liberal; he supported Napoleon III until 1860, when the Emperor allowed the Piedmontese to overrun the Papal States. After that event he opposed the Emperor bravely and his paper was duly suppressed, though he soon started a new one *Le Monde*.

The fight between Montalembert and Veuillot, that is between Catholic liberalism and Catholic authoritarianism, may be taken as representative of a conflict which was growing within the bosom of the Church, not only in France but in the whole of the West. At bottom the issue was whether or no the Church could be reconciled with the "Principles of 1789," principles which, with the revolutions of 1848, had won wide acceptance. To Montalembert, to Bishop Dupanloup of Orleans, and to many of their way of thinking, it seemed vital that the Church should embrace and ally herself with the new political liberalism, and in order to give wide publicity to their ideas and to create, it was hoped, a really effective Liberal Catholic movement, a great congress of archbishops, bishops, regulars, and laymen was called to Malines, in Belgium, in the summer of the year 1863, and Montalembert was invited to be the principal speaker.

In two great speeches he poured forth his ideas. The *ancien régime* of throne and altar, guaranteed by concordats, Montalembert argues, "had its great and beautiful side: I do not pretend to judge it here, still less to condemn it. It suffices for me to recognise in it one defect, but that a capital one: it is dead . . ." The protection the Church in France had enjoyed under Charles X (the last of the Bourbons) he claimed had been fatal to her; under Louis Philippe, who had been religiously indifferent, the Church had been reborn. He quoted Dupanloup: "We accept, we invoke the principles and liberties proclaimed in '89 . . . you made the Revolution of 1789 without us and against us but *for us*, God wishing it so in spite of you." The great purpose was to Christianise democracy. "The more one is a democrat the more it is necessary to be a Christian; the fervent and practical cult of God made man is the indispensable counter-balance to that perpetual tendency of democracy to establish the cult of man believing himself God." And finally, toleration. Spain and Naples, "those paradises of religious absolutism," had become the "scandal and the despair of all Catholic hearts." Protestant governments, he was quick to point out, had been just as guilty as Catholic ones in this respect; indeed they had often been more guilty. In his day the Catholic Church was still far from free in the Scandinavian countries, for example, or in Switzerland, where the civil war of the Sonderbund in 1847 had crushed the independent liberties of the Catholic cantons. But he was specially concerned with French history, and in particular with the revocation by Louis XIV of the Edict of Nantes, the edict which had guaranteed the liberties of the

French Huguenots. And he condemned, in his own day, the attitude of his enemy Veuillot, of *L'Univers*, who had demanded liberties for the Church under Louis Philippe, but who went on to support Napoleon III, although the Emperor was taking away the liberties of other institutions.

Montalembert's speeches at Malines were greeted with immense enthusiasm; but the shrewder spirits who heard them, and especially the papal nuncio, knew they could never be approved at Rome. They were too reminiscent of *L'Avenir*, and they seemed to approve the sort of thing that was being done in Italy, although Montalembert was explicit in his condemnation of the Turin government. In February of the following year he duly received a brief from Rome, courteous and friendly, but reminding the orator of Gregory's condemnation of *L'Avenir* in *Mirari Vos*. And in the following December the publication of the Syllabus of Errors, with its very different teaching on the relations of Church and State, silenced and embittered Montalembert and put an end to his campaign in the *Correspondant*.

The Syllabus also checkmated a growing Catholic intellectual movement which was particularly strong in Germany. The habit of holding Catholic congresses in Europe was growing, and the congress Montalembert had addressed at Malines was immediately followed by one at Munich, where the leading spirit was the historian Ignaz Döllinger, a professor of the University of Munich, and the subject under review was free intellectual enquiry and especially the scientific study of history in its relation to the Church. This congress was mainly patronised by theologians, philosophers, historians, and scientists from the German universities. From the start it was looked upon with some misgiving by Rome, because no permission had been obtained from the hierarchy to hold it, and because Döllinger was already regarded with suspicion, especially by his own archbishop, Reisach. The issue at Munich was the independent rights of history, reason, and science, and their relations with theology. Döllinger and his friends were claiming that, save for the few matters of faith, dogmatically defined, free intellectual enquiry need have respect for no teachings, certainly not those of the ordinary magistracy of the Church, of the Roman congregations (including the congregation of the Index), or of the accepted theologians. Furthermore he believed that a sound theology must rest upon a proper understanding of history and philosophy. He showed a fine contempt for contemporary Italian scholarship and a characteristically Germanic belief in the transcendent superiority of the German universities. Pio Nono replied to the findings of the congress with a brief in which he asserted that Catholic thought must be guided by just those elements whose authority Döllinger denied.

It was a brief pregnant with consequences, for not only did it prevent the holding of further congresses along the lines of that of Munich but it silenced the leading English Catholic scholar and historian, Sir John (later Lord) Acton, who was a pupil of Döllinger, and whose journals, first the *Rambler*, and then the *Home and Foreign Review*, had been arguing the case for independent, lay, Catholic intellectual enquiry, which should have regard for no authority save dogma. Acton felt unable to continue his work; instead, as Regius Professor of Modern History at Cambridge University, he pursued the paths of secular history. Soon the Syllabus duly confirmed the verdict of the brief by stating, in Proposition 12, that it was an error to say that "the science of philosophy and morals can and should be independent of divine *and ecclesiastical* authority."[2]

It will never be possible to estimate the consequences of the checkmating by the Syllabus of the whole movement loosely called "Liberal Catholic," or of the various analogous papal pronouncements which belong to the 1860s. Certainly it was they, rather than the later Vatican Council, with its decree of the dogma of Papal Infallibility, that drove Döllinger into an attitude which led to his apostasy, that silenced Acton and Montalembert, that dismayed Dupanloup. The cost was tremendous; yet it may have been necessary to pay it. The Syllabus was welcomed by Louis Veuillot, by W. G. Ward of the *Dublin Review*, by Queen Isabella of Spain, by Henry Manning, the new Archbishop of Westminster (1865). It has always to be remembered that the nineteenth-century liberals were inclined to assert that freedom was the *one* good, that it was *all* that was necessary; and their hostility to all authority, even to necessary and legitimate authority, was often exaggerated and—in the Italy of the Risorgimento or in the France

[2] The italics are mine. By philosophy we must, of course, understand what are now termed history and science as well as philosophy in the narrow sense.

of the French Revolution—often impious. Looked at in its entirety, the Syllabus, while it nowhere condemned free governmental institutions, was a reminder that the liberties invoked by the liberals were not in themselves the sources of truth and grace, that they might be beneficial or they might be harmful, according to place and to circumstance; and that, whatever might be said for or against the "Principles of 1789," the Church could never regard it as the *goal* of society that error should be freely taught to the young. As Pio Nono put it in October 1863, "The Church will never admit it as a benefit and a principle that error and heresy should be preached to Catholic peoples." In other words, absolute freedom of speech and of the press could not be regarded as everywhere or always desirable.

The Syllabus of Errors was not an infallible papal pronouncement; since it was a summarised classified index to previous pronouncements it could not be. If the infallibility lay anywhere it lay with the documents to which the Syllabus made reference; but since these, for the most part, were concerned with particular people, books, and occasions, it was not likely that they, either, would fulfil the traditional conditions of an infallible pronouncement, namely that it must be made by the Pope "when exercising the office of pastor and teacher of all Christians." All the same, it was very widely, though very loosely, taken to be the dogmatic teaching of the Church, and it was held to imply that she was opposed to modern liberties generally and was determined to assert the superiority of Church to State.

That was why the campaign conducted by the ultramontanes, especially in France in the later 1860s, in favour of a dogmatic definition of Papal Infallibility, aroused such enormous excitement and such grave apprehensions. In the popular view the Pope had just condemned modern liberties, and had reasserted the superiority of Church to State in terms reminiscent of Pope Boniface VIII in the fourteenth century. If, then, he were now declared infallible, where did the governments stand, and what would be their relations with their Catholic subjects? That these fears were not confined to emotional radicals may be gathered from the fact that they exercised very seriously Mr. Gladstone in England and the Protestant chancellor of Austria, Beust, together with the governments of Napoleon III and Bismarck, and of many of the lesser states

of Europe. In fact a *démarche* by the governments, to pre‹
vent the discussion of either the Syllabus or the Infallibilit
at the Vatican Council (opened on December 8, 1869), wa‹
only prevented by the good offices of the British representa‹
tive to the Holy See, Odo Russell, who explained the tru‹
state of affairs to Gladstone, and by the good sense of Napo‹
leon's Protestant premier, Emile Ollivier.

CHAPTER ELEVEN

The Vatican Council and the Loss of Rome (1870)

Since almost every government was hostile, and since it was supposed that an occupation of Rome by the Piedmontese army, or else by Garibaldi, was imminent, it is really rather remarkable that those concerned had the courage to go through with the vast project of holding a General Council of the Church at Rome. For it involved bringing to the city more than eight hundred ecclesiastical and other dignitaries from all over the world; and the scope of the agenda (the nature of the Church, and of her teaching authority, together with her relations with the State) suggested that the proceedings might well last as long as those of the previous General Council, that of Trent, in the sixteenth century, which had extended over eighteen years. Was this really a moment when Rome might expect so long a period of tranquility and security? Cardinal Antonelli, who disliked the whole idea of the Council because it was likely to exacerbate relations with Napoleon, thought the summons very rash. But Pio Nono went ahead, encouraged somewhat by the victory of his own troops in 1867, under Kanzler, over Garibaldi at Mentana, and also by the firmer attitude of the French, now back in Rome and determined to withstand the Piedmontese.

The purpose of the Council of Trent had been to define more precisely the beliefs of the Church, so that men might perceive and know what was erroneous and heretical in the tenets of the various reformers, in the period of the Reformation, and what might be accepted. The purpose of the Council of the Vatican was to define the nature of the Church herself. But, before it could do that, it was necessary for it to reassert the fundamental dogmatic basis of Christianity itself, since this was now, for the first time, being called in question. Whereas in the sixteenth century men had still believed in the idea of Christian authority and differed only as to its form, by the nineteenth century the very basis of Christianity, namely faith in Christ Himself, was being denied. Or, to put the matter in another way, whereas in the sixteenth century the practice and doctrine of the Church had been under at-

tack, by the nineteenth century faith in the Christian revela
tion itself had been called in question as a result of the
speculations of the eighteenth-century philosophers of the En
lightenment. It was therefore necessary for the Council, at the
outset, to counter the various non-Christian philosophies an
beliefs which had grown up since the previous Council had
met, and this it proceeded to do in the early months of 1870 to do
The result was the constitution *Dei Filius*, which rejected
rationalism (i.e. the belief in the sufficiency of reason withou
faith), pantheism (i.e. the belief that God is somehow im
manent in nature and not to be sought outside it), an
naturalism (i.e. the denial of what is not evident to the
senses). Unanimously agreed by the middle of April, *De
Filius* was duly approved by the Pope on April 24, 1870
and secured the basis of Christianity by reasserting th
unique, exclusive, and supernatural character of the Christian
revelation.

There had not been much argument amongst those as
sembled concerning this constitution. It was otherwise con
cerning the main task of the council, namely the definition o
the nature of the Church, of her authority, and of her relation
with the State. Here there was plenty of highly explosive ma
terial for argument, material upon which not only the world
outside but the Fathers of the Church themselves held dif
ferent views. Not all of the subject matter, however, was con
troversial. There were some early chapters in the proposed
draft which were concerned with the intrinsic nature of the
Church as a "perfect," "spiritual," and "supernatural" society
entrusted with a peculiar mission, and guided by the Holy
Spirit; about these things there was general agreement. Bu
the later chapters of the draft were concerned with matter
about which, broadly speaking, there were two diverging view
held by two distinct parties, the ultramontanes (the majority
and the liberals (the minority). These chapters concerned
the nature of the authority of the Pope, the nature of the
Papal States, the rights and duties of governments, and the
relations between Church and State. Some of these were mat
ters which had been touched upon in the Syllabus and had
already caused a storm. But the most controversial of them
the nature of the authority of the Pope—had not formed par
of the Syllabus, it had only become the chief topic of contro
versy in the later 1860s.

It would hardly be an exaggeration to say that <u>in the opinior</u>

of Catholics generally, as well as of those outside the Church,
the Council had been called with a view to defining the dogma
of Papal Infallibility. That this was not in fact the case will
be evident from what has just been said about its agenda. In
the first draft there were chapters on the papal authority, as
there were on the authority of bishops, parish priests, and
others. But there was nothing about the Infallibility. The
Pope's view was that it would be improper for him to introduce the topic; if the Council, after it had met, chose to
introduce it then it might do so. It soon became apparent that
a large proportion of the Council did so choose, and a draft
chapter on the Infallibility was already in circulation by March
6. By the end of April the Pope had agreed not only that
this chapter should be debated but that it should be taken
immediately and out of its turn. Logically, the first ten chapters of the draft should have been taken before the chapters
about the papacy were reached. But if this procedure had
been followed, it might well have been as much as a year before the chapters on the papacy came up for consideration,
and this was a delay which the keen ultramontanes were loth
to face. Their leader, Manning of Westminster (Wiseman's
successor), who knit them together as a party, was a man of
powerful and persuasive personality; a convert from Anglican-
ism, he was a passionate believer in the most authoritarian
interpretation of papal prerogatives. And, in his campaign to
have the matter of the Infallibility debated forthwith, he had
the support of two hundred members of the Council. When
the president of the Council refused to alter the order of the
agenda, or to introduce the Infallibility out of its turn, he
appealed directly to the Pope.

Pio Nono acceded to Manning's request, and the chapters
on the papacy were introduced forthwith. Although at the
opening of the Council the Pope had been so scrupulously
neutral, and although he remained outside the Council—the
one bishop without a seat—he had begun by March to make
his own personal attitude clear and to favour a settlement of
the Infallibility issue in an ultramontane sense. This was because he had been profoundly provoked by the attitude of the
liberals during January and February. Dupanloup of Orleans
had been responsible, with Darboy of Paris, for trying to secure
an intervention by Napoleon III to prevent the draft from
being debated at all. Acton, as we have seen, had been active
in the same sense in London, and Döllinger at Munich, and

both had their friends at the Council. In March the dying Montalembert had particularly incensed the Pope by publishing a very injudicious article in which he talked about the ultramontanes "setting up their idol in the Vatican." The controversy centering around the Infallibility was becoming a real menace to the Church, because the Catholic press, and very often the secular press as well, was whipping up passionate feeling about it. It seemed to the Pope that the Council had better settle the matter, once and for all, as soon as possible. It seemed unlikely that it would do effective work on the authority and duties of the other orders of the priesthood until it had settled those of the head.

Dupanloup, however, who led the liberal party at the council, could muster some 140 supporters who were all opposed to the introduction of the burning topic. But it is important to recognize that this does not mean that these opponents did not believe in the Infallibility of the Pope. The attitude of one or two may have been uncertain; but the general attitude of the liberal opposition—or, as they were generally called, the minority—was that of their leaders Dupanloup, Darboy, and Ketteler of Mainz. These churchmen believed very sincerely in the Infallibility of the Pope in matters of dogma; the old Gallican attitude, still current in the days of Louis XIV, which asserted the superiority of General Councils to the Pope, even in matters of faith, was little in evidence. The papal definition of the dogma of the Immaculate Conception in 1854 had been generally accepted without question, although on that occasion the Pope had only made such informal consultation of the Church as he chose. It would certainly not be true to say that the opposition considered a papal pronouncement, ex cathedra, on a matter of faith or morals, to be other than infallible.

The anxieties of the opposition revolved rather around the question whether so subtle a concept was capable of precise definition and whether, even if it could be defined, it was opportune that it should be. Thus Dupanloup, before the council had opened, had published a pamphlet in which he raised the question whether it could be exactly demonstrated when the Pope spoke only as "doctor in a particular case" and when as "universal father." He feared that "digging around the roots of the tree" of ecclesiastical authority, to try to find the "life-giving gland," might end by killing the tree itself. Behind this nervousness lay the fear that, stampeded by the more extreme ultramontanes, the Council might define the Infallibility in terms which would suggest that everything the Pope said was infallible. Some of the ultramontanes were saying dangerous things. The *Civiltà Cattolica* was talking about liberals of the school of Dupanloup and Montalembert as though they were not fully Catholics, and was asking for a "definition by acclamation" at the Council, while Veuillot was reminding his readers that the Holy Ghost had no need of the assistance of "lengthy deliberations." The attitude of Veuillot, of W. G. Ward in the *Dublin Review*, and even of Herbert Vaughan in the *Tablet*, was only less disquieting to sensitive souls than was that of the *Civiltà* in as much as those papers had less influence than had the Jesuit organ at Rome. The leading English theologian, John Henry Newman, perhaps the greatest Catholic thinker of the day, felt no difficulty at all in accepting the whole traditional infallible papal authority in matters of dogma, as it had been exercised throughout the centuries, but felt very keenly that it was unnecessary and unwise to make a dogmatic definition at that time on the matter. He did not believe that the spiritual authority of the Pope was at that date being called in question by the Church; and unlike Manning (who thought that a definition of Papal Infallibility would rally English Protestants to the Church) he thought that such a definition would discourage conversions.

It was noticeable that, on the whole, the opposition bishops came from countries where Catholics were either in a minority or were at least up against the constant criticism of Protestants, or of the Greek Orthodox, or of those who professed no Christian allegiance. Thus at least two thirds of the American bishops at the Council, led by the able Kenrick of Saint Louis, were opposed to the definition because they felt it would make their task in spreading the Faith more difficult, and at least a dozen of the German bishops, some twenty of the French bishops, a substantial proportion of the Austrians, and of those in the eastern Mediterranean, together with all the Hungarians, took a similar line. On the other hand it is noteworthy that the English bishops, with the exception of Clifford of Clifton, followed Manning in support of the ultramontane or majority party.

Finally there was the purely political consideration. This weighed heavily with the French bishops. No government liked the idea of the definition, following so closely upon and seeming to reinforce the Syllabus. But Napoleon III was particularly sensitive on the matter. His relations with the Church in France were still governed by the Concordat and Organic Articles of his uncle and, although he had been generally friendly to the Church in France, he was as jealous as any previous French ruler of "the encroachments of Rome." And the leading French bishops were very close to the Emperor. It would be a pardonable exaggeration to say that in 1869 Dupanloup and Darboy were closer to the Emperor than they were to the Pope; for this reason Pio Nono had refused to confer upon Darboy the red hat of a cardinal although, as Archbishop of Paris, he might expect this honour. And the political anxieties of these bishops were reinforced by Cardinal Antonelli, who understood better than anybody else how dependent was the Pope, politically speaking, upon the Emperor, and to whom it seemed folly to cause offence in Paris. But the Secretary of State was far beneath the spiritual level of his master the Pope, to whom the Secretary's political cautiousness seemed unworthy, and his relations with the opposition disloyal. From this time must be reckoned an increased cooling in the relations between Pope and Secretary, relations which, on account of a certain coarseness in the Secretary's character, had seldom been very cordial.

The lengthy debates of May and June 1870 upon the papacy centred around two major questions. The first was what was called the primacy of the Pope, by which was meant his primacy of jurisdiction. Some of the minority argued, with some force, that it was wrong to assert that the Pope held a universal primacy of jurisdiction because, in their own dioceses, the bishops exercised ordinary jurisdiction and they derived this authority not from the Pope but from God. This, however, was not Pio Nono's view of the matter. He had been in the habit of encouraging appeals to Rome, and on certain occasions had reversed the decisions of bishops, lifting cases out of the local ecclesiastical courts and bringing them directly under papal jurisdiction. So, far from yielding to the will of the minority in this matter, he insisted upon the assertion, late in the proceedings, of a statement that the Pope held "the full plenitude of this supreme power." The settlement of this ancient quarrel in the Pope's favour, at the Vatican Council, was one of the most important steps in that centralisation of ecclesiastical authority in the hands of the papacy which was so conspicuous a feature of this pontificate, and so ardently desired by the ultramontanes.

The second debate concerned the Infallibility itself.

Having failed to prevent this subject from being discussed, the minority concentrated upon trying to secure that the terms in which the dogma was defined should be such as would make it as clear as possible that only a very limited category of papal pronouncements could be regarded as infallible and therefore irreformable. In this they were successful to the extent that the wording finally adopted was a disappointment to some of the ultramontanes, and it disposed of the absurd claims of some Catholic journalists that the Pope was infallible in his every utterance. The agreed text reads that the Roman Pontiff is infallible only when speaking "*ex cathedra, that is, when exercising the office of pastor and teacher of all Christians,* he defines with his supreme Apostolic authority a doctrine concerning faith or morals to be held by the universal church. . . ."

But to many of the minority, including Darboy of Paris, Dupanloup, and Ketteler, this definition was still unsatisfactory, and eighty-eight of them voted against it at the committee stage. They wanted somehow to secure that a clause should be inserted showing that the Pope was bound to consult the Church before defining a dogma. In a last-minute effort to secure general agreement Darboy drew up a memorandum, at the Pope's request, in which he pleaded on behalf of the minority that, after the phrase "when exercising the office of pastor and teacher of all nations," there should be inserted the phrase "the bishops not being excluded." He also asked that the statement that the Pope held "the full plenitude" of the juridical primacy should be removed. He and Ketteler went to the Pope and begged him on their knees to accept these two changes; if they were made, the two bishops assured him the minority would vote with the majority. The Pope was moved, but Manning pressed for the text as it stood, and as it had been agreed by the majority, and the Pope said he must leave the matter to the Council. So, rather than appear at the final meeting and vote to his face against the known wishes of the Pope, most of the minority followed the advice of Dupanloup and left Rome and, when the final vote was taken on July 18, 533 of the fathers voted *placet* and only two *non placet*, the dissidents coming from Cajazzo, in southern Italy, and from Little Rock, Arkansas, U.S.A. As soon as the Pope had read out the new constitution, *Pastor Aeternus*, in St. Peter's (by flickering candlelight and during a thunderstorm) the two dissidents fell at his feet and gave their full filial assent. The new definition, recently the subject of hot debate, was now a dogma of the Church, and therefore commanded the assent of the minority as much as of the majority. Dupanloup and his friends had always made it clear that they would joyfully accept the general verdict, and letters of assent poured into Rome from those who had left before the final vote. By the end of the year almost all the bishops had written, mostly expressing the joy with which they accepted the verdict of the Council. The last to do so were Haynald of Kalocsa (Hungary) and Strossmayer, from Croatia.

It was very widely argued at the time, and it is sometimes repeated to this day, that the Council of the Vatican was no true Council of the Church because improper pressure was brought to bear upon the bishops, especially by the Pope. This was widely believed in London and in Paris as well as in Germany and in America. No doubt in part the wish was father to the thought; but the writings of Acton, who was in Rome, and of Döllinger, both of whom were bitterly hostile to the ultramontanes, together with the more sensational despatches of the journalists, such as Mosley of the London *Times*, provided the texts for the beliefs. Unfortunately the secrecy imposed upon those actually participating, who were not allowed to write home about what was happening, and the delay before the Vatican made the relevant papers available (they were only fully published in the year 1927) caused a very long interval before the criticisms could be effectively countered by the truth.

Was there any substance in these accusations?

In some respects the ultramontanes, and particularly their leader Manning, laid themselves open to criticism by their tactics; but the suggestion that the Council was not truly oecumenical or free, and that the Pope "coerced" the bishops is absurd. If the proportion of Italian bishops was large, that was because of the traditionally small size of Italian bishoprics—and a fair sprinkling of the Italian bishops were to be found amongst the minority. If the "guillotine" was imposed, late in the proceedings, to restrict the volume of debate, it was not done with the intent of suppressing criticism, but in response to a general petition, because the interminable repetition of the same arguments was becoming intolerable to all. If the Pope influenced votes by letting his own opinion be known, there was no reason whatever why any bishop should allow himself to be so influenced—the Pope's closest friend, de Mérode, his chamberlain, voted with the minority and was never rebuked for doing so. It is certainly true that the Pope dispensed hospitality; charitable as ever, he helped to pay the expenses of many of the poorer bishops who came from a distance. ("I don't know whether the Pope will emerge from this council fallible or infallible," he said, "but he will certainly be bankrupt."[1]) But the suggestion that the beneficiaries felt obliged to vote as he wished was both absurd and unworthy. Many of the poorer bishops came from America, and they were certainly not amongst the more docile. Nor does a scrutiny of the names of those who received the cardinal's hat in the years following the Council show any preference for those who had belonged to the majority; rather the reverse. And Manning, the leader of the majority, was kept waiting for his hat until the year 1875, even though he was Archbishop of Westminster.

The stories about papal pressure are in fact without foundation; the person who did employ tactics which might at times be called unscrupulous was Manning. The Archbishop of Westminster was not above packing committees with his friends, whereas the Pope was careful to try to see that all points of view were represented on the committees. In Manning's defence, however, it is fair to remember that an assembly of seven hundred and more, with a practical job to do, would never have achieved anything without a party organisation. Nor did the minority leader, Bishop Dupanloup of Orleans, yield many points to his colleague at Westminster in the matter of party manipulation.

Yet it is also true that the Pope's attitude played a very important part in the outcome. This was because his prestige and popularity had become so enormous throughout the Catholic world by the year 1870, and because his generosity, his sense of humour, his personal interest in all the members of the Council, and his bonhomie endeared him even to his opponents. There can be no doubt that there was a real reluc-

---

[1] The joke is more pointed in the Italian: *Non so se il Papa uscirà di questo Concilio fallibile od infallibile; ma questo è certo che sarà fallito.*

tance to "vote against the Pope," and that this was why some members of the minority left Rome rather than do so.

The growth of the prestige of the papacy in the decade before 1870, which was certainly a factor at the Council, was to prove to be the beginning of a movement so important in the development of the Catholic Church during the following hundred years that it is worth while trying to see how it came about. Its origin may be traced to the accession of Pius IX in 1846 when, in contrast to the practice under the régime of Gregory XVI, numerous visitors were welcomed to the Quirinal, and the Pope might almost be said to have courted popularity. One cannot easily imagine Pio Nono treating Lamennais in the chilly way in which the Breton had been treated by his predecessor. With the new Pope began the modern custom by which almost any visitor to Rome, whether Catholic or no, who wanted to see the Pope, could secure an audience. But, while this development tended to bring the Pope more into the public eye of the world, his authority within the Church was being strengthened rather by his encouraging the bishops to make frequent journeys to Rome, *ad limina*, and especially by the great gatherings of the year 1862, when more than three hundred bishops attended the canonisation of the twenty-six missionaries martyred in Japan in 1597, and in the year 1867, when more than five hundred were assembled there for the eighteenth centenary of the martyrdom of Saint Peter and Saint Paul. The great modern world-wide movement of the Church in pilgrimage towards Rome had begun—facilitated, of course, by improved communications.

It would be wrong, however, to suppose that Pius IX personally created the ultramontane movement. In the realm of ideas it went back, as we have seen, at least as far as Lamennais and De Maistre. And it grew throughout the nineteenth century as men came to appreciate clearly that the growing omnicompetence of the State carried with it the subservience of the Church unless she countered by asserting her own independent authority. Each new danger to the Church (and the new emotional nationalism, dating from the time of Napoleon, was a very serious danger) she tended to meet by developing her own powers in a new direction, and the new pretensions of state governments, seeking to control every aspect of life, she strove to counter by a strengthening of her own government. The necessity for such a development, though hidden from the wise, even from the very wise—the Actons, the Döllingers, the Montalemberts—was yet felt by the Church and was implemented by a Pope who, while he never claimed to be an intellectual, was peculiarly sensitive to what the Church was requiring of him. So Pius IX deliberately facilitated the process of centralisation, conferring, for example, more widely the Roman title of Monsignor, insisting upon the general adoption of the Roman liturgy (save by the Uniates), and extending the scope of the Roman jurisdiction. The length of his reign was itself an important factor in this process because it meant that, in his later years, the majority of the bishops had been invested by himself personally. By nature a humble man, he was not afraid to have greatness thrust upon him. He was willing to play the rôle marked out for him by the "manifest destiny" of the Church.

Meanwhile the political developments in Italy, while they led the anti-Catholics to hail the approaching end, not only of the Papal States, but even of the papacy itself, served to endear the resolute and unyielding sufferer to his Church. His long pontificate was regarded as a living martyrdom, even though his personal sufferings were not to be compared with those of Pius VII.

The final crisis in the liquidation of the Papal States came just after the Council had been prorogued. In one dramatic week of July 1870 Napoleon declared war upon Prussia, Dupanloup and other minority leaders left Rome (excusing themselves that they might stand by their flocks on the outbreak of the Franco-Prussian War), and the Council voted the constitution *Pastor Aeternus* defining the Papal Primacy and Infallibility. These were events pregnant with consequences for the twentieth century and they all occurred between July 14 and July 18.

On August 4 Napoleon, in dire need of every soldier he could muster, started to embark his Roman garrison from Civitavecchia; on September 2 he suffered the disaster of Sedan, on September 4 his empire was at an end. The hour for which King Victor Emmanuel and his Piedmontese army had waited had now struck. The King sent an envoy to the Pope to say that he proposed to take over key places within the Patrimony of Saint Peter to "maintain order"—this although he was detaining Mazzini at Gaeta and Garibaldi on the island of Caprera and the papal army, now thirteen thousand strong, was perfectly capable of meeting any internal disturbance which might be occasioned by the departure of the French.

The Pope rejected the ultimatum and calmly awaited the outcome. On September 19, from the top of the *Scala Santa*, which—an old man now with flowing white hair—he had ascended upon his knees, he addressed his troops assembled in the piazza of the Lateran. It was a farewell, and the last act of a papal ruler in the city of Rome. That night he shut himself up in the Vatican and moved no more in the city. Very early the next morning the bombardment began around the walls. The Pope had given orders that there was to be only a token resistance, sufficient to show that he was yielding to force. Nevertheless there was fighting, and there were casualties at the Porta Pia, which was where the Piedmontese General Cadorna effected his entry. By afternoon Cadorna and Kanzler had concluded an armistice. That night the papal Zouaves slept under the great Bernini colonnade of the Piazza San' Pietro; next day they were disbanded. In the following year Rome was officially proclaimed to be the capital of the new Kingdom of Italy.

Pius IX, now seventy-eight years old, still had more than seven years to reign, a month more in fact than his supplanter, the much younger King Victor Emmanuel who, in July 1871, established himself in the papal palace of the Quirinal. No word or sign or act would the aged Pope allow which might seem to imply that he condoned what had occurred. When, in November 1870, the Italian Government introduced the Law of Guarantees to regulate the new position of the papacy and the relations between Church and State in Italy, he ignored it and, although he was in dire need of money, he rejected what the law offered him in compensation for his temporal losses. He would not have back a "portion of what had been seized." None of the changes, not even the loss of the Legations, which dated from 1859, would he recognise.

All the same, the Law of Guarantees did in fact regulate the position of the papacy, and also of the Church in Italy, until it was superseded by the treaty negotiated between Pope Pius XI and Mussolini in 1929, which created the Vatican State. The Pope had no hand in the shaping of the law and the *Civiltà Cattolica*, the *Osservatore Romano*, and the rest of the Catholic press assailed it bitterly, though no more bitterly than the anti-clerical Italian press of the Left assailed it for its "leniency to the Church." The great problem was how to give the Pope sovereignty if he had no territory. Sovereignty without territory, argued the *Civiltà*, was unknown to Italian or to any other law; clearly it was only a fiction designed to satisfy opinion abroad. The Pope would remain at the mercy of the Italian Parliament. This was true, but what the law achieved, and not without success, was to confer upon the Pope what can best be termed "honorary sovereignty." It declared him to be possessed of the same immunities from the interference of ordinary Italian law as were enjoyed by the King of Italy or by other governments. He was to have his own postal, telegraphic, and diplomatic services, together with the exclusive use (but not ownership) of the Vatican, St. John Lateran, and Castel Gandolfo. He was allowed to keep his personal guard.

All this was in recognition of the Pope's peculiar position as Head of the Catholic Church throughout the world. But it was also necessary to regulate the position of the Church in Italy, and especially in those territories which had belonged to the Papal States. Here an attempt was made by the Law of Guarantees to introduce Cavour's "free Church in a free State." No longer would the State nominate bishops. No longer would papal missives and directions be subject to the State's *placet* or *exequatur*. But—and this was to prove crucial—no bishop or priest could be invested with his temporalities without the consent of the State. Thus did the New Order maintain a stranglehold which enabled it to control the Church far more closely than it had been controlled in Italy before.

Broadly speaking, the remaining years of the century were to see the Law of Guarantees somewhat differently honoured in its provisions regarding the Church and in its provisions regarding the papacy. In regard to the Church there ensued in Italy a persecution of the remaining religious orders and an anti-clerical programme of secularisation second in its stringency only to the policies of Bismarck in his famous Kulturkampf, or of the Third Republic in France. But in regard to the Pope, who was an object of world concern, the new Italian Government, by contrast, was at pains to behave with scrupulous correctness. The new State was indeed far too insecure at first to behave otherwise. It owed its unity to Bismarck's defeat of the Austrians in 1866, which had enabled it to seize Venice, and to his defeat of Napoleon III in 1870, which had enabled it to seize Rome. It certainly could not afford to ignore Bismarck, and the German chancellor, with an eye on the Catholics of the Rhineland and Bavaria, was insisting that the dignity and independence of the Head of the Church must be maintained—he would speak somewhat differently at the time of his own Kulturkampf. Even Gladstone, much as he disapproved of both the Syllabus and the work of the Vatican Council, declared his concern about the independence of the Head of the Church. All governments with large numbers of Catholic subjects were concerned. It is true that the government of Victor Emmanuel had no need to fear a military intervention at Rome on behalf of the Pope, such as had occurred in 1849, because the two governments which had been accustomed to intervene in Italy were now sadly embarrassed. Both Austria and France had lost wars against Bismarck and, although in both countries the Catholics were strong, and the ultramontanes openly urged intervention, neither the Protestant premier of Austria, Beust, nor the Head of the Provisional Government of France, Jules Favre, was in a position to act effectively in Italy even if either had been much inclined to do so. Yet the new Italian State was very insecure and there were many, including the Pope, who did not think it would last. It could not afford to estrange those Catholics at home who would accept the new régime only if it treated the Pope properly, or those Catholics abroad who might prove strong enough to persuade their governments not to recognise Victor Emmanuel's rule at Rome.

Looking back from the twentieth century it is easy to argue that the Pope was well rid of the encumbrance of his temporal power, and that the spiritual position of the papacy has, in the long run, been strengthened by the loss. But we have seen why Pius IX took a different view, and the immediate consequences of his defeat were very serious. The Church has always drawn strength from defeat, but a defeat this was, and to argue that Pius IX should have voluntarily yielded central Italy and the Eternal City itself, to a secularist anti-clerical rule, is as unreasonable as to say that no resistance should have been offered to the emergence of a Lutheran Church in Germany, or to the proscription of the Mass in England, because, in the long run, the Catholic Church in Germany and in England would be reborn from defeat to a purged and more vigorous life. How serious the defeat in Italy was may be judged from the treatment the Church received all over Europe in the following decades, a treatment which she had to endure largely because it was assumed, after the fall of Rome, that she was moribund. The prestige of the Pope within the Church may have been very high after 1870; but outside the Church, and especially in the chancelleries of the great states, it was desperately low, and governments felt free, as never before, to attack both the Church and her head with impunity.

CHAPTER TWELVE

The Church in America Before the Irish Immigration (to 1830)

With the year 1870 we have reached a moment in the history of the Church, and indeed of Western civilisation, when it is profitable to pause and to reflect upon where we stand. For we are in a position where, however briefly, we should take in the view upon either side if we are to acquire any idea of the land in which we dwell in the twentieth century. In this one year, more evidently than in any other, may be seen the growing centralisation of the Church and the rising authority of the new State. In this one year there had appeared: the dogma of Papal Infallibility, together with the clear recognition of the supreme authority of the Pope; the disappearance of the Papal States; the effective uniting of the Kingdom of Italy; the victory which established the new Germany; the total defeat and occupation of France. All these events meant a reorientation of the politico-religious world of Europe. They meant a more brutal and violent assertion of the claims of the State, now entering nakedly upon imperialistic ambitions which would lead towards the First World War. And, as though in reply, we see the Church Universal, now more centralised, always tending to assert her cosmopolitan character in order to redress the balance, and thus courting the cruel persecutions most often associated with Bismarck's Kulturkampf in Germany, and with the secularist governments of the Third Republic in France, but by no means confined to those two countries.

And in another respect we have reached a watershed. For we have reached an age when the rapid expansion of an industrial society was thrusting the social question into the foreground, so that Pius IX's successor, Leo XIII, would be compelled to preoccupy himself with the new economic problems which it raised.

Yet before we go on to consider this new era in Europe it is right that we should turn away, for a time, from that continent which has so largely preoccupied our attention and should consider the significance of what was happening in the

New World across the Atlantic. For already what was happening in America held much significance for Europe. If, with the pontificate of Leo XIII (1878–1903), we enter an epoch when Rome became for the first time in modern history very largely preoccupied with social and economic questions, the extraordinary expansion in numbers and wealth of North America in the middle of the century, and the sufferings of her workers, were an important influence in thrusting these questions upon Leo's attention. Moreover, in the field of politics and ideology, American experience was becoming important. It was becoming important and it was being unduly neglected. Looking back from the middle of the twentieth century, from a time, that is, when the disestablishment of Churches, together with a very wide measure of liberty of speech, of the press, and of association, has come to be accepted in most Western countries with the acquiescence and even with the encouragement of the Church, it is permissible to regret that the example in these matters already set by America in the nineteenth century was not given closer attention. For although it was probably inevitable that the programme of Lamennais in his *L'Avenir*, which had advocated these things, should have been condemned by Gregory XVI in 1832—at a time, that is, when Catholic opinion in France and Europe was not prepared for such ideas, and when any countenancing of them would very likely have led to a resurrection of the horrors of 1789–99— it still remains true that wonderful progress had since been made by the Church in America under much those conditions advocated by Lamennais. And it is at least arguable that Pius IX, by the year 1864, when he published the Syllabus of Errors, could usefully have made it clear that under some conditions such freedoms were very valuable. Although it might be an error to assert that disestablishment, free speech, and free choice of religion were everywhere necessary, it had become clear by then that they could, nevertheless, in certain circumstances be very advantageous to the work of the Church and to the cause of truth. It might have saved embarrassment to the hierarchies of America and of England had he done so; certainly it would have borne witness to a fact which was becoming increasingly evident in the nineteenth century and would be almost axiomatic in the twentieth.

Although in a variety of ways, and especially by the encouragement of missionary endeavours, Rome materially assisted in the growth of the Church in America, and although it gave Pius IX peculiar pleasure to create the first American cardinal (Cardinal McCloskey, Archbishop of New York, in 1875), it cannot be said that the climate of opinion at Rome was such as to encourage the notion that the Church Universal had much to learn from the experience of the Church in North America. That Church was a missionary Church, governed by the Congregation of the Propaganda; the conditions in which it had to operate were regarded as abnormal, and even as un-civilised. To Cardinal Antonelli it seemed rather outrageous to contemplate the creation of an American cardinal, and even the more generous and warmhearted Pio Nono was surely taking a rather distant, bird's-eye view of the New World when he said that his visit to Chile, as a young priest in 1821, caused him to have a special pride in making the Archbishop of New York a cardinal in 1875! It is true that he was the first Pope who had crossed the Atlantic. But his doing so had not brought him much nearer, even geographically speaking, to the United States.

But, in truth, before the "hungry forties" brought the hugely increased immigration of the Irish to seek a new life in the land of opportunity, the Church in North America was, numerically speaking, a very small affair. It was strongest, rela-tively, in Canada, since Canada had been settled by the French and had only been acquired by conquest by the British in the middle of the eighteenth century. Though subject to the penal laws operating throughout the British Empire before the Emancipation Act of 1829, the Catholics of Quebec and Montreal had been strong enough to resist and to retain their identity, and Pius VII had rewarded them by raising to metro-politan status the bishopric of Quebec and providing for a hierarchy. The liberal policy of Lord Elgin eased further the lot of French or Catholic Canada (i.e. the lower St. Lawrence Valley) while, after the Act of Union in 1840, there followed an exploration of the North and West, undertaken largely by French Canadians, which by 1860 had led to the establish-ment of bishoprics at Winnipeg and Vancouver and to the first conversions amongst the Eskimos.

These pioneer French Canadians were following a great French tradition in the New World. The first serious attempt to convert North America to Christianity had been made by the French Jesuits of the sixteenth and seventeenth centuries, who sailed up the St. Lawrence River (named by Jacques

Cartier in 1534) and, with Quebec or Montreal as their base, penetrated the regions of the Great Lakes, ultimately reaching, with their light canoes, the mighty Mississippi, and thus establishing contact with New Orleans. The remarkable story of the missionary work of these men amongst the Indians, a story associated with the names of Saints Isaac Jogues, Brébeuf, and other martyrs who suffered tortures in the course of their missions, belongs to an earlier age than the one with which we are concerned in this book. Yet it is necessary to bear it in mind because the tradition of French direction of the Catholic Church in North America lasted for a long time, and in Canada it still remains. It ceased, however, to be Jesuit. Disbanded in 1773, the Society of Jesus had already seen its pioneer efforts on the Great Lakes and the great rivers brought to nothing by the termination of French rule in North America in 1763. But, if the great missionary effort was over, the seminaries, and often the parish work, too, of Quebec and Montreal, were carried on by the Sulpicians of Saint Olier's foundation of Saint-Sulpice in Paris, that college from which, with the coming of the French Revolution, M. Emery sent many a young priest, not only to the St. Lawrence, but also to the state of Maryland further south on the east coast.

For many decades after the French had lost America, after the Jesuits had been silenced, and after the thirteen British colonies had won their independence, the flame of the Faith was kept alight by these Sulpicians, and by those priests who emigrated from France as a result of the persecutions there. They were men of learning, and they left their mark, even if their frequent failure to master English and their foreign culture limited their capacity to operate effectively amongst the Anglo-Saxon settlers.

And at this time, too (the end of the eighteenth century), another work which manifold destiny had seemed to have assigned to the Jesuits, the extension of the Faith northwards from Mexico up the Pacific coast, was in fact carried out, on account of the suppression of the Society, by their old-time rivals the Franciscans, who planted their famous mission stations, with their fine Franciscan names, as far up as San Francisco, Sacramento, and beyond.

At the time of the American Revolution, and when the Founding Fathers drew up the Constitution, Catholicism was a plant of very slender growth in the thirteen colonies. Quebec and Montreal, as well as the Pacific coast, lay, of course, outside the new Union. The only firm footing the Church had within the Union was in Maryland, originally settled by Catholics and other refugees from England. The penal laws, emanating from England, but intensified by the various state assemblies, kept not only the Puritan colonies to the north clear of the "infection of Popery" but the southern states as well, even including Maryland, where a law of 1704 "to prevent the growth of Popery" prevented the Jesuits or anybody else from starting Catholic schools. It is estimated that in 1791 there were not more than thirty-five thousand Catholics altogether in the Union; there was only one bishopric, that of Baltimore. One may, perhaps, be surprised that there were as many Catholics as there were, for only in Pennsylvania did they enjoy religious liberty. But during the American Revolution a new attitude towards Popery was born amongst the colonists, one which was to be enshrined in the Constitution and never quite to be forgotten, even during the wildest outbreaks of bigotry in the following century. The reason for this change was that the Revolution had need of the Catholics. It was not merely a matter of gaining the support of the handful of them to be found amongst the colonial population —though these had their usefulness, since they showed themselves to be "good citizens," as ready for the fray as were their Puritan fellows. It was rather because of Catholic Quebec and Catholic France.

The Revolutionary Congress had some reason to hope for Canadian support in the struggle with Britain, for had not Canada only just come under British rule, by virtue of conquest from the French? What love should she have for Westminster? Yet, oddly enough, she proved to have more love for Westminster than she had for Congress. More realistic, if not more tolerant than the colonial governments, the British Government had just granted, by the Quebec Act, what amounted to home rule to the French Canadians, including the Establishment of their Catholic religion. Faced with a choice between union with the intolerant Puritans of New England and the maintenance of their rather loose connection with Britain, the men of Quebec followed their stalwart bishop Joseph Briand in resisting all overtures from the Congress. But it was a close thing. There were volunteers from Canada for the Revolution, and there was a pro-Congress party at Quebec. What turned the scale was the publication

in Canada of the *Address to the People of England* in which
Congress, in October 1774, remonstrated with the British
Parliament for consenting to the Establishment in Canada of
"a religion that has deluged your island in blood and dis-
bursed impiety, bigotry, persecution, murder and rebellion
through every part of the world." After that it was useless for
Congress to protest (in the same month!) to Quebec that
"difference of religion" would prove no barrier to "a hearty
amity"; even a delegation from Congress, headed by Benjamin
Franklin himself, and including leading Catholics, could effect nothing at Quebec. It is a curious circumstance that her
Catholicism helped to keep Canada within the British Commonwealth!

The high cost of religious bigotry in the Quebec negotiations no doubt helped to determine Congress upon a different
attitude when it came to an alliance with France. The appearance of the French Navy off the American shores was the
signal for a general relaxation of Catholic disabilities lest offence be given to His Most Christian Majesty; and when Spain,
too, became an ally Congress was even to be seen attending a
Requiem Mass for the Spanish representative, lately dead! But
in any case, with Catholics now shouldering arms alongside
their Protestant brethren, it was difficult to maintain the discriminatory laws against them.

After the victory came the drafting of the Constitution of
the new federation, the drawing up of that charter of liberties
which has served the United States so well and has proved a
beacon light to the modern world, guiding the way to a wider
freedom. And since Presbyterians and Unitarians, Congregationalists and Episcopalians, besides a host of others—including the Catholics—were to be found in the different states, it
was inevitable that the new federal government should separate Church and State and should grant an equal toleration to
all religions. So we read in the First Amendment that "Congress shall make no law respecting an establishment of religion
or prohibiting the free exercise thereof; or abridging the freedom of speech or of the press . . ." And likewise, by the Sixth
Article, although all representatives and officers, whether of
the federal or of the state legislatures, were required to swear
an oath of loyalty to the Constitution, it was laid down that
no religious test should ever be required of a federal representative or employee.

Thus was established the "indifferent," "impartial," or

"neutral" State; some would say also the "secularist" State, but this appellation is inaccurate. The Revolution appealed to God, not to Reason. The Declaration of Independence, which owed much to that religiously minded philosopher John Locke (whose own thought may be traced back through the Anglican theologian Richard Hooker to Saint Thomas Aquinas), talks about the "laws of Nature and of Nature's God," and holds that all men "are endowed by their Creator with certain unalienable rights." It is a far cry from this recognition of the primacy of the "Creator God" to the aggressive secularism of the Jacobins of the French Revolution, or to the specifically anti-religious intention of the Russian Revolution.

The American Revolution was markedly religious, a quality which may be found amplified in the constitutions of the several states. Thus we read in the constitution of Massachusetts (1780): "It is the right as well as the duty of all men in Society publicly and at stated seasons to worship the Supreme Being, the great Creator and Preserver of the Universe." This, it may be argued, is merely the deistic religion later displayed by Robespierre. But Robespierre's religiosity, as we have seen, stood in marked contrast to the atheism of his fellow Jacobins, and stands still more opposed to that of Lenin. The American Revolution said, in effect, that God was real, was the author of justice, and ought to be worshipped. And, to quote the Massachusetts constitution again, the citizen was free to worship God "in the manner and season most agreeable to the dictates of his own conscience." So far from being secularist, the implication of the American Constitution was that a man ought to worship his Maker and, in those states which established toleration for Catholics, there was the further implication that (since a man was expected to worship his Maker according to the dictates of his own conscience) the Catholic *ought* to attend Mass! The governments, whether federal or state, came to be regarded as neutral in respect of religion, benevolently protecting every Church; but they assumed that there would be, indeed that there *should* be Churches. We may compare the different outlook of the agents of the Paris Convention of 1793, or that of the Supreme Soviet, conducting anti-religious crusades in its endeavour to create a truly secularist State. And though it is true, as George Washington said, that the Union was not founded upon the Christian religion, as the ancient states of Europe were, the

Union was certainly not founded upon atheism, as Communist states are.

Despite the lingering discrimination (in New York religious tests were still enforced, to exclude Catholics from office; in Massachusetts Congregationalism remained established and endowed), it may be said that by the year 1800 there was, federally speaking, religious equality before the law in the United States. How had such a situation come about in advance of the rest of the world? Clearly it had come about because no one religion had been strong enough to dominate the rest. Can we suppose that an overwhelmingly Congregationalist or an overwhelmingly Anglican country would have allowed such toleration? Certainly not to judge from the laws pertaining in 1770 in Massachusetts on the one hand or in Maryland on the other. Nor, it is fair to add, would the laws of Quebec, in 1750, suggest that the Catholics would have been more tolerant. It is true that in the days when the Catholic Baltimore family had owned Maryland they had established toleration; but they could hardly do otherwise when they held it from the English Crown. No; religious equality in the United States was the outcome of the play of historical forces; the union of so religiously divergent a people permitted no other solution. And even despite the religious equality established by the federal Constitution, it is likely that intolerance in some of the states, and especially in Massachusetts, would have persisted had it not been that already the rigours of Puritanism were yielding to the vague generalities of Unitarianism and Deism. The upper classes were beginning to become "enlightened."

So we must picture, in the first two decades of the nineteenth century, a very small Catholic community, still relying for the most part upon priests from France, but growing, and possessed of a new hope on account of the removal of the penal laws. Until the year 1808 there was only the one bishopric, Baltimore; but in that year the dioceses of New York, Philadelphia, Boston, and Bardstown were created, to be followed soon by Richmond, Charleston, Cincinnati and St. Louis. Under the patient and wise guidance of Bishop John Carroll, who had played his part in the Revolution and who occupied the See of Baltimore from 1790 to 1815, the colleges of Georgetown at Washington and Mount St. Mary's at Emmitsburg were founded, and a cathedral was begun at Baltimore. But priests remained few; trained, native, English-speaking priests were desperately needed and it was to produce them that the Sulpicians came from their Paris seminary and founded their own American seminary at Baltimore. But the students were very slow to appear and, by the year 1804, M. Emery, of Saint-Sulpice, was so disillusioned by the few fruits of his American venture, and the loss of most of his Society's savings upon it, that he was planning to withdraw his Sulpicians. It was none other than Pope Pius VII, in Paris for the coronation of Napoleon, who caused Emery to allow them to remain.

It was one of the great advantages of the separation of Church and State, effected by the American Revolution, that the Pope could make his dispositions as he chose, without having to reach an agreement with the temporal government or having to undergo the humiliation of obtaining a ruler's *placet* for his episcopal appointments or an *exequatur* for the publication of his orders. The rapid development of the young Church across the Atlantic, under Pius VII and his successors, owed something, at least, to the freedom with which the Pope could create new dioceses, institute bishops, and establish seminaries and colleges to meet the changing conditions. It was a striking contrast to the position in France where, as we have seen, the different rulers, whether Napoleonic, Bourbon, or Orleanist, interpreted their title of "Most Christian," and the privileges which they accorded to Catholicism, as conferring upon themselves an almost unlimited power to intervene in the affairs of the Church. Once more one is puzzled, at first, as to why Rome rejected so sharply in Europe a policy which was proving advantageous to the Church in America— one which had, indeed, been adopted more than a century before the American Revolution in the Catholic colony of Maryland. Only a clear recollection of what the Revolution meant in Europe, of the gulf, religiously speaking, which separated it from the Revolution in America, can explain the alarm which the liberal ideas created in the Church in Europe at a time when John Carroll's successors were thriving upon them in America.

It has been argued by the distinguished historian of the Catholic Church in America, Dr. Theodore Maynard, that religious freedom of the kind adopted in America "has never been considered by the Catholic Church as being, absolutely considered, the best basis, though American Catholics will not

wish any change so long as our society is constituted as it is."[1]
As a statement of the attitude of American Catholics this
is admirable. What is more questionable is his further
statement: "according to Catholic doctrine, however, the
union of Church and State is still affirmed to be the most
perfect solution in itself." "Union of Church and State" is
perhaps an unfortunate phrase; even in the Middle Ages there
was no union, indeed there was a very clear distinction. But if
there has not been union there has generally been Establishment, and co-operation; and in support of the view that this
has been regarded as the natural state of things the historian
can quote Pius IX's Syllabus of Errors as well as his silencing
of Montalembert and Acton. But there is, in fact (as Bishop
Dupanloup of Orleans was able to show), no reason to derive
from Pius IX's pronouncements anything more than a condemnation of the view that disestablishment and complete religious equality are *always* desirable. And although it is a matter of history that the characteristic Catholic pattern has, in
fact, been one which has associated closely together the
temporal and the spiritual power (a pattern which derives
from the Middle Ages and was accepted by Saint Thomas
Aquinas or Dante as a "norm") it should be recognised, as
Father John Courtney Murray has so cogently argued,[2] that
the relations of Church and State are governed by historical
contingencies, and this means that it is premature to say that
"the legal establishment of Catholicism as the religion of the
State" should be regarded as "a permanent and unalterable
exigence of Catholic principles governing Church–State relations." It would seem a mistake to speak of "doctrinal
absolutes" in this matter. Pius IX, as we have seen, even in
the Syllabus, was defining no absolutes. He was rather condemning others who did so. He was condemning those who
taught, as absolutes, their own liberal views about the relations of Church and State.

We shall have to return later to this interesting but vexed
problem, which holds so much contemporary significance, not
only in America but also in the rest of the world. All that it is
necessary to notice now, while we are concerned with the nineteenth century, is that American Catholicism was developing

[1] *The Story of American Catholicism* (Macmillan, 1941), p. 152.
[2] E.g. in "The Problem of Pluralism in America" in *Thought*, No.
29 (1954), and in "The Problem of State Religion" in *Theological
Studies*, No. XII (1951).

rapidly, under conditions of freedom which the Liberal Catholics of Europe were advocating strenuously, but which Rome, surely with reason, thought it would be very dangerous to introduce into old-established Catholic countries.

CHAPTER THIRTEEN

The Church in America After the Irish Immigration (1830–1890)

The rapid expansion of the Church in America in the 1830s and the 1840s was a result of immigration. That a high proportion of the immigrants were Catholics was due to the fact that a high proportion of them were Irish. The great Irish invasion was during the "hungry forties," but there had always been Irish immigration, especially into New England and New York, and many of John Carroll's problems had been presented by the pitiful plight of some of these immigrants who were under every inducement, economic and social, to forget about their faith, and for whom it was often impossible to provide priests or even an annual Mass. Moreover to the Irish, a priest of French or German origin, even if he could be found, seemed a very strange being indeed. But after the great invasion of the '40s the situation became rather different, anyhow in New England. In Maryland, Virginia, and Pennsylvania, and the region of the Great Lakes, there would be complaints from French and German priests who found themselves put under Irish bishops; occasionally these even resulted in small schisms. But soon not only New England but the whole country, save for the Carolinas, Georgia, and the Deep South, came to be so permeated by the Irish that the government and ordering of the Church acquired a distinctively Irish quality, except in a few pockets, such as were provided by the German or Polish Catholics of Chicago and beyond.

It is estimated that by 1850 there were one and three quarter millions of Catholics in the United States, and by 1860 twice as many. The total immigration into the country between 1830 and 1860 was about five millions, and nearly half of it was Irish. By 1855 there were forty-one bishoprics and most of them, naturally enough, were occupied by Irish bishops. The great Italian invasion did not occur until the last two decades of the century.

It is not really surprising that so great a flood of immigration, and one which was so largely Catholic, should have created alarm amongst the old inhabitants. There could, of

course, be no question of restricting the inflow, since it sup
plied the labour which was opening up the West, building u
the new factories, and making possible the new fortunes. Bu
particularly in New England, and most of all in Massachusett
(proud home of the Congregationalists, and spearhead of th
Revolution), it was asking a lot of human nature to expec
that those who had only lately, and with difficulty, accepte
the idea of religious equality, and who had been accustome
to look with alarm across the hills to Catholic Quebec, shoul
contemplate with equanimity what was fast becoming
Catholic majority in their own state. And if their own Purita
zeal was beginning to flag, with the development of Deism
there were those from the Orange Lodges of Ulster who wer
ready to revive it. The Irish immigrant, moreover, was no
only a Catholic, he was also poor; and although it might seen
admirable that pioneers should live in log cabins away on th
frontier, it was objectionable to good Bostonians to see squat
ters living in shanties on the outskirts of their city. So it wa
that right down the eastern seaboard, as well as inland, ther
sprang up in the '30s and '40s the violent anti-Catholic move
ment known as nativism, which reached its culmination in th
'50s in the highly disciplined and dangerous society known
as the "Order of United Americans," and commonly called
the "Know-Nothings," with a secret ritual of its own, and
with such great political influence that it acquired for a time
actual control of Massachusetts, Delaware, Rhode Island
Connecticut, Maryland and Kentucky, as well as great influ
ence in the majority of states.

The main political objective of the nativist movement was
to keep Catholics out of power and position; its most lasting
effect has been to prevent any religious instruction of any kind
from being given in state public schools (which were generally
started in those years) lest public money might be found to
be spent in support of Catholic teaching. The peculiar
American arrangement by which Catholic or other religious
groups wishing to give a religious education to their children
must pay the whole cost of their own schools, whilst also sup
porting those of the State, takes its origin in these decades
when feeling ran so high; it is at least possible that more
equitable arrangements, analogous to those worked out in
European countries of mixed religion, might have taken root
also in America, had the more tolerant attitude of the years
following the Revolution been maintained. It would be wrong,

however, to attribute the severely secular character of American public education solely to the nativist determination to avoid any state aid for Catholic teaching. There were many religious schools besides the Catholic schools at the time that the free public-school system was being adopted by the different states. Clearly the State could not provide for public support for all of them, since any attempt to subsidise all sectarian schools must have led, on account of the multiplicity of sects, to a sense of hardship on the part of those who were obliged to send their children to a school of a different religious complexion from their own. On the other hand, it is possible that the differences between the Protestant Churches had decreased so markedly by the middle of the century that what in England is now called an "Agreed Syllabus" (i.e. a "Highest Common Factor" of agreed religious doctrine) might have received their mutual support, so enabling them to receive state money, and ensuring that public education should have *some* religious basis.

The view of the redoubtable Bishop John Hughes of New York, who occupied that see from 1842 to 1864, was that it was logical and right that public funds, to which Catholics contributed in the same way as others, should be used in support of Catholic schools for Catholic children, Jewish schools for Jewish children, Protestant schools for Protestant children. And on the limited area of Manhattan, which was then in question, this solution might have been possible. At all events, the argument which weighed with the Common Council at New York, and which defeated John Hughes' strenuous endeavours, was not the argument that it was *impracticable* for the State to provide for everybody in the way in which he was suggesting, but rather the argument of the Protestant ministers, who took the line that it was *immoral* for any public money to be spent in any way that might assist Popery. "If the fearful dilemma were forced upon me," said one of them, "of becoming an infidel or a Roman Catholic, according to the entire system of Popery, with all its idolatry, superstition, and violent opposition to the Bible [the Catholics were demanding the approved Douay version of the Bible for their children], I would rather be an infidel than a Papist." A fair reading of the arguments which were used during the great education controversy compels the view that it was not so much the impossibility of satisfying all the religious sects as the determination, at the height of the nativist and Know-

Nothing agitation, not to satisfy the Catholics, which led to the "easy way out" of saying that all public education must be absolutely secular. In short, the reverend gentleman who preferred to see men infidels rather than Papists had his way; infidels they became, but to the undoing of the Protestant Churches even more markedly than the undoing of the Catholics, since the latter endeavoured, with mixed though marked success, to provide their own schools out of their own exiguous resources.

John Hughes was a fighter. He lost the battle of the schools, but he won the bloodier battle against the incendiaries. The wilder elements which supported the Know-Nothings took a particular pleasure in the burning of churches and convents. In Baltimore the mild and saintly Archbishop Francis Kenrick preferred to turn the other cheek, in obedience to a pacifism of which he had already given clear proof when Bishop of Philadelphia. In that city not only had churches been destroyed but there had been pitched battles, in one of which thirteen lives were lost while the police stood helpless or openly acquiesced. It is arguable that, against a hooligan mob, the Catholics would have been better advised to defend their property by force. At all events Bishop Hughes, at New York, thought so. His threats of retaliation were taken seriously, and the Catholic churches were not attacked; but he was in the advantageous position, enjoyed also by his brother Bishop of Boston, of having a substantial body of Irishmen at his back!

A salacious side line of the anti-Catholic campaign was the circulation of stories of immorality in convents. They purported to be written by nuns who had renounced their vows or had "escaped," and they were intended to imply that convents were no better than brothels for priests. The most notorious of these "disclosures" were those of Maria Monk, which were later discovered to be entirely without foundation; she had never been inside the convent whose life she described in her *Awful Disclosures*. But this did not prevent the book from providing a handsome income for its true author, a clergyman for whom she provided a nom de plume. To this day new editions of this book are still to be found in shops which provide pornography, long after its uses in religious controversy have disappeared. That a real horror and even fear of convents was aroused at the height of the campaign is evident enough; even the eminently respectable Ursuline convent of Charlestown, outside Boston, was burned to the ground by the mob, pupils and nuns being left to escape as best they could. For this event only one man was brought to trial, and he was acquitted. But the Massachusetts legislature saw fit to set up a committee for the inspection of convents.

The middle of the nineteenth century is generally spoken of as having been a peculiarly crude era in America, when the main idea of most men was to "get rich quickly." At all events foreign visitors, such as Charles Dickens, made the point with some emphasis. But while this might account for the violent behaviour which the reaction against Popery often displayed, it would not seem a satisfactory explanation of what was a very deep-seated superstition on the matter. It would be wrong to doubt that many intelligent men were genuinely afraid of what might happen as a result of the "Catholic invasion." Such a man, for instance, was Samuel Morse, the inventor of the code which bears his name; we need not suppose that it was only his preoccupation with secret communications which led him to think that there was an underground conspiracy on the part of the Catholics to take possession of America. Another was Lyman Beecher, a prolific Presbyterian preacher and writer of great power, and the father of a gifted family, which included Harriet Beecher Stowe, the author of *Uncle Tom's Cabin*. It was one of his favourite themes that the Pope was planning to take over the Mississippi Valley, and thus to encircle and strangle the United States. This sort of view was common currency amongst the enlightened intelligentsia of the eastern seaboard, and it should be remembered that the intelligentsia of Boston and New Haven were very intelligent indeed—this was the age of Ralph Waldo Emerson and of Margaret Fuller.

It should also be remembered that events in Europe in the '50s encouraged Americans to take a highly coloured view of the situation. It is too easily forgotten with what passionate interest American liberals concerned themselves in the revolutions of 1848–49—was not Margaret Fuller herself a nurse in one of Mazzini's hospitals in Rome? The general collapse of the European revolutions, the reinstatement of the Pope in full authority over the Papal States, the crushing by the Austrians and Croats of the national movements in Hungary and Italy, with the re-establishment of centralised authority under the young Emperor Francis Joseph, and the *coup d'état* by which Napoleon III suppressed the Second Republic in

France—all these things appeared, from the American point of view, to add up to the defeat of those liberal and national movements with which it was natural that Americans should sympathise. We have already seen the effect of these events upon the politically more mature and more stable population of England, the hysteria with which the re-establishment of the Roman hierarchy was greeted there in 1850. If Lord John Russell seriously supposed that English political and religious liberty was threatened by the Pope, we ought not to be surprised that American leaders took alarm. They were even less well placed than were the British to understand the true position in Europe, namely that Napoleon III and Francis Joseph, so far from being the Pope's henchmen, were really his gaolers in the Papal States; or that their mutual rivalry—alas!—was very much more powerful than their mutual Catholicism. What Americans heard about was what they were told by the exiled revolutionaries, and notably by Louis Kossuth from Hungary, and by the apostate priest, Alessandro Gavazzi, from Rome, whose mission was to save the Americans, after he had saved the English, "from the joint snares of Rome and Oxford" (!). Few more effective or popular lecture tours in either country have been carried out than were conducted by Gavazzi, although those of Felice Orsini must be reckoned amongst those few in England. Gavazzi's campaign in America was largely directed against Monsignor Bedini, the papal legate at Bologna, whom Pius IX had sent on a fact-finding mission to the United States, including consultations with President Pierce. Gavazzi accused Bedini of hanging Garibaldi's friend, the Carmelite friar Ugo Bassi, at Bologna, which was untrue because he was hanged by the Austrians. But with this and similar scares he achieved his object of hounding the Pope's envoy out of the country, a fate which Cardinal Wiseman had only avoided in England by the most consummate skill and courage.

It has been argued that during these troubled years Rome, preoccupied with events and movements upon the continent of Europe, was insufficiently sensitive to the true state of affairs both in England and in America, and was not always wise in her handling of them. Admittedly she showed herself a little imperceptient in the flourish of trumpets with which she restored the hierarchy to England, and also in her unqualified support, a little later, of the ultramontane element in the shape of Archbishop Manning and of W. G. Ward of the *Dublin Review*, and in her disapproval of Acton and her chilliness towards Newman. But in America she was very cautious, if not always very well informed. It was her steady policy to let those on the spot fight their battles in the way they thought best, and even when they disagreed violently with each other she shrank from intervening. The battles against nativism and the Know-Nothing movement were fought under the leadership of John Hughes of New York, who was not inclined to look over his shoulder for orders from Rome. And by the time he died, in 1864, the crisis of that contest was over, though whether the defence of the Catholics and their worship owed more to his militant efforts or to the influence upon public opinion of those saintly men his brother bishops, Kenrick of Baltimore and John Neumann of Philadelphia, will never be known. Perhaps the different genius of both types of Catholic was needed.

Perhaps, too, events themselves served to kill the persecution, for in the '60s came the Civil War. A major crisis in a nation's history generally makes for religious toleration; it is unwise to persecute a minority if you want its help. Except when there is a fear that the Church is in secret sympathy with the government's enemies (as the French revolutionaries feared), a national emergency tends to draw Catholics and their fellow citizens together. Thus was the agitation against Cardinal Wiseman and the restored hierarchy in England quietened by the Crimean War, and especially by those nursing nuns who accompanied Florence Nightingale to the hospital at Scutari. Thus was the violent anti-clerical campaign of the French Third Republic shipwrecked on the rock of the curés' fortitude in the trenches of the Somme. And in the Second World War, in England as in America, a common purpose drew together the hierarchy and their critics of other denominations.

There would also seem to be a tendency for periods of prosperity and security, such as America enjoyed between 1830 and 1860, to promote outbreaks of anti-Catholic agitation. Such an age England certainly was enjoying when Cardinal Wiseman landed at Dover to face the storm; and it was a friendly sun that shone upon the newly united Bismarckian Germany of the Kulturkampf, and upon that prosperous France of the *fin de siècle* which banned the religious orders. However this may be, it was certainly the sharp shock of the Civil War in America that changed the climate of opinion about the Catholics. Nobody could seriously pretend (although the attempt was made) that either secession or slavery in the South was being supported by the Pope to enable him to take over the Mississippi Valley; and the outbreak of war provided a crisis, both in the North and in the South, of the kind which draws Catholics and their fellow citizens together. Catholics fought on both sides, but there were many more Catholics in the armies of the North than in those of the South because there were many more Irish in the North. They fought shoulder to shoulder with their Protestant brethren, and the impression made by their courage, and especially by the devotion of their priests in ministering to the wounded and the dying, and by the nuns of many orders who nursed in the field hospitals, went far to sweeten the bitter bigotry.

But it was natural that the Catholic workers of the North should feel some scepticism when invited to join the emotional campaign for emancipation of the slaves. Suffering as they were from the militant Puritanism of Lyman Beecher, they were sometimes a little cynical about the torrents of tears shed over the pages of his daughter's book, *Uncle Tom's Cabin*. They were in a better position than their compatriots to perceive, at the time, what only came to be generally acknowledged much later, namely that the profits and future prosperity of their masters in the North were very much involved in the outcome of the war. And if the states of the South were fighting to avoid being dominated by the powerful employing classes of Pennsylvania or Massachusetts, that was a sentiment which the Irish in the North were in a better position to understand than were their masters. Moreover, if the Negro were suddenly to be emancipated would he not flood the northern states with his cheap labour? It was asking a lot of the Irish, in the lamentable condition in which they found themselves, to espouse wholeheartedly the cause of the Negroes. And if it be argued that the priests and the bishops, at least, should have risen above such considerations and should have joined their voices more loudly with those of the Protestant pastors in a holy crusade against slavery, it has to be noticed that those eloquent pastors were from New England and New York, not from the Carolinas or Georgia.

By and large the Catholic bishops, both in the North and in the South, took a more consistent and judicial view of the matter. The official attitude of Rome was to condemn the slave trade as a sin, as she had consistently condemned it, but only to treat slavery as a "social evil," as a social status, that is, which should be ameliorated (as it had been ameliorated by Christianity in Europe until it had disappeared there) but which did not in itself, necessarily and always, carry with it the spiritual ruin either of the owner or of his slaves. This attitude was repeated by Gregory XVI in 1839, in his letter *In Supremo Apostolatus.* Slavery, as such, was not *absolutely* condemned by Rome, any more than it was by the American Constitution; it was treated as a condition to be improved with a view to its ultimate removal. This was the line followed by the great bishops of the South, namely John England of Charleston, Patrick Lynch of the same see, and Kenrick of Baltimore. Catholic leaders in the North, such as Bishop Hughes of New York, or the publicist Orestes Brownson, though they felt freer to denounce the evils of slavery, threw their influence into the cause of moderation and adjustment, and against emotional extremism, and so were fundamentally at one with responsible Catholic opinion in the South. Their attitude had a great deal in common with that of Abraham Lincoln (until the President was driven into proclaiming the edict of emancipation), and the unjust ruin of the South and the appalling evils of "reconstruction" after the war might well have been avoided, and harmony between the races have been furthered, if this more moderate programme had been pursued.

It would be wrong to suppose that the spirit which lay behind the nativist or Know-Nothing campaign died altogether with the Civil War, or indeed that it ever died. What the anti-clerical of the 1850s feared as "foreign superstition," or "Popish plots," the anti-clerical of a later age called "divisism" or "the intrigues of the Vatican." The fear of the foreigner in the guise of the priest is common to all countries, and at least as old as the England of the thirteenth century. The "dual allegiance" of the early Christians was the reason why the Roman emperors persecuted them. "Render unto Caesar the things that are Caesar's, and unto God those that are God's" is teaching which Caesar has always found it hard to tolerate and no doubt always will, and the conflict is bound to continue, with greater or lesser force, in all countries, so long as a spiritual and a temporal order both continue to claim men's allegiance. No doubt it is not always the State, or secular society, which oversteps the proper limits of its authority; it is fair to remember Pope Boniface VIII. But in the America of the nineteenth, and even of the twentieth century, the Church found herself in the position of striving to maintain the barest minimum of those rights necessary to safeguarding her spiritual liberty; and in some vital matters, such as education, she had to put up with even less than the minimum.

The peculiar violence, however, of the pre-Civil War attacks upon the Church did not make its appearance again. The American Protective Association of the '80s and '90s, though sometimes successful in keeping Catholics out of political office, or in sponsoring the pornographic literature of "ex-Roman Catholic priests" or "ex-nuns," was a mere shadow of the earlier nativist movement. "The pallid ghost," Dr. Theodore Maynard has called it, of Know-Nothingism. Not only the size of the Catholic body—some ten millions by the turn of the century—but its proved loyalty gave the lie to this sort of hysterical fanaticism. The leaders of the American Church were now becoming friends of Presidents, and pulling their weight in the public affairs of the nation. We have reached the era of Cardinal Gibbons, Archbishop of Baltimore from 1877 to 1921, whom President Cleveland described as "a good citizen and first-rate American," whose "kindness of heart and toleration are in striking contrast to the fierce intolerance and vicious malignity which disgrace some who claim to be Protestants." We have reached the times of John Ireland, Archbishop of St. Paul, from 1888 to 1918, and friend of liberal statesmen the world over. And if it is true that the huge Italian immigration at the end of the century tended to reawaken in some quarters, and particularly in New England, alarm about a "foreign Catholic invasion," the United States had by then become a continent whose whole face had been covered by successive waves of immigrants, so that it was becoming increasingly difficult for a handful of New Englanders, of Pilgrim Father descent, to claim that they alone were "true" or "good" Americans.

CHAPTER FOURTEEN

The "American Heresy" (1890–1900)

In guiding the Church in America, Rome showed a marked reluctance to intervene directly. It was a prudent caution, having regard to the distance of America, the rapidly developing
situation there, and the anti-papal prejudices. When Pius IX's
envoy, Monsignor Bedini, met with his hostile reception in
1853 he was quietly withdrawn, and the idea of establishing
an apostolic nunciature at Washington was not pursued. Not
until 1893 did the Pope have his own representative in the
United States; it was in that year that Monsignor Satolli became apostolic delegate. Throughout the century the affairs of
the Church in America, like those of England, remained the
concern of the Congregation of the Propaganda at Rome. Both
were regarded as missionary countries; it was only in the year
1908 that they were admitted to the normal direct relations
with the different congregations and with the *Curia*.

But despite this caution Rome did in fact intervene not
infrequently, and generally with good effect, in settling some
of the problems which beset the growing American Church.
Thus Bedini was sent by Pius IX with the primary purpose
of straightening out the difficult "trustee" problem, which was
a constant source of trouble in the first half of the nineteenth
century. It was his task to insist upon the absolute control,
in all matters spiritual, of the bishops and clergy in their
own dioceses and parishes; the trustees who administered the
Church buildings and temporalities on behalf of the congregations had often acquired powers of control over their pastors
more consonant with Presbyterian practice, or with the Constitutional Church of Revolutionary France, than with Catholic tradition. Another peculiarity of the American Church,
which presented a serious problem for Rome to decide, was a
Germanic move for its reorganisation along racial lines. At
bottom this was part of an endemic quarrel between the Germans and the Irish. The Germans resented the fact that large
numbers of their parishes found themselves under Irish bishops, and sometimes under Irish parish priests as well. To this
state of affairs some attributed many losses to the Faith; and
at Lucerne, in Switzerland, Peter Paul Cahensly, of the Saint

Raphael Society for the protection of German Catholic immigrants, sponsored a memorandum in 1890 appealing to the Pope to prevent this cause of lapsing amongst the immigrants by setting up what were likely to become independent autonomous Churches in America. But whatever the need for German priests for German parishes, and the justice of the demand for more German bishops, it is clear that such a plan as Cahensly's would, in practice, have divided and weakened the American Church; and that in refusing to support the Cahenslyist agitation Pope Leo XIII, prompted by Cardinal Gibbons, was acting in the best interests of American Catholicism.

The same may be said for the Pope's intervention, two years later, in favour of the more moderate party in the vexed educational question. The issue here was whether the attitude of the extremists, headed by Archbishop Corrigan of New York and Bishop McQuaid of Rochester, who denounced the public schools, root and branch, and wanted to insist upon independent parochial schools for every Catholic child, should prevail against the more moderate attitude of those like Archbishop John Ireland, who tried to reach a compromise with the state system. Leo XIII approved Ireland's compromise, and although both he, and his delegate, Monsignor Satolli, were at pains to support the drive launched by the Third Council of Baltimore, of 1884, for parochial schools for all Catholic children, his influence was exerted against the indiscriminate denunciation of the public schools, and he insisted upon a cessation of the polemics hurled to and fro by brother bishops.

Consistently with his policy of accommodation, Leo XIII sent Monsignor Satolli to represent him at the Chicago Columbus Exhibition of 1892, in honour of the fourth centenary of the discovery of America. Still more remarkable, he allowed Cardinal Gibbons to share with the Chief Moderator of the Presbyterian Church the organisation at the exhibition of an extraordinary affair known as the "Parliament of Religions." The idea behind this parliament was to show the basic unity of men's religious beliefs by inviting representatives of all the great world religions to share, for ten days, in a public affirmation of basic religious truths—God, immortality, the soul—and to explain their own peculiar tenets without attacking those of the others. Thus Cardinal Gibbons found himself alongside Buddhists, Hindus, and Moslems, leading the recitation of the "Our Father" (upon which all were agreed) and giving the apostolic blessing at the conclusion of the proceedings.

Perhaps this occasion marks the highest watermark ever attained in the history of Catholic co-operation with non-Catholic religions. It was generally supposed to be a great success, but the attempt to stage a similar demonstration shortly afterwards, at the Paris World Exhibition, was defeated by the opposition of the Archbishop of Paris and the majority of the French hierarchy. It was one thing to organise such an affair in that melting pot of humanity which was the Chicago of the 1890s; it was quite another thing to organise it in an historic capital, where men were either Catholics or *incroyants*. In France such a proceeding could only have served to swell the numbers of the sceptics.

The Chicago Parliament of Religions was only the most colourful example of a tendency in American Catholicism to go to greater lengths than Catholicism elsewhere in conciliating its opponents. But whilst it would be absurd to suppose that American bishops were prepared, as some of their European critics pretended, to "soft-pedal" some articles of faith, so as not to give offence, it was nevertheless true that they were prepared to go far along the road of common action and common platforms with their rivals. From this there arose very naturally, in the minds of some, the attitude that different religions were different roads to God, equally valid for different kinds of people, an attitude which leads to a state of mind which the Church calls indifferentism and which Pius IX denounced in the Syllabus of Errors. Obviously such an attitude is heretical, because it denies the unique and divine nature of the Church.

But the circumstances of immigration into America made it very natural that a vigorous party of progressives in the American Church should strive, by all the means in their power, to lift Catholics out of the social status of pariahs and should endeavour to bring them into the public life of the community, thus breaking down the hostility which had expressed itself in the nativist movement, and which, in the '90s, was being renewed in the Protective Association. Moreover, if Catholics were to fulfil their mission to evangelise the whole country, they had to acquire as full a knowledge of it as possible and hold positions of responsibility, to become, in short, "good Americans"—which indeed was what they most of all desired to become. Those who felt most strongly about these

matters, like Archbishop John Ireland of St. Paul, or Bishop
Keane, first rector of the new Catholic University of America,
saw that it was vital to have American trained priests to prevent the kind of segregation which some of the Germans of
Milwaukee aimed at, and not to lose sight of the possibility
of co-operation with the public-school system, where such co-
operation might prove possible. Their activities, however, and
those of their friends in the Missionary Society of Saint Paul
the Apostle (which the apostolic Father Hecker had founded)
or of Monsignor O'Connell (who was rector of the American
College at Rome) soon came under suspicion in many quarters, and eventually at Rome itself, until in 1899 Leo XIII
was compelled to address his letter *Testem Benevolentiae* to
Cardinal Gibbons, drawing attention to the errors "called by
some Americanism."

The Pope's letter had particular reference to the preface to
the French edition of a life of Father Hecker, a preface which
had been written by a French *abbé* named Klein. And the
ideas singled out by the Pope for condemnation were the notions that to win converts the Church should adapt herself to
the age in respect of her discipline, and even her doctrine;
that spiritual direction was less necessary than it used to be
(more attention being needed to the voice of the Holy Ghost
within); that the natural virtues, such as honesty or temper-
ance, were more important than the supernatural virtues—
whereas the latter were really the result of grace acting upon
the former; and that the active external life was more important than the passive inner life of those who bound themselves by religious vows and devoted themselves to prayer and
penitence.

It is not difficult to see from this papal letter what it was
that bothered many able and religious critics in what they understood to be Americanism. And although the American
bishops unanimously accepted the ruling of Rome and protested that nothing had been further from their minds than
to teach those errors which the Pope was condemning, and
which they held in the same horror as Rome held them, it
was not altogether true to say that Americanism was a figment
of the French imagination, invoked by those who hated the
Abbé Klein, or that the campaign against John Ireland and
the American Church generally was inspired by those at Rome
or at Paris who hated America or who hated republicanism.
The bishops of the province of Milwaukee, and also those of

the province of New York, thanked the Holy Father for thus explaining the errors which existed in their provinces, and for calling back the erring; and an even more vigorous warning would have been welcomed by Bishop McQuaid of Rochester. It has also to be remembered that Leo XIII felt it necessary to remove Monsignor O'Connell, in 1895, from his post as rector of the American College in Rome, and Bishop Keane, in the following year, from his as rector of the Catholic University of America; and in 1895 he specifically condemned inter-Church congresses. Satolli, whom he recalled in 1896 from his post as legate at Washington to make him a cardinal, returned to Rome a disillusioned man. He had started as a friend of John Ireland and the liberals and had greatly offended those of the McQuaid-Corrigan outlook, but his growing appreciation of the secularist tendencies in America had ended by reversing his attitude, so that it was he who was in part responsible for Bishop Keane's removal from the Catholic University, and he who sponsored at Rome a condemnation of Americanism. It seemed to him that there was "nothing of the supernatural" in the American Church.

We should therefore be chary of regarding the agitation against the American heresy as merely a French plot, or a monarchist plot, or as something invented by the Jesuits or the Dominicans. There was some fire in America as well as in France and in Rome that gave rise to the smoke of agitation—indeed there was some in the biography of Father Hecker, and in Archbishop Ireland's preface to the American edition of it. But when everything has been said that can be said about the dangers to the Faith inherent in the attitude of some American Catholics, who wanted to minimise their differences from Protestants, it still remains true that the American bishops, including Archbishop Ireland, were absolutely loyal to Rome and to the Catholic faith in its traditional entirety. As Leo XIII himself said, the condemnation was needed rather to clarify opinion in France than opinion in America. Archbishop Ireland had been educated in France, and he was fond of giving addresses in Paris, which were very popular with those of a liberal outlook in Church matters and a republican outlook in political matters. He was therefore very much disliked by those of the neo-ultramontane school, many of whom hoped to see a restoration of the monarchy, and who detested Leo XIII's policy of *Ralliement* in support of the republic.

Further, he was regarded with some reason as an opponent of the religious orders, because of his consistent advocacy of the claims of the seculars, and especially of the primacy of the bishops. It is not difficult to imagine the feelings of the Jesuits when he told them that the Church in Japan would not have collapsed if the successors of Saint Francis Xavier had petitioned Rome to appoint bishops and secular clergy, and—much more remarkable—that the English Jesuits of Queen Elizabeth's time were to blame for opposing the appointment of bishops in the England of the sixteenth century![1] It is not to be wondered at that his views did not commend themselves to the *Civiltà Cattolica* at Rome, or to a large part of the French Catholic press, and although he came in for some unkind attacks, especially from the Abbé Maignen, in his *Le Père Hecker est-il un saint?*, which added greatly to the excitement of the controversy, he could also give as good as he got and did not hesitate to castigate his opponents' criticisms as "the vile attacks of ignorant and vengeful bigots."

Indeed, although issues of orthodoxy were at stake, the main concern of Leo XIII with America in the later part of the nineteenth century was the same as Pius IX's main concern at a rather earlier date with England, namely how to pour oil on the furious feuds within the native hierarchy. He was not so much afraid that heresy would develop in America as he was of the deplorable effect of quarrels between bishops about education, or about the racial organisation of parishes. Just as Pius IX had given the English bishops, assembled before him, a severe talk, in which he told them to put a mountain "the size of the Alps and without a tunnel through it" upon their quarrels, so Leo XIII, confronted with the spectacle of Ireland and Keane on the one side, and Corrigan and McQuaid on the other (with Gibbons of Baltimore somewhere in between, and striving to maintain the peace), politely ordered them all to stop arguing about the education issue. And his persistence with the policy of sending an apostolic delegate to Washington (for which he has been much criticised) was precisely to enable him, from outside, to impose his own settlement of issues which divided the metropolitan archbishops of America so deeply that no one of their own members could end the controversy. Even Gibbons was in no position to assert any au-

[1] Sermon of April 19, 1896. Presumably such bishops would have had to operate in disguise and in hiding.

thority. He enjoyed, as Archbishop of Baltimore, only an "honorary precedence," and he was regarded by McQuaid of Rochester as belonging to Ireland's party and as trying to set up an "American Vatican." Leo can fairly claim to have saved the unity of the American Church in the nineteenth century, for whatever the mutual disagreements of the American bishops, and however much they may have disliked the appearance of an apostolic delegate, the loyalty of all of them to the See of Peter was absolute, and this enabled the Pope to still the storms.

The reason why it was in Europe, and especially in France, that Leo XIII saw the special need to settle the issue of Americanism was that it seemed likely to lead there to more serious consequences. One has to remember the peculiar *élan* which attached to the movement launched by Lamennais, and the invocation by his disciples of just those liberties which flourished across the Atlantic, and most of all the separation everywhere of Church and State, which had been the *cri de coeur* of Montalembert. The Liberal Catholics had made much of America, if only as a stick with which to beat Napoleon III, with the result that the writings of Archbishop Ireland had been translated into French and widely read, and the distinguished American liberal prelate enjoyed a *succés fou* during his visit to Paris in 1892–93. No doubt his popularity was bound up with his republicanism, and with his rather vague appeals to democracy and individualism, which fitted in at Paris with the temper of the supporters of the Third Republic. No doubt, too, the opposition to him was monarchist as well as religious. But his religious outlook, with its enthusiasm for the separation of Church and State, for the active as opposed to the contemplative virtues, and for broad and original approaches to the Protestants, appeared to be altogether too like that of Montalembert at Malines, and was quite out of harmony with the more authoritarian temper which had followed the Vatican Council and the increasing ascendancy of the Jesuits. Leo XIII, who preserved excellent relations to the end with John Ireland, and who was famous for his policy of accommodation, was nevertheless at one with his predecessor Pius IX (of the Syllabus) and his successor Pius X (of the condemnation of Modernism) in the rigour with which he maintained the integrity and the entirety of the Faith, and in suspecting anything that might lead to any dilution of doctrine, or to undue respect for the spirit of the times. In the face of the rationalism and naturalism which, following Strauss' life of Jesus, *Das Leben Jesu*, in Germany, or the books of Ernest Renan in France, were all the vogue in the Europe of the '90s; in the face of the Old Catholic schism in Germany, which had followed the defection of Döllinger and was at bottom a revolt against legitimate authority; in the face of important, if isolated, defections in France, of which the apostasy of the very popular Notre Dame preacher Père Hyacinthe was the most important, Leo stood firmly behind those Jesuits and Dominicans in Paris who raised the cry of alarm against Americanism. Never, since the defection of Lamennais, had Rome given much encouragement to what was very vaguely and loosely called Liberal Catholicism; much less was she inclined to do so in the secularist atmosphere of the 1890s and on the impulse of a westerly wind from across the Atlantic.

It was the Abbé Maignen, of the Congregation of Saint Vincent de Paul, author of *Le Père Hecker est-il un saint?*, who was the spearhead of the attack upon Americanism in France, an attack which ranged over a wide variety of topics and received supporting fire from more than one of the Jesuits in the pulpit of Saint-Sulpice, or of the new Sacré-Coeur of Montmartre. But the point of special importance to us, in our attempt to pursue the interconnection of the various storms which have buffeted the barque of Peter in modern times, is that Maignen launched his attack against what he called "the partisans of Americanism and Modernism,"[2] thus directly associating the American heresy with that wider and more important movement which so preoccupied the attention of Rome in the pontificate of Leo XIII's successor, Saint Pius X (1903–14). It is for this reason that we shall do well to pursue our study, in the next chapter, into the Modernist movement, and its condemnation, before we return to those social and economic issues which were so important a feature of the pontificate of Leo XIII.

The most striking event in the American movement, within the American Church, had been the participation of Cardinal Gibbons in the Parliament of Religions at Chicago, and it has already been mentioned that this was followed by a movement

[2] Cf. his *Nouveau Catholicisme et nouveau clergé* (Paris, 1902), p. 77.

in France in favour of a Parliament of Religions at the projected Paris Exhibition of the year 1900. The idea was vigorously, but most indiscreetly and prematurely publicised by Père Charbonnel, in defiance of the Archbishop of Paris, Cardinal Richard, who secured its condemnation by Leo XIII. Continuing his campaign, Charbonnel left the Church in 1897, becoming a militantly anti-clerical Protestant, and helping to cover Americanism with increased suspicion by referring to it as "a sort of neo-Protestantism." The significance of this little episode is that it helped to put Rome still more on her guard against any minimising in the realm of dogma, discipline, and obedience, especially when it was reinforced by the warm but unwelcome approval extended by leading Protestants to the ideals of Father Hecker and Archbishop Ireland, and by the reception they accorded to the apostasy of Charbonnel.

It will, however, have been seen that, even though what was called Americanism may have paved the way for what was called Modernism, the former had in fact no dogmatic content. At worst Americanism was a false emphasis in the realm of public relations and an unbalance between the interior and the exterior life and between private inspiration and religious authority. It never denied any article of faith. It only advocated a way of life which was liable to lead towards secularism and indifferentism, and these dangers were firmly but very courteously pointed out in Leo XIII's *Testem Benevolentiae.* It was far otherwise with Modernism. When Pius X condemned Modernism, in the famous and bitter phrases of the encyclical *Pascendi Gregis* of the year 1907, he was condemning a heresy which cut right at the root of the Christian revelation and the deposit of faith.

CHAPTER FIFTEEN

Modernism (1893–1907)

What then was Modernism?

At bottom it was an attack upon authority, both in Church and State, and that is why it is very relevant to our theme in this book. But those who recognised themselves as condemned by Pius X's denunciation of it said it was something invented by the Pope, having no real relation to their writings—here we have an echo of the indignation of American Catholics at being saddled with "Americanism." And there is, indeed, this analogy between the two condemnations, that what the Pope did in both cases was to crystallise certain related ideas which were "in the air," bring them together, and demonstrate that they were false. But, just as in condemning Americanism Leo XIII had prominently in mind a particular writing, namely the Abbé Klein's preface to the *Vie de Isaac Hecker*, so, in condemning Modernism, Pius X was preoccupied with the writings (without mentioning them by name) of Alfred Loisy and of George Tyrrell.

If, then, we want to understand what was Modernism—that potentially most powerful of all heresies—we shall do best to consider what was being taught by Loisy and Tyrrell, although we shall need to remember that there were other important figures in the background, such as the German-British Catholic, the Baron Friedrich von Hügel, a close friend of both the principals, and the Italians Romolo Murri (whom we shall meet as a founder of Christian Democracy) and Antonio Fogazzaro (author of that world's best seller *The Saint*) and likewise the French Protestant pastors and publicists, Paul and Auguste Sabatier, who strove for the cause of Modernism, urging its adherents not to apostatise from Rome but to remain within the Church the better to "rejuvenate" her with their ideas.

How widespread the movement was within the Church generally it is quite impossible to say. Paul Sabatier was certainly exaggerating wildly when he said that "almost all the young clergy in certain dioceses of France and Italy had embraced it," or that "perhaps a half" of the whole Church had done so.[1] Any estimate of its strength depends upon the test of orthodoxy. If, as its supporters were fond of claiming, Modernism was an "orientation of thought" rather than a doctrine, how shall an estimate of its extent ever be made? But if, more correctly, we reckon only those who specifically believed what Pius X condemned, the number concerned must have been very limited, if only because the philosophical and historical ideas in question were not easy. To the claim that fifteen thousand priests in France alone were Modernists, Loisy (who was in the best position to judge) replied that not fifteen hundred were. Probably the number of those who were more than vaguely attracted by the Modernist ideas was very much less. The heart of Modernism was only a handful of enthusiasts, but that did not lessen its chance of effectiveness when so much in the spirit of the age was in its favour.

Alfred Loisy was a pupil of Louis Duchesne, who was himself a pupil of the great Italian archaeologist the Cavaliere de Rossi. This intellectual genealogy is important because Rossi, patronised by Pius IX, had excavated the catacombs and the Colosseum, and so had laid the foundations for a new scientific study of the Early Church, while Duchesne had subsequently devoted himself to the same period, bringing the strictest Germanic historical scholarship to bear upon early Roman and Greek texts. Duchesne taught at the Institut Catholique de Paris, where Loisy was his pupil; but the pupil soon became the colleague, devoting his own acute historical scholarship to the study of the Old and New Testaments.

We have seen already how Pius IX, at the time of the Congress of Munich (1863), had refused to allow that science—historical or any other—was independent of the authority of the Church in matters concerning the deposit of faith, and how uncongenial to scholars like Acton or Döllinger was his ruling. Leo XIII demonstrated in his encyclical *Providentissimus* (1893) how wide were the bounds within which scholarship could, and indeed should operate, even within this sacred realm. The study of the New Testament could hardly be undertaken as though it were an historical document of precisely the same order as any other. For those accepting any traditional form of Christianity this was clearly impossible, because the acceptance of the divinity of Christ involves an

[1] *Contemporary Review* (London), March 1908, Vol. CXIII, pp. 301–303.

interpretation of His life and teaching which must necessarily be partly the province of the theologian. Loisy, however, continued his studies and publications without regard for the teaching of the Church or for the special character of his subject matter, and they lost him his Chair at the Institut Catholique. This was in 1893, by which year, on his own later showing, he had already lost his own faith, having rejected the unique nature and eternal truth of the revelation contained in the New Testament. But it was part of his technique as well as that of George Tyrrell in England to remain— even though they knew that what they were teaching was entirely unorthodox—within the visible unity of the Church. They so disguised their doctrines that their heretical character should not be apparent; in this way they hoped to alter the course of Christianity from within. To this end Loisy shaped his most important book, *L'Evangile et l'Eglise*, which he published in 1902, so that it appeared to be a brilliant Catholic refutation of the celebrated German Protestant scholar Adolf von Harnack, and it was at first given a friendly reception, because of the reputation of its author and its pretence to complete orthodoxy.

Harnack had been arguing that the pure doctrine of the Gospels had later been corrupted by the Church. Loisy was concerned—ostensibly—to demonstrate the essential and opposite Catholic truth that the Church, through the guidance of the Holy Spirit, "developed" the implications of the deposit of faith contained in the New Testament. "Developed." This word covers the crux of the matter. It is perfectly orthodox, indeed it is necessary to recognise that Catholic tradition, from the days of Saint Paul down to those of the Vatican Council, and on to the dogma of the Assumption of the Blessed Virgin Mary, defined in 1950, has continued to develop. It is clearly bound to develop so long as the Church has life. This theory of development had been already expounded by John Henry Newman, the great English convert, in his *Essay on the Development of Christian Doctrine*, and it is clearly of fundamental importance. But Loisy's exposition of it changed, as he fully intended, the very basis of the matter, and led logically to the disappearance of the whole dogmatic foundation of the Faith. For Loisy, pretending to be strictly historical, and not theological, sought to demonstrate that, just as Jesus was the Messiah prophesied by Isaiah and the Prophets, so He was concerned only to herald the Last Judgement and the coming of the Kingdom, and to call men to repentance and to salvation through Himself. Loisy argued that He was not concerned to impart any final truths, but to impart a spirit, to initiate a religious movement. The language of the Gospel, according to Loisy, necessarily belonged to the age and circumstances in which it was preached; and Jesus Himself, because He belonged to that age, because He was Himself only a part of history, could not impart the ultimate truths of God. He, like everybody else, was limited by His context in the development; He might be the Son of God, but (Loisy avoids saying this in so many words) He was evidently not God Himself, but part of history. All teaching and dogmatic formulation, Loisy insists, is conditioned by its times, and this rule applies to the times of the Gospel as well to any other. So he does not treat of the New Testament as of a *depositum fidei*, to be explained and developed but never *changed* by the Church, he treats it rather as something in itself subject to change, and it was in treating *development* as though it were *change* that the essence of his heresy consisted.

It was Loisy's concern to remain purely the historian. It was as historian that he had been able to undermine Harnack, by showing that the Protestant was in a dilemma, since any commentator on the Gospel must consider the subsequent growth of the Church, which demonstrates the Holy Spirit within her, or he will not be able to deduce any recognisable Christian religion at all. But it was also as historian that he expounded an evolutionary theory of religion in which the very subject matter treated of by the Gospels took its place merely as one phase like any other phase in historical development.

It will readily be appreciated how heretical this latter proposition was, although disguised as part of an attack upon Protestantism. Loisy's book was duly condemned by the Archbishop of Paris and although he "submitted," in the specious sense that he said his work was "purely historical" and that, if it contained theological error, he repudiated the error, he went on his way explaining his position further, in later books, and developing the relativism of his evolutionary arguments, until Pius X's encyclical of 1907, so clearly aimed at him, made it impossible for anybody to suppose that his thought could any longer be regarded as orthodox. A scholar and an intellectual, proud and persistent, he had always found it very hard to bow his spirit to the daily devotional exercises required of a priest, and he spent much of his protracted old age in cynically explaining for how long and how deliberately he had deceived the world about his fundamental agnosticism.

If Loisy was the intellectual, historical luminary of Modernism, George Tyrrell was its "soul." Tyrrell was an "original." A Dublin Protestant who, in his search for truth, reached Rome and the Society of Jesus via the Anglican High Church, he found himself teaching moral theology at the Jesuit College of Stonyhurst in Lancashire. But, in spite of his thorough grounding in scholastic philosophy, a strongly individual mystical tendency led him to a preoccupation with the interior quality of faith and to a suspicion of the logical definitions of theology; and this made him see dogma as wholly relative and subordinate, as a merely transient and always inaccurate and incomplete way of rationalising and preserving from error the living idea of Christianity. Dogma, instead of enshrining eternal truths, seemed to him merely an instrument reshaped by each age according to its knowledge and understanding. In any case it was unimportant, a mere "intellectual interpretation," whereas revelation, which was the real vision of truth, was the work of "inspired imagination." Through the influence of his friend Von Hügel, Tyrrell was introduced to the German thinkers and to Loisy. Never an historical scholar in the sense that Loisy was, his chief debt to continental Modernism was the doctrine of "Immanentism," the idea, that is, of the in-dwelling Spirit of God always developing in humanity, but never able to express itself in any final dogmatic terms. It goes without saying that these views were not compatible with Tyrrell's remaining a member of the Society of Jesus; in the year 1906 he was expelled from the Society and also suspended from performing his priestly offices. Even Loisy affected to be shocked by Tyrrell and pointed out that his doctrine of religious inspiration had a strong analogy with Protestant ideas.

Yet nothing angered Tyrrell more than to have his views confused with the liberal Protestantism of his age. Actually, there was an analogy, and it consisted in Tyrrell's want of respect for any ecclesiastical authority and in his disbelief in the possibility of valid dogmatic definitions. But the vital difference between Tyrrell and liberal Protestantism was that he believed profoundly in the mystical union of the "community of the Faithful," an essentially collective concept, "a union

with God by way of humanity, with humanity by way of
God."[2] It is the Church, he insists, and the Church alone
that enables us to enter into relation with the divine goodness, but only on condition that we recognise that her dogmas
are imperfect and crude images, deficient symbols, yet "our
only means of approach to God and God's only means of
approach to us."[3] Communion with the visible Church is an
efficacious sacrament but only "a means, a way, a creation, to
be used so long as it is useful and abandoned when it becomes
an obstacle."[4]

Tyrrell has boundless scorn for the liberal Protestant, who
sees in Christ merely a "moral teacher," who fails to perceive
the profound significance of His acceptance of institution-
alised religion, of His insistence upon incorporation into His
mystical body, of His institution of sacraments, of His teaching about the Kingdom, salvation, damnation. So far from
disbelieving in these things, the true Modernist, according
to Tyrrell, wants to infuse new life and reality into them. So
far from accepting the unhistorical and invalid distinction
made by Protestants between the Gospels and the Church
(as though the latter were not the very object and offspring
of the former), the Modernist wants to give more life and
reality to the latter. Tyrrell believes that the current expression "of religion, of revelation, of institutionalism, of sacra-
mentalism, of theology, of authority . . . is inadequate to
their true values." He thinks that the Catholic Christian idea
"contains within itself the power continually to revise its
categories and to shape its embodiment to its growth . . .
To suppose then that such Modernism is a movement away
from the Church and is converging towards liberal Protestantism is to betray a complete ignorance of its meaning . . .
With all its accretions and perversions Catholicism is, for the
Modernist, the only authentic Christianity. Whatever Jesus
was, he was in no sense a liberal Protestant. All that makes
Catholicism most repugnant to present modes of thought derives from Him. The difficulty is not Catholicism but Christ
and Christianity."[5]

Tyrrell's pet aversion was Protestant criticism of the school
of Harnack, self-satisfied German pundits who "wanted to

[2] *Lex Credendi* (London, 1906), p. 74.
[3] *Ibid.*, p. 80.
[4] *Ibid.*, p. 86.
[5] *Christianity at the Cross-Roads*, London, 1910, pp. XX, XXI.

bring Jesus into the nineteenth century as the incarnation of its ideal of Divine righteousness, i.e. of all the highest principles and aspirations that ensured the healthy progress of civilisation. They wanted to acquit Him of that exclusive and earth-scorning otherworldliness which had led man to look on His religion as the foe of progress and energy . . . They could only find the German in the Jew; a moralist in a visionary; a professor in a prophet; the nineteenth century in the first; the natural in the supernatural. Christ was the ideal man; the Kingdom of Heaven the ideal humanity . . . The Christ that Harnack sees, looking back through nineteen centuries of Catholic darkness, is only the reflection of a liberal Protestant face seen at the bottom of a deep well."[6]

No wonder that Tyrrell suffered more acutely from the "good-natured pats on the head" of Protestant "supporters" than from the censures of Rome. "I own . . . to intense irritation in reading some of their well-meaning critiques. Their line of argument is almost stereotyped. They begin by dilating on the lethal stagnation and immobility of Rome. They then announce the outstanding discovery of a little Goshen of enlightenment amid the waste of Egyptian darkness; of a group of Roman Catholics who, in spite of the Index and the vigilance of the terrible Inquisition, had dared to read and think for themselves, with the inevitable result of developing strong Protestant and rationalistic sympathies."[7] Then it is pointed out to them that they are on the right track and need only push on courageously and abandon, like good Protestants, their childish dreams about the papacy, and "with a pat on the head of final benediction they are good-naturedly dismissed."

We can now understand how, so far from Modernism being a form of Protestantism, Loisy and Tyrrell were agreed in the view that the Protestant break away from the Church at the time of the Reformation was the root of the contemporary trouble because it produced, by reaction, an authoritarian Rome. In Tyrrell's view Rome should have welcomed Loisy's principle of change, on the grounds that the French historian was teaching a true view of "integral" and "developmental" Christianity. But, "Rome (profoundly ignorant of the critical movement, its current and tendencies) thought that even a

[6] *Op. cit.*, pp. 41–44.
[7] *Op. cit.*, p. XVIII.

victory over the Protestant might be purchased at too great a cost, and repudiated a notion of development different from that of her theological dialecticians and disastrous to their idea of orthodoxy."[8]

She did indeed!

On their own showing Loisy and Tyrrell and, to a greater or lesser extent, their many intellectual friends in every Western country, were undermining every dogma of the Faith, destroying the whole structure and trying to replace it by an indefinable and unknowable flux. Powerful to destroy, but powerless to build, they represented a greater threat to the Faith than any other heretics in the Church's whole history, because their attack was aimed not at a single point of dogma or doctrine but at the entire edifice. They were also more dangerous because they operated from within, writing under pseudonyms and disguising their heresy. It was for this reason that Rome, though she recognised and publicly acknowledged that some of them were in good faith, nevertheless reacted against them with a sharpness of language uncommon even in papal condemnations.

Two months before the issue of the encyclical *Pascendi Gregis* (September 8, 1907) Pius X published the decree *Lamentabili*. In this he explained that, on account of the "fever for novelties" which characterised the times, a number of errors were being taught and attended to "under the colour of science and progress." They belonged to two main groups, those concerned with the interpretation of Scripture and those concerned with the mysteries of the Faith. He was therefore charging the "Holy Inquisition Roman and Universal" with the task of noting and reproving the principal of these errors. There follows a list of sixty-five erroneous propositions, drawn up by the Congregation of the Inquisition after receiving the assistance of consultors. The model is clearly Pius IX's Syllabus of Errors, but this new Syllabus covers only errors belonging to the two categories mentioned. Numbers 1–38 concern the interpretation of the Scriptures, and Numbers 39–65 the interpretation of dogma. In so far as these interpretations were repetitions of previous censures and definitions, pronounced by Pius IX and Leo XIII, they had as their object to reaffirm the fundamental idea of an objective revelation, dis-

[8] *Ibid.*, p. 44.

closed in Scripture, and safeguarded by the Church. In so far as they were new, they were <u>concerned to insist upon the integral truth and historical authenticity of the Gospels</u> (especially that of Saint John), of the sacraments of the Church, and of the primacy of the Holy See. These historic dogmas were the skeleton of the Faith; they might be capable of development, in Newman's sense of the word, but they could not be *changed*, since they owed their principle and origin to the teaching of Jesus Himself.

The encyclical *Pascendi Gregis* was the natural complement of the decree *Lamentabili*. In the decree a large number of specific but not organically related propositions were condemned as erroneous. In the encyclical a body of related ideas was isolated, labelled Modernism, and pronounced to be a fallacy cutting at the very roots of the Faith. No less than two thirds of the encyclical itself were devoted to expounding the basic principles underlying the Modernist standpoint. It might be possible for any one individual Modernist, even for Loisy or for Tyrrell, to say that the Pope was inventing a heresy to which no particular person adhered—just as nobody "owned up" to being an "Americanist." But the Pope was constructing, or was causing to be constructed, a composite picture, composed from the principal ideas of Loisy, Tyrrell, and their friends, in the realm of philosophy, belief, theology, history, criticism, apologetics, and reform, and was thus arriving at an idea which could truly be called "Modernism," and which he characterised as not merely a heresy but as "the poisonous juice of all heresies."

The Pope finds two errors at the root of Modernism; one is agnosticism, according to which God is "unknowable," so that reason has little to offer in finding a grounding for faith, its arguments and constructions being mere "intellectualism." The other is the paramount role of "Vital Immanence," a need for the divine deep down in our nature, which not only makes us seek but enables us to find God; and which has its counterpart in humanity as "Divine Permanence," which is the religious tradition of mankind, expressed in the sacraments and teaching of the Church. Both these notions were Tyrrell's, with whose ideas, indeed, the encyclical is at least as much concerned as it is with Loisy. Taken together, they represented a playing down of the rational element in religion and a playing up of the intuitional, subjective, and romantic element. The encyclical notes that they leave science (including his-

orical criticism) free from all religious control, even when
he science of history is treating of the Gospels or the sacraments. "Complete freedom for science in relation to faith;
rather, indeed, enslavement of faith to science."

The description of Modernism contained in the encyclical
concludes with an outline of the reforms demanded by the
Modernists: reform of the history, theology, and philosophy
taught in the seminaries; a purging of the dogmatic content
of the catechism; a reduction in the number of devotions; reform of ecclesiastical government to bring it "into harmony
with men's conscience, which is turning towards democracy";
reform in the realm of morality, by adoption of the principles
of the Americanists, which assert the superiority of the active
virtues; return of the clergy to their "ancient humility and
poverty."

To these beliefs, denials, and recommendations, the encyclical proceeds to reply by a reassertion of the traditional
teaching of the Church, a reassertion which ranges from the
Council of Trent on the sacraments, to the Council of the
Vatican condemning agnosticism. Immanentism is condemned
by reaffirmation of the defined Catholic faith in an external,
objective, supernatural order. Associated with the condemnation of agnosticism, on the one hand, and of immanentism, on
the other, is the denunciation of the Protestant idea of the exclusive validity of "inward illumination," an idea which had
filtered from Protestantism into some Modernist teaching.

But it is necessary to read the encyclical itself in order to
obtain some idea of the indignation felt at Rome concerning
the work of the Modernists. "Lost to all sense of modesty . . .
with sacrilegious audacity . . . the most pernicious of all the
adversaries of the Church . . . because they are within her
and because they lay the axe to the root not the branches."
They "ascribe to a love of truth that which is in reality the
result of pride and obstinacy . . . it is one of the cleverest
devices of the Modernists to present their doctrines without
order and systematic arrangement, in a scattered and dis-
jointed manner, so as to make it appear as if their minds were
in doubt or hesitation, whereas in reality they are quite fixed
and steadfast . . . they say that 'in the religious sense one
must recognise a kind of intuition of the heart which puts man
in immediate contact with the reality of God and infuses such
a persuasion of God's existence and His action, both within
and without man, as far to exceed any scientific conviction

. . . it is this experience which makes the person who acquires it to be properly and truly a believer.' How far is this position removed from that of Catholic teaching! . . . What is to prevent such experiences from being found in any religion? Will they claim a monopoly of true experiences for Catholics alone? . . . For the Modernists to live is a proof of truth, since for them life and truth are one and the same thing . . . so all existing religions are equally true, otherwise they would not survive." So we read that the Modernist position is a "delirium," an "insanity," an "audacious sacrilege," a "monstrosity."

Finally, after recalling that Leo XIII had endeavoured, but without success, to fix the proper limits to biblical criticism in his encyclical *Providentissimus*, and had likewise recommended the renewed study of the scholastic philosophy of Saint Thomas Aquinas, Pius X declares that it is now necessary to take more drastic measures to safeguard the Faith. These he adumbrates in certain articles:

1. *The scholastic philosophy is to form the basis of all sacred studies.*

2. *There is to be strict censorship of the opinions of the professors and directors in the seminaries. The regular course in scholastic philosophy is to be required of all candidates for the doctorate of theology or canon law.*

3. *The bishops are to assist the work of the censor by prohibiting the reading in seminaries of any Modernist literature which, owing to the quantity published, may have escaped the attention of Rome.*

4. *The bishops must appoint censors in their dioceses to examine all books and periodicals. Their signed nihil obstat must precede the granting of an episcopal imprimatur.*

5. *Vigilance committees are to be set up in each diocese to collect any evidence of Modernist writing or teaching, and are to meet every second month and deliberate secretly.*

6. *These committees are to keep their eyes especially open for Modernist treatment of social questions and social institutions.*

7. *Bishops are to report to Rome every three years, and under oath, on the doctrines current amongst their clergy.*

To soften the rigour of these articles, and to meet the "ancient calumny which portrays the Church as the enemy of science and progress," the Pope announces the foundation of an International Catholic Institute of learned men who, "with Catholic truth as light and guide," shall "foster the progress of all that could rightly be called science and erudition." Little has as yet come of this project; but the precautionary measures outlined in the seven articles were undertaken with some industry.

The issue of *Pascendi Gregis* belonged to the tradition of the condemnation of Lamennais in *Mirari Vos* and of Pius IX's Syllabus of Errors. It was one of the most decisive acts ever undertaken by the papacy, for the Modernist movement simply expired as a result of it. Loisy and Tyrrell became isolated exiles supported only by a handful of personal friends. Waverers like Von Hügel accepted the verdict of Rome with better or with worse grace. The action of Pius X was very successful; but the cost of the victory in terms of those who became estranged from the Faith, or of those, from outside, who, as a result, could no longer contemplate submission to Rome, can never, of course, be computed.

We have seen that it was an important part of the Modernism condemned by the Pope that it demanded reform of the government of the Church to bring it "into harmony with men's conscience, which is turning towards democracy," and that it asked for a return of the clergy to their "ancient humility and poverty." At bottom this was an attack upon the whole idea of authority, whether in State or in Church. Undoubtedly a profound suspicion of "Rome," in the sense of the higher ranks of the hierarchy, and especially of the *Curia*, played a very important part in the Modernist attacks. It had been a commonplace of Döllinger and his friends, in the German intellectual movement, that Roman scholarship was third rate, and it seemed intolerable to their successors of the Modernist movement that such men should wield the weapons of the Index and the Inquisition.[9] How should a "pure intellect," like that of Loisy, bow to the intelligences of the *Curia* on matters of biblical scholarship? And why should this anachronistic medieval aristocracy exercise absolute power in the century of democracy?

To these Modernist criticisms there were sufficient answers.

[9] The Roman Congregation of the Inquisition should, of course, be distinguished from the ancient Spanish court of that name!

It has yet to be demonstrated that Roman scholarship, in the second half of the nineteenth century, guided by men like the Jesuit Fathers Curci or Taparelli d'Azeglio, or, a little later, Cardinal Zigliara (who planned Leo XIII's social encyclicals), was of an inferior quality. Yet even if it were inferior to German scholarship, especially to German historical scholarship, it clearly remained the case that, on matters directly touching the Faith, the last word must rest with the Church. This would not necessarily mean that her scholars were always the best scholars. The authority of Roman decrees derives not from the scholarship of the theologians who prepare them but from the authority of the Holy See itself. Moreover, decrees usually have the limited role of safeguarding the deposit of faith by pointing out what is dangerous. If, for instance, the Biblical Commission at Rome, of which much complaint was made, ruled that some new historical interpretation of the Scriptures was unacceptable, it did not necessarily mean that the new interpretation would not ultimately be accepted; it only meant that, since it conflicted with traditional interpretations, time would be needed—sometimes quite a long time—for considering the new theory in all its aspects, and especially in its bearing upon the rest of the tradition and upon the unalterable deposit of faith.

Mistrust of the scholarship of the Roman congregations was paralleled by apprehensions about Roman "privilege." Such apprehensions, however, were losing their force at the end of the century. It might have been all very well at the time of the Renaissance to invoke a return of the clergy to their "ancient humility and poverty," but this return had been very effectively accomplished by the Risorgimento, just as it had been accomplished at Paris by the French Revolution. Many of the bishops at the Vatican Council were so poor that they had to walk to and fro from St. Peter's in the rain. The "greed and luxury" of the Roman *Curia* was one of those myths which had been nurtured by men reading about the days of the Borgia and Medici Popes of the sixteenth century. Most of the Sacred College, at least from 1860 onwards, were men of simplicity, purity and charity, and some, such as the aristocratic Cardinal Altieri (who gave his life ministering to those stricken by the plague at Lake Albano) or the humble Martinelli (who was the candidate preferred by some when Leo XIII was elected), were possessed of saintlike quality. Perhaps it was because he was so ignorant of the continent of Europe that Tyrrell but-

tressed his Modernist arguments with the wildest charges of
Roman corruption and exploitation. "Will the Roman bu-
reaucracy that exploits even the Papacy," he asked, "ever resign their revenues and their ascendancy . . . ?"[10] It was a
curious question to ask in the year 1909, because they had already resigned most of their revenues in 1870 when they lost
their state, and when the Pope refused the subsidy offered by
Victor Emmanuel's government. The picture of a sort of
Renaissance court at Rome was peculiarly inept in the days of
Pius X, a Pope who was a saint and had been born a peasant.
But we should not underestimate its influence, especially at a
time when the social question was coming decisively into the
foreground. In the struggle for the allegiance of the workers,
which was then being waged between the Social Democratic
movement, springing from Karl Marx's First International,
and the Christian Democratic movement, it was easy for her
enemies to portray the Church as undemocratic.

Easy, but erroneous. By the time of Tyrrell the Church in
Europe was no longer wealthy. Nor was she taking sides against
democracy. Leo XIII had been at special pains to repeat what
his predecessors had said, namely that the Church believed,
certainly, in social order, and therefore in obedience to legiti-
mately constituted authority, but as to forms of government
she was neutral. She did not side with monarchy as such (as
the French of the Right were urging her to do after 1870)
or with republicanism as such. Leo XIII had been prepared
to praise the American Constitution, and to urge support for
the Third Republic in France, because they were the legally
constituted authorities. But he had been prepared to do the
same for the Hapsburgs at Vienna. In his encyclical *Immortale
Dei* of 1885, he had reminded the world that power is given
not by men but by God; it has therefore to be exercised by
rulers in accordance with God's principle of justice and equity,
and obeyed by subjects with the obedience due to such legitimate rule. If, however, rule was unjust, in the sense that it
ignored or violated God's law, then it might be necessary to
oppose it: ". . . if, in administering public affairs, it (the
government) is wont to put God aside and show no solicitude
for the upholding of moral law it deflects woefully from its
right course and from the injunctions of nature; nor should

---

[10] *Christianity at the Cross-Roads*, p. 280.

such a gathering together of an association of men be accounted as a commonwealth, but only as a deceitful imitation and make-believe of civil organisation."[11]

It was not, therefore, a matter of the Church supporting in all circumstances, or as a matter of faith, monarchy, or aristocracy, or any ruling class as such, however much the behaviour of some churchmen (reproved by the Pope) in the French Third Republic might make it appear so. It was a question of the Church supporting a just and legitimate order. And the question which imposed itself with ever greater urgency, as the nineteenth century drew to its close, was whether the existing order, in its social and economic aspects, could possibly be regarded as legitimate or just, having regard to the dire poverty and excessive working hours of the many, and the mounting wealth of the few. Was there any answer to the "problem of the working class" other than the pitiless *laissez faire* of the classical economists, on the one hand, or the blindly materialistic violence of the First International on the other? The question takes us from Modernism to Marxism.

[11] *Sapientiae Christianae* (1890).

CHAPTER SIXTEEN

Leo XIII and the Social Question:
Rerum Novarum (1878–1903)

It was the peculiar merit of Leo XIII that he was prepared
squarely to face the social problem; he saw how serious it had
become. He also saw that the real issue was justice, and the
true principles of justice were the heart of that scholastic philosophy which was so dear to him. An intellectual, as Pius IX
had not been, he sought first to combat false social philosophies by a return to the reassessment of Saint Augustine and
Saint Thomas Aquinas, and he founded universities, and gave
guidance to seminaries, with this end in view. He believed
that if men were well grounded in a sound philosophy of the
State (Aquinas, deriving from Aristotle), they would not so
easily be misled. With Aquinas the first end of man is
the worship of God and the salvation of his soul, and the
first purpose of the Church is to minister to that end. The
State is secondary but necessary. Just as Aristotle had recognised that man was by nature a political animal and therefore bound to live in a society, so the scholastic philosophy
had assigned to the State a necessary although a subordinate
place. Leo XIII defined the matter in this way: "Nature did
not fashion society with the intent that man should seek in
it his last end, but that in it and through it he would find
suitable aids whereby to attain to his own perfection."

This, then, is the framework within which Leo XIII saw
the social question, and it ruled out the utopian, evolutionary-
perfectionist philosophy, born of the eighteenth and running
to seed in the nineteenth century. Society was not, as the
starry-eyed supposed, the last end of man; heaven would not
be built upon earth, because man remained imperfect. Society
existed because man was sociable; because he needed it to
"find suitable aids whereby to attain to his own perfection."
But if it were to provide these aids it must provide for his
livelihood and for that of his family. It must not so exploit
him as to leave him utterly without either leisure or the means
of subsistence. Such a society would be both unjust and use-

less to him. Here was no question of socialism[1] or of economic equality, ideas castigated by the Pope in the first years of his pontificate in *Apostolici Numeris* (1878). (". . . spurred on by greedy hankerings after things past . . . [the Marxists] attacked the right of property sanctioned by the law of nature; and with signal depravity, while pretending to feel solicitous about the needs and to be anxious to satisfy the requirements of all, they strain every effort to seize upon and to hold in common all that has been individually acquired by title of lawful inheritance through intellectual or manual labour or economy in living . . .") No, it was a matter of justice rooted in liberty, a matter to be settled if possible between those immediately concerned, rather than by the State, and to be settled peacefully. Diversity of class function and wealth in society was natural, but the whole rested upon the principle of mutual obligation; exploitation was a sin.

Before we go on to see how the Pope summed up his social teaching in the famous encyclical *Rerum Novarum* (1891) we may notice his public action on social questions.

It brings us back again from Europe to America. In Europe it was hardly likely that Rome could lend any support to the radical movements which emerged before Christian Democracy seriously entered the field in the 1880s. She might, and did, support the individual efforts of relief societies and savings banks, but she could only denounce the European Socialist movement, with its false philosophy. How should she countenance the atheism of Proudhon or the materialism of Marx and Bakunin? The early Socialist movements in France, in Switzerland, in Belgium, and in Germany, unlike those in England, were rooted in materialist philosophy and bitterly attacked the Church for seeking to "turn men's eyes to heaven." Only in England was there a strong religious element in the social movement, an element visible in the ideals of Robert Owen and his friends, as later in those of Charles Kingsley, William Morris, or Ruskin. But these English religious radicals were nevertheless earthbound in their vision; little concerned with the transcendental and the supernatural, their movement could never greatly commend itself to Catholics.

[1] The theories which the Pope was attacking were not what we should now call socialism, but something much more extreme. Indeed the teachings of Marx and his followers, with which Leo XIII was concerned, were further reaching than many Communist régimes have proved to be.

In America, however, there existed by the 1880s a powerful workers' organisation which contained a strong Catholic element, and which was beginning to achieve something for the workingman. It was called the Knights of Labor and it was the forerunner of the American Federation of Labor. Its president, Terence Powderly, was a Catholic, as was a large proportion of its membership; it avoided the conspiratorial and ritual elements of a secret society, and so was not open to the objections raised by the Church to the teaching and activities of the Carbonari or Freemasons. It did not aim at revolution or violence but at mutual benefits and collective bargaining. However, so powerful was the suspicion in which the Church, as a result of her European experience, held revolutionary societies, that a society in Canada organised on the same basis as the Knights of Labor was rebuked from Rome (at the instigation of the Archbishop of Quebec) and the American society was for some time in serious danger. The pleadings in its favour of Archbishop John Ireland of St. Paul, or of Bishop Keane of the Catholic University of America, were not calculated to further its cause with some of those at Rome; and it was only the energetic action of Archbishop Gibbons of Baltimore and the personal interest of Leo XIII which saved the day for the Knights of Labor.

In his memorial to the Pope, Gibbons included a paragraph giving a picture of the position in which the workers found themselves in America which is as illuminating as it was probably influential: "There already exists an organisation which presents innumerable attractions and advantages, but with which our Catholic workingmen, filially obedient to the Holy See, refuse to unite themselves; this is the Masonic Order, which exists everywhere in our country, and which, as Mr. Powderly has expressly pointed out to us, unites employers and employed in a brotherhood very advantageous to the latter, but which numbers in its ranks hardly a single Catholic. Nobly renouncing advantages which the Church and conscience forbid, our workingmen join associations in no way in conflict with religion, seeking nothing but mutual protection and help, and the legitimate assertion of their rights. Must they here also find themselves threatened with condemnation, hindered from their only means of self-defence?"[2] The Church, he pleaded, must be true to her glorious title of "Friend of the

[2] Much of the memorial is reprinted in Soderini, *Pontificate of Leo XIII*, transl. of 1934 (Burns, Oates and Washbourne), Vol. 1, p. 172.

People," and he quoted Cardinal Manning of Westminster: "A new task is before us. The Church has no longer to deal with Parliaments and Princes, but with the masses and with the people."

Leo XIII was convinced by Gibbons and the Knights of Labor were never condemned. By the year 1887, when Gibbons' memorial was presented at Rome, the Pope had already made a habit of meeting workers' deputations. This was the year when Count Albert de Mun led from France the first of those pilgrimages of workers and employers to Rome for which he, and that model employer Léon Harmel, soon became famous. The matter of the Pope's discourses on these occasions was mostly the errors and dangers of Marxist teaching, and the advantages of that mutual assistance and protection which had characterised the ancient guilds. But what some saw as most significant about these audiences was the solemn consecration of labour and management to Christ which occurred at them. As one observer said, a "new social power made solemn entrance into Saint Peter's; these workers were new claimants to the Empire coming, as Charlemagne, Otto, and Barbarossa had come, to seek consecration and investiture."

If the social movement, for a time, was less conspicuous in Italy, this was because of the painful preoccupation of Italian Catholics with their fight against the new government of their country, a fight into which they entered to win the most elementary rights of the Church such as freedom for the religious orders, for the schools, or for the disposition of the funds bequeathed to the Church for charitable purposes. Objectives of this kind dominated the thinking of those Catholic congresses which, beginning in 1874 at Venice, were held in the different Italian cities, to draw up programmes of Catholic action to protect the Church. Nevertheless, the fourth of these great congresses, that held at Bergamo in 1877, devoted itself to the social question, pleading that children under twelve should not be employed in the factories, that women and children should not work more than a nine-hour day, and that women should continue to be paid their wages during their periods of confinement. A modest beginning indeed! It was with the eighth congress (Lucca, 1887) that the low level of wages and the advantages of a guild or corporate organisation became a main topic of discussion.

In 1890 the young German Kaiser, William II, took the

initiative, summoning an international conference to Berlin to discuss industrial legislation and workers' insurance. He wrote to Leo XIII about it because the Pope, he said, had "always used his influence in favour of the poor and forsaken of human society," and he asked for his co-operation. Leo XIII did not send a personal representative to this conference, as the Kaiser suggested he should, but he wrote a cordial letter reminding the German ruler of the important rôle of the Church in these matters, and he expressed his satisfaction that the prince bishop of Breslau was to attend. No doubt the Kaiser's cordiality was bound up with his aversion to the Socialists; he saw in the German Catholic workers' associations a preferable alternative to the Marxist International. But what we need to notice here is the existence of these Catholic associations, that there was in being, by the 1880s, a very extensive non-revolutionary religious network of unions, sometimes of workers only, sometimes of workers and employers, designed to save the workers and their families from the horrors of exploitation and to knit together a society ravelled by the ruthlessness of "rugged individualism." These endeavours owed most to one of the greatest of all ecclesiastics of the nineteenth century, Bishop Ketteler of Mainz, whom we last met amongst the minority at the Vatican Council. His *Christianity and the Labour Question* (1864) was a pioneer volume, and it gave the Germany Catholics a programme. Even in Britain, the most advanced nation industrially at that time, but the least Catholic, the Church was striving to awaken men's conscience in the matter. Though she was preoccupied there with the difficult task of maintaining her own position, after the excitement following the restoration of the hierarchy, and with the economic effort involved in building churches and schools, yet her often squalid little presbyteries were frequently the chief agencies of relief for the poor Irish immigrants of Liverpool and Manchester, of Newcastle and Glasgow, amongst whom the Sisters of Charity were working ceaselessly. And the English Church's new leader, Archbishop Manning of Westminster (who had succeeded Cardinal Wiseman in 1865, and was himself elevated to the purple in 1875), saw it as his mission to strive to do something to alleviate the horror of the London slums. In his view, as in the view of the Free Churches, the Established Anglican Church had failed to face the new problem of the proletariat. He saw that the hours men, women, and children were spending at work made family life impossible; if the home, the very foundation of the life of both individuals and society, were ruined, the whole of civilisation must be undermined. He wrote warmly in praise of the German Kaiser's initiative, and he urged the Pope to tackle boldly the problem of pauperism. His unceasing labours, in pamphlets and on platforms, especially in London, earned him the workers' respect and made it easier for him than for any other religious leader to intervene effectively in the great London dock strike of 1889.

It will be seen then that when Leo XIII issued his social encyclical *Rerum Novarum* in 1891 he was not merely expressing his own convictions or those of a part of the *Curia*. In the papal tradition, he was pronouncing upon a matter which had already become one of the deepest concerns of the Church in every industrialised country. The real purpose of *Rerum Novarum* was not so much to introduce new teaching on the social question as to bring the Church Universal, through her authoritative voice, into line with the efforts which were coming here and there to have the generic name of Christian Democracy. And this was very needful, if only because men like Gibbons and Ireland, Manning, Ketteler, or Count Albert de Mun, had their outspoken opponents amongst the social conservatives. It was not so easy then as it is today to distinguish between what was reform and what was revolution, and the fact that the Church was properly perturbed about those heresies called "Americanism" and "Modernism" sometimes confused the issue, because a Modernist or an Americanist might also be a social reformer. Thus the Abbé Maignen in France, who stigmatised Archbishop Ireland and Isaac Hecker, and who almost created the Americanist heresy by the bitterness of his writing, was also the sworn opponent of the social reformer Count Albert de Mun. Likewise Tyrrell was not the only Modernist to take up the social question. Further, if Christian Democracy had to be carefully distinguished from the heresies which were tending to deify humanity, it had also to be distinguished from Social Democracy, which was the name then given to the materialist and revolutionary Socialists of the First and Second Internationals. So clearly did Leo XIII see the importance of this distinction that he was reluctant to use the term Christian Democracy at all, and it does not appear in the encyclical *Rerum Novarum*. That he ultimately approved it in *Graves de Communi*

(1901) seems to have been due to its gaining such wide currency that Catholics would hardly have understood what he was talking about if he had used any other.

Rerum Novarum (1891), which embraced the whole social problem in its context as part of religion, politics, and the right ordering of society, was not merely the most important pronouncement of Leo XIII, but has provided the basis for Catholic teaching on social justice ever since. And because it emanated from a Pope deeply imbued with traditional Catholic philosophy, but also sensitive to the economic realities of his own day, it treated of these matters on the highest level with a serenity and authority, but also a warmth and sympathy, which blend to make it one of the great documents of history. We can best judge of the scope of its teaching by a few quotations.

The subject is introduced with a breadth of vision proper to its magnitude:

"That the spirit of revolutionary change, which has long been disturbing the nations of the world, should have passed beyond the sphere of politics and made its influence felt in the cognate sphere of practical economics is not surprising. The elements of the conflict now raging are unmistakable: in the vast expansion of industrial pursuits and the marvellous discoveries of science; in the changed relations between masters and workmen; in the enormous fortunes of some few individuals and the utter poverty of the masses; in the increased self-reliance and closer mutual combination of the working classes; as also, finally, in the prevailing moral degeneracy . . . there is no question which has taken a deeper hold on the public mind . . ."

The ruthlessness of modern exploitation, in Leo XIII's view, has been accentuated by the abandonment of the ancient Christian order. Thus the work of the secularist "enlightened despots" of the eighteenth century, and of the Malthusian economists, are by implication condemned: ". . . Some opportune remedy must be found quickly for the misery and wretchedness pressing so unjustly on the majority of the working class: for the ancient workingmen's guilds were abolished in the last century, and no other protective organisation took their place. Public institutions and the laws set aside ancient religion. Hence by degrees it has come to pass that workingmen have been surrendered, isolated and helpless, to the hard-heartedness of employers and the greed of unchecked competition. The mischief has been increased by rapacious usury which, although more than once condemned by the Church, is nevertheless under a different guise, but with the like injustice, still practiced by covetous, grasping men. To this must be added that the hiring of labour and the conduct of trade are concentrated in the hands of comparatively few; so that a small number of very rich men has been able to lay upon the teeming masses of the labouring poor a yoke little better than that of slavery itself."

But the remedy proposed by the Socialists (by whom, we must remember, the Pope means rather those whom we would now call Communists) is no answer.

"To remedy these wrongs the Socialists, working on the poor man's envy of the rich, are striving to do away with private property, and contend that individual possessions should become the property of all, to be administered by the State, or by municipal bodies. They hold that by thus transferring property from private individuals to the community the present mischievous state of things will be set to rights, in as much as each citizen will then get his fair share of whatever there is to enjoy. But their contentions are so clearly powerless to end the controversy that, were they carried into effect, the working-man himself would be among the first to suffer. They are, moreover, emphatically unjust, because they would rob the lawful possessor, distort the functions of the State, and create utter confusion in the community."

The worker will be the first to suffer under such socialism.

"Socialists, by endeavouring to transfer the possessions of individuals to the community at large, strike at the interests of every wage earner, since they would deprive him of the liberty of disposing of his wages [in the form of savings] and thereby of all hope and possibility of increasing his resources and of bettering his condition in life. What is of far greater moment, however, is the fact that the remedy they propose is manifestly against justice. For every man has by nature the right to possess property as his own. This is one of the chief points of distinction between man and the animal creation . . ."

After several paragraphs on the right to private property in land, no doubt intended to refute the followers of Henry George, who had caused some stir in America, the Pope goes on to consider private property in relation to the family.

"No human law can abolish the natural and original right of marriage, nor in any way limit the chief and principal purpose of marriage ordained by God's authority from the beginning: increase and multiply. Hence we have the family; the 'society' of a man's house—a society very small, one must admit, but none-the-less a true society, and one older than any State. Consequently it has rights and duties peculiar to itself, which are quite independent of the State. . . . For it is a most sacred law of nature that a father should provide food and all necessaries for those whom he has begotten; and similarly it is natural that he should wish that his children who carry on, so to speak, and continue his personality, should be by him provided with all that is needful to enable them to keep themselves decently from want and misery amid the uncertainties of this mortal life. Now in no other way can a father effect this except by the ownership of productive property, which he can transmit to his children by inheritance . . . the family has at least equal rights with the State in the choice and pursuit of the things needful to its preservation and its just liberty."

Furthermore, undue state interference would defeat its own purpose:

". . . The sources of wealth themselves would run dry, for nobody would have any interest in exerting his talents or his industry; and that ideal equality, about which they entertain pleasant dreams, would be in reality the levelling down of all to a like condition of misery and degradation . . . therefore the first and most fundamental principle, if one would undertake to alleviate the condition of the masses, must be the inviolability of private property."

Proceeding to show "where the remedy to be sought for must be found," the Pope first draws attention to the primacy of the Church in the matter. ". . . all the striving of men will be vain if we leave out the Church." Next, the natural inequality of men must be accepted as a fact: "people differ in capacities, skill, health, strength; and unequal fortune is a necessary result of unequal conditions. Such inequality is far from being disadvantageous either to individuals or to the community." It has further to be recognised that there will never be a Utopia in this world; and "lying promises" about one "would only one day bring forth evils worse than the present. Nothing is more useful than to look upon the world as it really is . . . the great mistake in regard to the matter now under consideration is to accept the notion that class is naturally hostile to class, and that the wealthy and the workingmen are intended by nature to live in mutual conflict. So irrational and so false is this view that the direct contrary is the truth . . . Each needs the other: capital cannot do without labour nor labour without capital. Mutual agreement results in the beauty of good order . . ."

He then outlines the requirements of religion in the sphere of social relations:

"Religion teaches the labourer and the artisan to carry out honestly and fairly all equitable agreements freely entered into; never to injure the property nor to outrage the person of his employer; never to resort to violence in defending his own cause, nor to engage in riot or disorder; and to have nothing to do with men of evil principles who work upon the people with artful promises of great results and excite foolish hopes which usually end in useless regrets and grievous loss. Religion teaches the wealthy owner and the good employer that their workpeople are not to be counted as their bondsmen; that in every man they must respect his dignity and worth as a man and a Christian; that labour for wages is not a thing to be ashamed of if we lend ear to right reason and to Christian philosophy, but is to a man's credit, enabling him to earn his living in an honourable way; and that it is shameful and inhuman to treat men like chattels to make money by, or to look upon them merely as so much muscle or physical strength."

The Church also enjoins Christ's Holy Law of Charity: ". . . it is one thing to have a right to the possession of money, and another to have the right to use money as one wills . . . Saint Thomas Aquinas teaches: 'Man should not consider his material possessions as his own,' in the sense of being only for his own use, but should be ready 'to share them without hesitation when others are in need.'"

And in certain worldly as well as spiritual ways the Church directly helps to alleviate the lot of the workers. Thus the Christian morality she teaches "leads of itself to temporal prosperity" by inculcating a better attitude to work; she sets up and maintains her associations for mutual support and for relief of all kinds; and she has established religious congregations devoted to works of mercy—"no human expedient will ever make up for the devotedness and self-sacrifice of Christian charity."

Turning from the Church to the State, the encyclical outlines the limited rôle of the latter:

"Whenever the general interest of any particular class suffers, or is threatened with harm which can in no other way be met or prevented, the public authority must step in to deal with it . . ." But such occasions are strictly limited. The Pope gives the following examples: "If by a strike, or by other combination of workmen, there should be imminent danger of disturbance to the public peace; or if circumstances were such that among the working class the ties of family life were relaxed; if religion were found to suffer through the workers not having time and opportunity afforded them to practice its duties; if in workshops and factories there were danger to morals through the mixing of the sexes, or from other harmful occasions of evil; or if employers laid claims upon their workmen which were unjust, or degraded them with conditions repugnant to their dignity as human beings; finally, if health were endangered by excessive labour, or by work unsuited to sex or age—in such cases there can be no question but that, within certain limits, it would be right to invoke the aid and authority of the law."

It is the poor more than the rich who need the defence of the State: "The richer class have many ways of shielding themselves and stand less in need of help from the State; whereas the mass of the poor have no resources of their own to fall back upon and must chiefly depend upon the assistance of the State."

On the other hand violence must be resisted. The strike is accepted as an inevitable, though regrettable, "last resort," but not violence:

"When workpeople have recourse to a strike it is frequently because the hours of labour are too long, or the work too hard, or because they consider their wages insufficient. The grave inconvenience of this not uncommon occurrence should be obviated by public remedial measures; for such paralysing of labour not only affects the masters and their workpeople alike but is extremely injurious to trade and to the general interests of the public; moreover on such occasions violence and disorder are generally not far distant, and thus it frequently happens that the public peace is imperilled. The laws should forestall and prevent such troubles from arising; they should lend their influence and authority to the removal in good time of the causes which lead to conflicts between employers and employed."

The State has a responsibility for seeing that labour is not protracted over too long hours of work, having regard to the nature of the work and especially to the employment of women and children; that children are not put into factories "until their bodies and minds are sufficiently developed"; and that women are not given unsuitable work—they are best employed in the home. And on the vexed question of wages the encyclical comes out quite clearly against the classical economists, who taught that wages could be fixed only in accordance with the laws of supply and demand. The Pope asserts the contrary principle of the "sufficient wage":

"Let the workingman and the employer make free agreements, and in particular let them agree freely as to wages; nevertheless, there exists a prior dictate of natural justice, more imperious and ancient than any bargain between man and man, namely that wages ought not to be insufficient to support a frugal and well-behaved wage earner. If, through necessity or fear of a worse evil, the workman accepts harder conditions, because an employer or contractor will afford him no better, he is made the victim of force and injustice. In these and similar questions—such, for example, as the hours of labour in different trades, or the sanitary precautions to be observed in factories and workshops—to avoid undue interference on the part of the State, especially as circumstances, times and localities differ so widely, it is advisable that recourse be had to Societies or Boards . . . the State being appealed to, should circumstances require, for its sanction and protection."

The workingman should be encouraged to save, and if possible to acquire land, and it is very important that "a man's means be not drained and exhausted by excessive taxation." But his chief support will be his Union.

"History attests what excellent results were brought about by the artificers' guilds of olden times. They were the means of affording not only many advantages to the workmen but in no small degree of promoting the advancement of art, as numerous monuments remain to bear witness. Such unions should be subject to the requirements of this our age—an age of wider education, of different habits, and of far more numerous requirements in daily life. It is gratifying to know that there are actually in existence not a few associations of this nature, consisting either of workmen alone, or of workmen and employers together; but it were greatly to be desired that they should become more numerous and more efficient." Some associations—the Pope was evidently thinking of the Freemasons and other secret societies—are to be eschewed because they are hurtful to religion and dangerous to the State, and should not be allowed; unfortunately governments, the Pope observes, are often inclined to support such societies rather than the Catholic associations.

Finally, the Pope concludes:

"Everybody should put his hand to the work which falls to his share, and that at once and straightway, lest the evil which is already so great becomes through delay absolutely beyond remedy. Every minister of holy religion must bring to the struggle the full energy of his mind and all his power of endurance . . ."

CHAPTER SEVENTEEN

Rerum Novarum in the Twentieth Century

So fundamental are the principles of *Rerum Novarum* to the modern social teaching of the Church that we shall do well, before returning to the general religious and political problems of the pontificates of Leo XIII and Pius X, to move far into the twentieth century in order to see how Leo XIII's social teaching has been developed.

And first we have to notice how Leo XIII himself, ten years after he had published *Rerum Novarum*, issued what may be called a supplementary encyclical on the same problems, in 1901, entitled *Graves de Communi*. In it he applauds the efforts that have been made, in the form of societies for mutual help, and the like, to give effect to his teaching, and he notes with pleasure that even non-Catholics are impressed by the way in which the Church shows herself careful of all classes of the community, and especially of the very poor. But the historical importance of this encyclical lies in its baptism of the name Christian Democracy. The rise of socialist parties in Europe, which were normally called Social Democrats, had, by the year 1901, given rise very widely to parties of political reformers opposed to the socialists, calling themselves Christian Democrats, and this appellation the Pope now felt compelled, if rather reluctantly, to accept. He only did so on the understanding that such parties did not adopt the policies either of the class war or of the upsetting of governments; all forms of government were acceptable to the Church, and obedience was the first necessity. Christian Democracy "must insist that the right to have and to hold be kept inviolate; it must maintain such distinction between classes as properly belongs to a well-ordered State; in short, it must assert that human society should have that form and character which its divine Author has imposed upon it." Its aim should be "to make the lives of labourers and artisans more tolerable, to enable them gradually to make some provision for themselves, to make it possible for them at home and in the world freely to fulfil the obligations of virtue and religion, to let them feel themselves to be men and not merely animals, Christian men and not pagans, and so enable them to strive with more facility and earnestness to attain that 'one thing needful, that final good for which we came into the world. . . .'"

In the year of Leo XIII's death (1903) his successor, Pius X, as anxious as his predecessor that Catholic societies should promote the objectives of *Rerum Novarum*, summarised his predecessor's teaching in a *Motu Proprio*, at the same time stressing that Christian Democrats should not, as a party, "mix in politics," that they must be "strictly bound to dependence on ecclesiastical authority by complete submission to the bishops and their representatives," and that in Italy (on account of the *non-expedit* which still ostracised the new Italian kingdom, usurper of the Papal State) they must, like all other Catholics, abstain from any political action at all. Before long, however, the rapid growth of socialism was becoming so marked, and the Social Democratic party was making such progress in the Italian Parliament, as well as elsewhere in Europe, that Pius X started to grant exceptions in the matter of the *non-expedit*, allowing Christian Democrats to contest parliamentary seats, as a check to socialism, and encouraging Catholic political parties in Germany, France, and wherever the Socialist and Communist parties were a menace, to do likewise. In 1919 Pius X's successor, Benedict XV, confronted with what appeared likely to be the seizure of power by the Communists in Italy, withdrew the *non-expedit* altogether, and Don Luigi Sturzo entered Parliament at the head of a substantial Catholic party—the *Popolare*. Thus had the danger of communism, so real after the First World War and the Russian Revolution, impressed itself upon Rome to such an extent that the liberal State, created by the Risorgimento, now appeared as a much lesser evil, indeed as an ally.

It is in the light of these events that we have to view the great social encyclical of Pius XI, *Quadragesimo Anno*, of the year 1931, in which, in the fortieth year after his predecessor's *Rerum Novarum*, he reiterated Leo XIII's social teaching, and tried to bring it up to date. We find the same insistence upon the evil of class warfare, upon the moral rather than the economic root of the problem, upon the value of voluntary associations, especially small associations, upon the error of seeing the remedy in wholesale nationalisation: "The State should leave to smaller groups the settlement of business of minor importance which otherwise would greatly distract it; it will thus carry out with greater freedom, power, and success the tasks belonging to it alone, because it alone can effectively accomplish these, directing, watching, stimulating, restraining, as circumstances suggest and necessity demands."

But we also find Rome recognising that much of what had been condemned in *Rerum Novarum* as socialism must now be called communism. As a result of the First World War and the Russian Revolution a clear practical distinction had appeared between communism and socialism. Communism Pius XI denounces in the kind of terms which Leo XIII or Pius IX used concerning socialism; a censure which its record in respect of religion and class persecution, together with its dedication to the destruction of the Church, made inevitable. But socialism, Pius XI recognises, has changed very much in its outlook. When one remembers that such moderately-minded men as Aristide Briand of France, or Ramsay MacDonald of Britain, belonged to the Second International, and that the Third International, owing to the policies of Lenin and Stalin, never commended itself outside the Communist party proper, one realises that by the year 1931 it had become natural for the Pope to recognise certain distinctions of attitude within that body of opinion hitherto loosely called socialist.

Pius XI's thought, in *Quadragesimo Anno,* is that unbridled individualism and *laissez faire* have led to monstrous monopolies, beyond the control of the State (here he is in agreement with Marx) which, in turn, have led to the still more monstrous inhumanity of communism, while Socialists, shocked by the excesses of communism, have tried to mitigate its worst features. "Free competition has destroyed itself; economic domination has taken the place of the open market. Unbridled ambition for domination has succeeded the desire for gain; the whole economic régime has become hard, cruel, and relentless, in a ghastly measure . . . since the days of Leo XIII Socialism too, the chief enemy with which his battles were waged, no less than the economic régime, has undergone profound changes . . . one section of Socialism has undergone approximately the same [monopolistic] change as that through which (as we have described) the capitalist economic régime has passed; it has degenerated into Communism. Communism teaches and pursues a twofold aim: merciless class warfare and complete abolition of private ownership . . . the other section [of Socialism], which has retained the name of Socialism, is much less radical in its views; not only does it condemn recourse to violence, it even mitigates class warfare and the abolition of private property and qualifies them, to some extent, if it does not actually reject them. It would seem as if Socialism were afraid of its own principles, and of the conclusions drawn therefrom by economists, and in consequence were tending towards the truths which Christian tradition has always held in respect; for it cannot be denied that its opinions sometimes closely approach the just demands of Christian social reformers. . . . If these changes continue, it may well come about that gradually these tenets of mitigated Socialism will no longer be different from the programme of those who seek to reform human society according to Christian principles. For it is rightly contended that certain forms of property must be reserved to the State, since they carry with them a power too great to be left to private individuals without injury to the community at large."

It is clear, then, that many of the objectives of Socialist parties met with papal approval. Yet to socialism as a doctrine, as an historical fact, or as a movement, Pius XI remained implacably hostile. We do not know precisely whether he had particularly in mind the situation in Italy, where Mussolini was in power, or in Spain, where the Republic, with Socialist support, had been proclaimed, or in the United States, where the Socialist party of Norman Thomas was small, or in England, where the principles of the Labour party were never philosophically defined and were in practice moral and humane, or (as seems probable) in Germany and France, where there were substantial and well-organised Socialist political parties, strongly marked by anti-clericalism, tending always towards communism, and holding many seats in their respective assemblies. What the Pope is concerned with is the "pure theory" of socialism, which he does not here distinguish from the "theory" of communism.

"According to Christian doctrine," the Pope explains, "man, endowed with a social nature, is placed here on earth in order that, spending his life in society, and under an authority ordained by God, he may cultivate and evolve to the full all his faculties to the praise and glory of his Creator; and that by fulfilling faithfully the functions of his trade or other calling he may attain both to temporal and to eternal happiness. Socialism, on the contrary, entirely ignorant and unconcerned about this sublime end both of individuals and of society, affirms that human society was instituted merely for the sake of material well-being. For, from the fact that goods are produced more efficiently by a suitable division of labour than they are by the scattered efforts of individuals, Socialists argue that economic activity, of which they see only the material side, must necessarily be carried on collectively, and that because of this necessity men must surrender and submit themselves wholly to society so far as the production of wealth is concerned . . . society therefore, as Socialism conceives it, on the one hand is impossible and unthinkable without the use of obviously excessive compulsion, and on the other no less fosters a false liberty since, in such a scheme, no place is left for true social authority, which is not based upon temporal and material well-being, but descends from God alone, the Creator and last end of all things."

The rôle of the State then, in economic affairs, remains in principle with Pius XI what it was with Leo XIII, namely a limited yet a regulating one. He is even more impressed than was his predecessor with the evils of rugged individualism, and with the necessary rôle of the State as "supreme arbiter, ruling in kingly fashion far above all party contention, and intent only upon justice and the common good," and he recognises explicitly that "certain forms of property must be reserved to the State, since they carry with them a power too great to be left with private individuals without injury to the community at large." It is sometimes said that he was enamoured of the Corporate-State solution, as evolved by Italian fascism, but this is a serious overstatement, much publicised for polemical purposes. No doubt he preferred Mussolini's economic structure, or Primo de Rivera's, and later on General Franco's, to that propounded by the Communists. But it was a choice of the lesser of two evils. In *Quadragesimo Anno* he treated specifically of the Corporate State and criticised Mussolini, at the height of his power and popularity in Italy. After describing the corporative structure he went on: "Little reflection is required to perceive the advantages of the institution thus summarily described: peaceful collaboration of various classes; repression of Socialist [meaning Communist-Revolutionary] organisation and efforts; the moderating influence of a special magistracy. But in order to overlook nothing in a matter of such importance . . . we feel bound to say that to our knowledge there are some who fear that the State is substituting itself in the place of private initiative, instead of limiting itself to necessary and sufficient assistance. It is feared that the new syndical and corporative organisations tend to have an excessively bureaucratic and political character and that, notwithstanding the general advantages referred to above, they end in serving particular political aims rather than in contributing to the initiation and promotion of a better social order."

That, of course, was precisely the trouble with Italian fascism. The syndicates and corporations, in principle sound enough, and superficially seeming to revive the medieval guild idea, so praised by Leo XIII in *Rerum Novarum*, were, in fact, controlled so closely by the Fascist party that, in so far as they functioned at all, they did so as the instruments of the party will.

As, during the 1930s, the Communist government in Russia entrenched itself more firmly, and the Third International spread its propaganda with ever more effect throughout the world, in Spain and in Mexico to the west, in India and in China to the east, the menace of communism became more and more a preoccupation of Pius XI until, in 1937, he published another lengthy encyclical *Divini Redemptoris*. In this he showed how people "of no ordinary worth" had been seduced by speciously presented half-truths, how the way had been prepared "by the religious and moral destitution in which wage earners had been left by liberal economics," how a "conspiracy of silence" on the part of the press had left the world in the dark concerning the enormous scale of the horrors perpetrated in Russia, in Spain, and in Mexico; and he went on to praise what had been achieved by the Church, and especially by Catholic Action (the latest form of Christian Democracy). He recalled the economic principles of *Rerum Novarum* and *Quadragesimo Anno*, denouncing in particular those Catholic employers who, "in one place succeeded in preventing the reading of the encyclical *Quadragesimo Anno* in their local churches." With more precision than Rome had used before, the Pope now stated: "The rôle of justice and charity, in social and economic relations, can only be achieved when professional and interprofessional organisations, based on the solid foundations of Christian teaching, constitute, under forms adapted to different places and circumstances, what used to be called guilds." To further this "it is of the utmost importance to foster in all classes of society an intensive programme of social education, adapted to the varying degrees of intellectual culture; and to spare no pains to procure the widest possible diffusion of the social teachings of the Church among all classes, including the workers."

It is to this powerful papal appeal for a social education that we may attribute the teaching of the social principles of *Rerum Novarum* and its successors in Catholic schools subsequently, as well as the development of the Catholic Unions. The growth of communism had served only to make the Catholic approach to the social problem, as Leo XIII had outlined it, of greater urgency and importance; subsequent Popes amplified his teaching in certain particulars, but the essential principles—the harmony of classes, the just wage, the spiritual basis of the social problem, the limited but very necessary rôle of the State—were already enunciated in *Rerum Novarum*, from which they passed into Catholic thinking and provided the framework within which the Church's approach to the social question necessarily proceeded.

CHAPTER EIGHTEEN

The Kulturkampf in Germany (1870–1890)

We have pursued the consequences of Leo XIII's social teaching far beyond the confines of his own lifetime, since it seemed necessary to do so for the proper development of his principles. We must now return to the period of his pontificate (1878–1903) in order to see how the unification of Italy and Germany into powerful nation states radically affected the fortunes of the Church in Europe. For the Italian Risorgimento, which had set up a hostile secularist state on the very threshold of Rome, was followed by a violent assertion of nationalist and secularist anti-clericalism throughout Europe, and in much of the New World as well.

It is well to remember that the concluding decades of the nineteenth century saw the rise of that unbridled nationalism of the great powers of the West which is often called imperialism. It was the age of Bismarck, the age of the "scramble for Africa," of the French dream of *revanche*, of D'Annunzio, of the Boer War, of the Spanish-American War. This phenomenon of emotional nationalism—jingoism—was, psychologically speaking, a rather natural corollary to the weakening hold of religion and to the current materialism, intellectual, social, and economic. It filled the psychological need for enthusiasm, devotion, and self-sacrifice. Thus, if the semi-educated Italian bourgeois of the cities now felt it beneath him to observe the restraints and pieties urged upon him by the Church, he could yet satisfy the quixotic element in him by spilling his blood, as D'Annunzio was urging him to do, in the sands of Libya, for the Italian tricolour—or at least by urging others to do so. The wildest of the new anti-clerical rulers of Italy, Francesco Crispi, was also the most reckless advocate and promoter of Italian imperialist adventures in Africa. Bismarck in Germany, or Clemenceau in France, whose devotion to the supremacy of their respective nations was so strong, were also the heaviest hammers of the Church.

At the same time it is necessary to make certain distinctions. First, it would certainly be wrong to see the later nineteenth century as a period of religious decline, whether in the Catholic Church or in Christianity as a whole. The extent of missionary and educational activity, the founding of new religious orders, the congresses promoted by the Liberal Catholics (and even the very heat of their controversy with the ultramontanes), the conversions in England, and the rapid growth of the American Church, would alone belie such an estimate. By comparison with the Church of 1780 the Church of 1880 was a very vital institution. Yet it remains true that the philosophical and scientific outlook, which derived originally from the Enlightenment of the eighteenth century, had helped to alienate a very large part (though by no means all) of the intelligentsia, especially in the universities, and that the rapid rise of the proletariat had produced a population not nurtured, as the peasant had been, in Catholic beliefs and pieties. The vitality of nineteenth-century Catholicism, though undeniable, and amounting almost to a rejuvenation, operated within a more restricted section of the population; statesmen, professors, and businessmen, in all the Western countries, were far more liable to leave the Church out of their calculations, and its impact upon the urban masses was only slight. It was to these new secular elements that the new religion of nationalism, with its lamentable resurrection of racial superiority, made its effective appeal.

But there is a further distinction to be made. The spirit of patriotism, love of one's country, and obedience to the State, are Catholic virtues, which have shone brightly throughout the ages, and have always been fostered by the Church. There is no conflict between a true patriotism and a true Catholicism; rather is the latter a guarantee of the former. It is only when the nation poses as the *sole* fount of morality and education for its members that conflict arises. But for many children, especially after the establishment of universal and free education, that moral monopoly was just what *was* arising towards the end of the nineteenth century, and one of the results was that the First World War was fought with the new ruthlessness of ideological totalitarianism. In Germany and Italy, and in other new nations, this tendency became even more marked in the age of Hitler and Mussolini; while in the Communist countries all pretence that there could be any limit to the moral authority of the government, any inner check of conscience, arising from belief in a God who is Father of all men, disappeared. It is because the year 1870 marked the emergence of the new Italy, the new Germany, and also a new nationalist French Republic, determined upon curbing the Church, that it must be seen as so important a landmark in the struggle between the spiritual and the temporal power.

Yet many believed that the State was on the defensive against the Church, because the new rulers made the proclamation of Papal Infallibility, at the Vatican Council of the same year, their excuse for "precautionary measures." The error may be understandable, but it remained nonetheless an error, for, as Cardinal Manning demonstrated to Gladstone, the new dogma did not alter "by one jot or tittle" the loyalty and obligation owed by Catholics to the State; it merely defined what had generally been believed, namely that the seat of dogmatic authority for Catholics lay at Rome. Any subject or citizen, be he Quaker or Baptist, Gentile or Jew, if he preserved any liberty of conscience, was bound to set a limit to the authority of the State in matters of faith or morals, and his guide in those matters, as Manning reminded his opponents, would commonly be his Church.

It was in Germany that the new struggle was sharpest and of greatest importance to the world. This was because, by the defeat of France in 1870, Bismarck's Prussia was enabled to absorb the other German states into the new Germanic empire, and so to create the strongest military power in the world, and one which would set the pace and the fashion to Europe in matters cultural and spiritual, as well as political, for the coming fifty years.

The startlingly rapid victories by which Prussia defeated Austria in 1866, and France in 1870, completely changed the political balance of power in Europe, and in a manner far from advantageous to the Church. It is necessary to remember that in the Germanic Confederation, set up in the year 1815, Austria was the premier power, and that the southern German states, and especially Catholic Bavaria, looked to Austria as their leader, and for the most part looked askance at Prussia. For long the Hohenzollern kings of Prussia had accepted their secondary position in the Germanic Confederation and had supported the Hapsburgs at Vienna; it was Bismarck's achievement to alter all this and to give to Prussia a lead which led to her supremacy in northern Germany, after the defeat of Austria in 1866, and to her supremacy in the whole of Germany (except Austria) after 1870. Thus the new Germany was really a greater Prussia, whereas many liberals and most Catholics had hoped that it would be a federation, in which

Austria would be the preponderant power. Clinging to the old idea of empire, and ignoring the new principle of nationality, the Hapsburgs had striven to maintain their traditional rule over Italian and German, Slav and Magyar, and had only succeeded in losing the two former, in 1859–70, just as in the twentieth century they would lose the two latter.

From the Catholic point of view Bismarck's victories were disastrous because the Catholic empires of Napoleon III and Francis Joseph were his victims. It is true that the behaviour of neither of the two defeated Emperors had been altogether Pope Pius IX's idea of what was to be expected of a "Most Christian Majesty" or of a "Catholic Majesty"; but they were much to be preferred to Bismarck, or to the anti-clericals of Paris and the anti-clericals of Rome, who assumed power in those two cities as a direct result of the Franco-Prussian War. Instead of a Europe suspended between an officially Catholic Paris and an officially Catholic Vienna, Rome was now confronted with a Europe revolving around a Protestant-Imperialist Berlin.

It was natural that their military victories should lead the Germans to a tremendous sense of their racial superiority, for they came at a time when in science and philosophy German ascendancy was pronounced. It is arguable that this age in Germany, the age of Nietzsche and Treitschke, was really much less golden than the age of Goethe and Hegel had been; but certainly it lacked nothing in self-confidence. "Enthusiasm for an exalted idea, consciousness of a great future, good fortune in arms, practical intelligence and control of the will by the categorical imperative of Kant—all continue to make Germany irresistible." So wrote the historian Gregorovius, who added that the time had come to renew the Lutheran onslaught upon Rome. The historian Mommsen likewise took the line that the work of the Reformation had been only partially achieved, and was now to be completed "even at the price of a new thirty years' civil war"; and the famous journalist Richter popularised the same idea. There was a general and not altogether unjustified belief in the superiority of German historical criticism, especially in the field of biblical study and Church history, and the fact that one of the leaders in this field, Ignaz Döllinger, of the University of Munich, had found himself unable to accept the decisions of the Vatican Council, led to important practical consequences, as we saw earlier, in causing the Old Catholic schism in Germany. The fact that Döllinger soon found himself entirely out of sympathy with the schismatics, as he had previously grown out of sympathy with Rome, did not prevent his name and academic reputation from being used as a shield to cover the nakedness of the new movement. Yet the Old Catholics merely sought to fossilise the Church by denying her modern representatives (at bottom because they disliked them so) the power to shape beliefs, a power which was treated as though it had lapsed after the first five, or at latest the first fifteen centuries.

Germanic pride, racial and intellectual, was the soil in which the Kulturkampf—Bismarck's attempt to subjugate the Church—took root, and it is likely that pride, too, in the soul of Bismarck himself, was the primary source of his campaign. For after 1870 the Church was the only force in Germany which still resisted him. The National Liberal party, which had hoped to create a democratic Germany, had capitulated after the defeat of Austria in 1866. The Emperor William I owed his new crown and his world prestige to his chancellor, and henceforth was his tool. The Lutherans, with their necessarily national view of the Church, saw nothing but advantage in a German prince, stronger by far than those princes to whose chariot wheels Luther had sought to "tie the Reformation." Only the Catholics remained, a body which disliked the political turn of events, and one Bismarck felt it difficult to dominate.

But it is also fairly clear that, in the years immediately following 1870, Bismarck believed Catholic political opposition to be a real danger to him. The fact that his new empire embraced the large Catholic populations of Bavaria, Würtemberg, and Baden, and those of Alsace and Lorraine, seized from France (as well as the Catholics of the Rhineland provinces, to the west, and of Polish Posen to the east, previously absorbed by Prussia), meant that he now ruled a country one third of whose population was Catholic, and that third belonged mostly to regions recently acquired and lacking in traditional respect for Berlin. Since it was also Catholic sentiment in France which was most eloquent on the subject of a war of revenge against Germany, and there was a danger of a Franco-Austrian alliance with this common motive, it seemed to Bismarck that the centre of his empire, Brandenburg, was surrounded by hostile elements within and without, and that these hostile elements were also Catholic. His fears are understandable. Had a crusade been started, as many Catholics hoped it would be, for the recovery of Rome for the Pope, with the consequent discomfiture of the new Italian State, forces might have been set in motion which would have endangered his own new State.

International anxieties, then, played their part with Bismarck, alongside personal pique and a readiness to give rein to nationalist passions which could be enlisted in support of his new political creation. The Old Catholic movement could be represented as "Germanic," so he gave it his support. The hierarchy, the religious orders, and most of all the Jesuits, could be represented as cosmopolitan in outlook, or what has since been called "divisist," so he determined to secure his own control over them. And he would find an excuse for doing so in the decrees of the Vatican Council.

It is interesting to notice that religious toleration in pre-Bismarckian Prussia was as fairly and as fully established as in any European state of the nineteenth century. Throughout the later struggles between the chancellor and the Church, it was the constant endeavour of Ludwig Windthorst, the leader of the Centre party (mainly Catholic) in the new Reichstag, to try to restore the toleration which had obtained before the year 1870. But Bismarck was determined, anyhow until the year 1877, upon establishing a control over the Church so close that he could be certain of its support in all his projects; in this he was pursuing the same objectives as Napoleon had pursued, and it may be added that he showed an ignorance of what was vital to religion, and therefore Rome could never sacrifice, as glaring as had been the ignorance of the Emperor.

Oddly enough, the conflict was precipitated in Catholic Bavaria, on account of the influence of Döllinger at the University of Munich. The anti-clerical government there actually prohibited priests from publishing the decisions of the Vatican Council and gave its full support to the Old Catholic movement. Thereupon Bismarck added fuel to the flames by nominating the Bavarian Cardinal Hohenlohe as the new German ambassador to the Holy See, thus attempting to "run the papacy" through a friendly and anti-papal cardinal, an attempt which may be compared with Napoleon's efforts to use his uncle, Cardinal Fesch, in the same way. Pius IX, who had not been consulted, could only refuse to accept the new ambassador, and diplomatic relations between Berlin and Rome were broken. There followed a press campaign throughout Germany which showed that the Protestant pastors were in alliance with Bismarck, whom they regarded as a new Luther, and that they were also in alliance with the agnostic and atheistic Liberals and Socialists, whose aim was the downfall of the whole Christian faith. Prussia soon became the centre of the struggle, which was fairly launched when Dr. Falk became the Minister of Cults there and issued, in February 1872, the first of the famous laws which bear his name. This first of the Falk laws subjected all schools to state inspection, even in respect of their religious instruction, and forbade any religious congregation from doing any teaching, even religious teaching. Next, the Reichstag expelled the Jesuits by forbidding them to say Mass in Germany. The Falk laws in Prussia, which followed in the month of May 1873, and were known as the May laws, placed the training of the clergy under state control, requiring them to study theology in a university, and to satisfy state inspectors as to their scientific, philosophical, and historical knowledge and outlook. All seminaries were subjected to state inspection, and could be closed at the will of the government, and disciplinary power over students and clergy was taken out of the hands of the bishops and put into the hands of the State. This was the heart of what was now christened the Kulturkampf or "cultural struggle"—a veritable new war on religion. The bishops tried to meet it by passive resistance, but for this they were hauled before the Tribunal of Ecclesiastical Affairs and either fined or imprisoned.

Yet in spite of the alliance of anti-Catholic forces which supported Bismarck and Falk, the remarkable result of three years of persecution was that the Centre party, led by the shrewd and courageous Windthorst, actually increased its representation in the Prussian Diet, at the elections of November 1873, from fifty-two seats to ninety, and at the Reichstag elections from fifty-nine to ninety-one. The fight was fairly joined. Windthorst tried to improve his position further by introducing direct as well as universal suffrage into Prussia; but in this he was defeated by the National Liberals, who had always favoured giving everybody the direct vote, but who fought shy of doing so when they found it would favour the Catholics.

Bismarck was not unduly concerned about parliamentary indications of popular feeling and his campaign continued. It reached its climax with the law of 1874 on the "internment or expulsion of recalcitrant priests." In the first four months

of the year 1875 a hundred and three priests were expelled
or imprisoned. In May 1875 all the religious orders (with the
exception of the Hospitalers, who were needed by the Army)
were dissolved. Monks and nuns followed the secular priests
into exile; some were drowned in the wreck of the ship
Deutschland, off the Thames Estuary, on a wild night in December 1875, a tragedy immortalised by the poet, Gerard
Manley Hopkins:

Loathed for a love men knew in them,
Banned by the land of their birth,
Rhine refused them. Thames would ruin them;
Surf, snow, river and earth
Gnashed: but thou art above, thou Orion of light;
Thy unchancelling poising palms were weighing the worth,
Thou martyr-master: in thy sight
Storm flakes were scroll-leaved flowers, lily showers—
    sweet heaven was astrew in them.

In February 1875 Pius IX denounced the whole legislation, root and branch, forbade Catholics to obey it, and
excommunicated those few clergy who had accepted investiture
by the State.

The consequences of the Kulturkampf were extremely serious
for the Church. More than a million Catholics were deprived
of the sacraments because thousand of priests were in exile
or in prison. There were no bishops available to ordain new
priests, because they had been relieved by the State of their
sees after their failure to secure the approval of the prefects
to their ordination; two archbishops (Cologne and Posen) had
been exiled. The government forbade parish priests to visit
other parishes than their own to give the sacraments. And,
as a sort of crowning insult, priority in the use of the churches
was given to the handful of anti-Roman Old Catholics, and
the government created a new bishopric which it bestowed
upon the leader of that sect.

It will be seen that Bismarck was attempting to create something very similar to the Constitutional Church of the French
Revolution, though the Old Catholic movement never assumed
comparable proportions and soon dwindled into insignificance
with the defection of Döllinger. Bismarck was also endeavouring to use his preponderant diplomatic position in Europe to
influence other countries to follow his example. In Switzerland

a similar campaign was already raging. Both the Belgian and the new Italian governments were the recipients of his advice on how to handle the Church, but in both countries the advice was resented, and in Belgium Disraeli countered from England with suggestions in a contrary sense.

After 1878 Bismarck began to retreat. By April 1887 the last of the really offensive legislative acts had been removed. But the religious freedom that had obtained in Prussia in pre-1870 days was not wholly restored. In particular, the priest was still in law supposed to satisfy the prefect with a modified form of "declaration" although this, in so far as it was insisted upon, became little more than a general oath of loyalty to the new régime. The old guarantees of administrative liberty and of free relations with Rome were not restored; but in practice the State ceased to stand upon its rights. The religious orders (except the Jesuits) were allowed to return, though the terms upon which they might do so were far from generous. Gradually they were able to resume their independent way of life in the same manner as previously; gradually, too, though the laws favouring the Old Catholics were not repealed, their dwindling numbers prevented any real problem from arising on their account. The vital point upon which the Church won an explicit victory was the restoration of the full authority of the bishops over the clergy, the abolition of the Royal Tribunal of Ecclesiastical Affairs, and the end of the state examination of intending priests, all of which was achieved in April 1886 in the Prussian Diet, with the acquiescence of Bismarck, and against the opposition only of the Liberals. This victory marked the real end of the Kulturkampf.

That an attack, of greater ferocity than any major branch of the Church had suffered since the French Revolution, was withstood and quelled in Bismarck's Germany was due primarily to the steadfast loyalty of the German clergy and laity, but also to the firmness of Rome. But that a reasonable peace was restored was also due to the good sense and cool-headedness of able men on both sides. On the side of the Church outstanding was the great leader of the Centre party, Windthorst. It was his leadership that enabled the Centre party not only to increase its parliamentary strength throughout the contest, but to keep the door always open for negotiation with Bismarck by steadily voting the budget presented by his government, and by supporting him when the interests of the Church were not at stake. The fact was that Windthorst very much preferred Bismarck to the Liberals, and not without good reason. But to have kept open the door to collaboration with him, at a time when the chancellor was making the issue of the *Kulturkampf* a personal one between himself and the leader of the Centre party, and was denouncing Windthorst as a *Reichsfeind*, or "enemy of the State," showed in the Catholic leader a balance and control, combined with tenacity, which must raise him to the highest rank amongst political leaders of the nineteenth century.

Leo XIII is often credited with having been the peacemaker in the contest, it being generally assumed that the election of a "conciliatory Pope" in 1878, in the place of the intransigent Pius IX, made it possible for Bismarck to negotiate a settlement. This is a superficial reading of the matter. It is true, of course, that Pius IX, in his last years as prisoner in the Vatican, was not an easy sovereign with whom to negotiate, and that the attitude of Bismarck's government towards the Old Catholics, of Döllinger descent, was necessarily very painful to him. But the essential ground of the Roman position in this contest remained what it always must remain in such conflicts, whoever may be the occupant of the Chair of Saint Peter, being none other than the maintenance of the spiritual independence of the priesthood. For this, to go no further back, Innocent XI had striven with Louis XIV, Pius VII with Napoleon I, and Pius IX with Napoleon III, just as Pius XI would have to contend with Mussolini, with Stalin and with Hitler. When Bismarck yielded on the essential issue in 1886 peace became possible; earlier it had been impossible.

Nevertheless it is true that there were points of divergence between the policy of Rome, in Leo XIII's time, and that of the German Centre party, with its mainly Catholic composition; Bismarck realised that Leo wanted peace, and he tried to play off the Pope against Windthorst. In order to understand what was happening it is important to notice what, by the 1880s, had become Bismarck's real preoccupation. He had ceased to be haunted by the spectre of a European Catholic alliance embracing France, Austria, and southern Germany, designed to restore the Pope to his State, and to destroy his own new Germanic empire. He was concerned now with three more realistic matters. He wanted to impose his own brand of social legislation in Germany; he wanted to secure his own control over foreign and military affairs by persuading the

Reichstag, in 1887, to vote him a seven-year military budget; and he wanted to subdue the perennial pan-Polish sentiments of the Prussian province of Posen. In each of these matters the Church and the Centre party were very much concerned.

In his social legislation it was Bismarck's aim to offer state-supported unemployment and sickness insurance, and other workers' benefits, as a *quid pro quo* to soften the blow of his measures against the trade unions and against the Socialists generally—"a good investment for our money," he said, "in this way we avoid a revolution . . ."! The aims of the Centre party were more sweeping. They included restriction of working hours for men, elimination of women and young children from the factories, a day of rest on Sunday, and proposals for corporate organisation, which the Liberals ridiculed as me-dieval, and which Bismarck regarded as impractical, but which were founded upon a religious view of man clearly contrasted with liberal *laissez faire* on the one hand and with exaltation of the State on the other. But although they were rooted in contrasted philosophies, there was enough in common between Bismarck's plans for meeting the social problem and those of the Centre party to make some useful co-operation possible, and it became important to the chancellor to have the support of the Catholic Centre, both against the Socialists and also against the Liberals.

It was not on this matter of the social programme that Leo XIII and the Centre party came to be at variance; sub-stantially the party stood for just those principles which the Pope was about to affirm in *Rerum Novarum*. Where the Pope and Windthorst were in disagreement was in regard to Bis-marck's second aim—to control military and foreign affairs. The crucial issue here was whether the Reichstag should vote the chancellor the seven-year budget he demanded in respect of military expenses. By the year 1887 Leo XIII was sufficiently satisfied with the progressive liquidation of the Kulturkampf to believe that the interest of the Church would best be served by supporting the chancellor, rather than by supporting the Reichstag, and he could see little advantage in weakening a statesman whose essential wisdom and ability even Wind-thorst acknowledged, in favour of a democratic assembly, in which the anti-clericalism of the Socialists was only matched by the anti-clericalism of the Liberals. The analogy here is with Pius VII's position in respect of Napoleon; a powerful states-man might be a constant danger to the Church, but at least he was likely to be a realist, and as a realist would recognise the *fact* of the Faith. He was therefore to be preferred to the utopian, iconoclastic, "idealist" type of reformer, who was seeking to replace the Church by an idea of his own. So we find Leo XIII telling the nuncio at Munich, through Cardinal Jacobini, that he hopes the Centre will favour Bismarck's project for a seven-year military budget, and we find Windthorst courteously refusing to do so, taking the line that the matter is purely political. Bismarck obtained and published the text of Jacobini's note to the nuncio, so as to show up Windthorst and the Centre as "more papal than the Pope," and as a self-constituted menace to Germany's true interests. It was an odd manoeuvre on the part of one who had been declaiming against the Centre for "obeying a foreign power." But it was effective, and in the event the majority of the Centre abstained from voting on the issue, while some of its right-wing members voted against Windthorst and in favour of the chancellor's proposal, which was duly approved.

Bismarck's third preoccupation was the Poles of Posen. He had come to pretend that the whole Kulturkampf had been waged to check the separatist Catholic nationalism of the Poles of Prussia's eastern provinces. This was far from true, but it was over Posen that the chancellor was least disposed to yield. Rome sought to secure that the millions of Catholic Poles should have an archbishop of their own race; but, after Bismarck had rejected no fewer than thirteen candidates put forward by the Pope, Leo XIII was obliged to accept a Polish-speaking German. Nor did Leo ever secure the return of the exiled Archbishop of Cologne. The compromises to which he felt compelled to agree, in the interests of restoring religious peace, seemed to Windthorst to go too far; the leader of the Centre always believed that with patience and fortitude the *status quo* could be secured. Whether he was right about that will never be known. But it is easy to understand and sympathise with his insistence that, in political matters such as the voting of the military budget, the party should be free from Roman advice, nor was it helpful to himself and to his followers that the Pope accorded to the chancellor, in the year 1885 (before any of the major measures of the Kulturkampf had been withdrawn), the coveted Order of Christ, with brilliants. Bismarck was the first Protestant to receive this order; it was conferred upon him after he had submitted to papal arbitration the quarrel between Germany and Spain over the Caroline Islands, and had accepted the Pope's award.

The Kaiser, William I, had always been uneasy about the Kulturkampf. A religiously minded Protestant, he had been able to see that the passions which had been unleashed militated against the basic interests of all religion. With the accession, in 1888, of the young Kaiser, William II, relations with Rome were not again seriously disturbed; we have seen how the new Kaiser's determination to push further the cause of social legislation commended itself to Leo XIII. The Church was now regarded as a useful ally against the Socialists, and it had been amply demonstrated that Catholics were good and loyal subjects of the new empire. It may indeed be argued that they became too good and too loyal. Now that the menace of a ferocious religious persecution seemed to be over, and the rise of an atheistic socialism appeared to be the chief danger to religion, there developed a tendency on the part of the Centre to support the government of William II, even when it developed increasingly militaristic and pan-Germanic qualities. Bismarck was dismissed by the Kaiser in March 1890; Windthorst died in the following March. For a time, under the leadership of Ernst Lieber, the party maintained its strict independence of the government, voting against increased military budgets, and often with the left-wing groups. But the appearance of a Catholic chancellor (Chlodwig Hohenlohe-Schillingsfürst) at the end of 1894, together with a member of the Centre party (the Baron de Buol) as president of the Reichstag, tended to keep it in a central position. The real difficulty which confronted the party, after the collapse of the Kulturkampf, was that there was too little to hold it together or to make it appeal to the electorate as a whole. It did not notably diminish in parliamentary strength before 1914, retaining around a hundred seats in the Reichstag, but it lost both in prestige and in tactical importance. Efforts were made to enlist non-Catholic political supporters, but they were ineffective because, politically and economically, the party seemed to have too indecisive a policy. The dominant National Liberals, having been transformed by Bismarck from a party standing for individual liberty and parliamentary democracy into a party standing for authority, pan-Germanism, and "Germany's civilising mission," were better suited to the increasingly chauvinistic jingoism which was taking hold upon public opinion, encouraged by the flamboyant political gestures of Kaiser

William II. The Socialists, on the other hand, had developed their own intransigent class-war and state-control policies and were uninterested in the Catholic social conceptions favoured by the Centre. And popular sympathy generally was a good deal estranged by the anti-Modernist campaign, which, by emphasising the supremacy of dogma over "free enquiry," seemed an especial affront to the work of the German universities. A policy of political compromise, intended to restrain the excesses of the pan-Germanists on the one hand, and of the Socialists on the other, was insufficient to attract effective support, even though it may well have been the policy of which Germany most sorely stood in need. The temperature of German nationalism was rising, and the violently anti-Catholic propaganda of the evangelical *Bund* served to fan the flames. It seemed increasingly intolerable that Germany's "manifest mission in the world" should be restrained by a party in the Reichstag which was supposedly "subject to the Vatican."

It was with the emergence of Chancellor von Bülow, in 1906, that the party ceased to hold a controlling position. A decline in the Socialist vote having freed the new chancellor from the need to rely upon the support of the Centre, that party found itself the uncomfortable bedfellow of the Socialists, in opposition to a government which was piling up the armaments that led to 1914; and many even of the Catholic votes were now going to the government parties.

Two questions, both of great consequence for the future, must readily arise in the mind of the spectator of the Catholic struggle in the new Germany of 1870–1914, the Germany of the Second Reich. The first is the danger to which an Established Church is exposed when the government proves hostile. Bismarck, in the Kulturkampf, was not trying to exterminate the Church, or even to restrict it, he was trying to *control* it, as Napoleon had tried to control the Church in France. He wanted to compel it, by his "culture examination," by supervision of the training of priests, and the rest, to teach what he wanted—to be a sort of auxiliary of his State. But none of this would have been possible had not the Catholic Church been one of the Established Churches of Germany, whose parish priests, as well as bishops, had to be approved by the State. The Catholic was not of course the only, or even the largest Established Church in Germany, but it was one of those approved and supported by the State, and such it remained even after the Kulturkampf. It was therefore subject to state pressure.

And the other question is whether, in a parliamentary régime, a Catholic political party is desirable. Political action in defence of the Church has no doubt been a frequent, indeed a constant necessity in all countries. The question is whether this defence has been best achieved by a Catholic political party, or by Catholics of either or of all parties combining (as in contemporary England or America) when issues affecting the Church are raised. No doubt this is a problem in which time and circumstances play a large part; there may have been occasions when a Catholic political party, such as the German Centre of Bismarck's time, is needed. But one can safely add that the experience of the pre-1914 German Centre showed that when the religious issue was quiescent, then divergent views on political, social, and economic matters made it impracticable to maintain a strong and effective Catholic political party in Germany.

CHAPTER NINETEEN

Anti-Clericalism in Italy and France (1870–1914)

In Italy the fierce contest inherited from the Risorgimento overshadowed everything. The persecution of the religious orders, extended from Piedmont to the whole country, would alone have been sufficient to set Pius IX against the new kingdom. But when it involved the seizure of the Papal States and Rome itself, and the deliberate encouragement of all the anti-Catholic forces of the country, and particularly the Freemasons, as well as divorce laws, abolition of feast days, secularisation of education, and the like, the elderly "prisoner in the Vatican" barricaded himself against all transaction, even against the money which the new government offered him in compensation for his losses.

Yet so long as the political Right, under the statesmanlike Marco Minghetti, held power, there was some hope that a more tolerable *modus vivendi* would be achieved. It was when the veteran Freemason, Agostino Depretis, leader of the Left, won power in 1876, that the more violent anti-clericals, like Giovanni Nicotera (sometime Garibaldian legionary), had their way. Religious processions were banned; the secret meetings of monks or of nuns, who assembled in little groups to continue to live their lives in accordance with their religious vows, were hunted out and suppressed; priests were conscripted for the Army; Catholic congresses were dissolved. But the most serious legislative act was that by which any criticism of the State by the clergy was declared a serious offence in the "Clerical Abuses Bill," passed by the Chamber in January 1877. Many of the Right were scandalised by this discriminatory interference with free speech, and the Bill was subsequently quashed by the Senate. But its effect upon the relations between Church and State in Italy were nonetheless calamitous, for it goaded the Pope into an allocution in which he roundly declared that the new Italy was incompatible with the independence of the Holy See.

From the year 1868, when Pius IX's *non-expedit* first advised Catholics not to take any part in the public affairs of the new kingdom (they were to be "neither electors nor elected"), until the year 1919, when Benedict XV lifted the ban, the Church was practically without direct influence in Italian politics. But she was far from inactive in the country. We have already had occasion, when discussing the social question, to notice how the great Catholic congresses of the last three decades of the century hammered out a social programme which had its bearing upon the issue of *Rerum Novarum*. But these congresses were not only concerned with the workers' problems, they strove to co-ordinate the entire range of Catholic activity, through a network of diocesan and parochial committees, and soon the younger and more ardent spirits, calling themselves Christian Democrats, were thinking in terms of service to the new nation by building up an organisation which would be strong enough to replace both the Socialist trade unions, on the one hand, and the centralised Piedmontese-controlled State upon the other. Though prevented by Rome from taking part in national politics, they were invading the world of local government and were preparing themselves for the day when Leo XIII should die and a new papal policy towards Italy would enable them to emerge, bearing the pattern of a new order for the country, an order which would decentralise her politically and restore some sphere of temporal power to the Pope. It was a bold conception, and in order to understand how it came to be so seriously entertained it is necessary to remember that the new Italy was a very precarious political structure, detested as "Piedmontese" in Naples and Sicily, and likewise by most Republicans and Socialists, and weakened still further by being ostracised by the Church. Italy, indeed, was at first held together by little more than the Piedmontese army and the Piedmontese civil service.

However, the death of Leo XIII in 1903, and the accession of Pius X, put an end to these ambitious dreams of the Christian Democrats. For the new Pope had decided that the danger from the Socialists had become so great that it was necessary, where they were particularly strong, for Catholic candidates to oppose them. It was thus that the *non-expedit* of Pius IX was at last relaxed, and in June 1905, in the encyclical *Il Fermo Proposito*, the election of Catholics to Parliament, in certain selected places, was regularised. The way was now open for the final abolition of the *non-expedit* by Benedict XV in 1919, as a result of which Luigi Sturzo found himself at the head of a substantial Catholic parliamentary party, the Partito Popolare Italiano. But it should be noticed that in 1905 Sturzo was a supporter of the Christian Democrat leader, Romolo Murri, and that the two men were intent upon a policy which would refashion the Italian State altogether. They were therefore distressed by Pius X's decision to allow a limited Catholic participation in the politics of the new Italian kingdom, for they had been hoping to create a new kind of Italy altogether. But the Pope did not care for their plans. Murri was a Modernist, and this spelt the ruin both of himself and of his instrument, the Lega Democratica Nazionale. It is also the explanation of those paragraphs in the Pope's encyclical *Pascendi Gregis*, of 1907, which particularly required that writings concerned with social questions should be examined for Modernist heresies.

In the new Italy then, as in the new Germany, we see the Church gradually driven by the threat of socialism into closer collaboration with a "liberal" and hostile State. But neither in Italy nor in Germany did she do so without first procuring elementary guarantees for her own survival.

These last decades of the nineteenth century and the years leading up to the First World War were times of heavy losses for the Church in the Western world generally. In Britain and the British Commonwealth (and notably Australia) and in the United States of America she was making steady progress; but in the rest of the world, and especially in the traditionally Catholic countries, she was being compelled to yield ground which had always been regarded as sacrosanct. One after another the states of the Western world took away from her control over aspects of life which she regarded as peculiarly her own, such as marriage, education, or the observance as public holidays of the great feasts of the Church. The banning of processions, and especially of the public veneration of the Blessed Sacrament, censorship of press and pulpit, and close control over monasteries, leading often to expulsion of the religious orders, became commonplace occurrences in countries which had hitherto been particularly noted for their Catholic devotion. Thus in Belgium, in 1879, a law was passed secularising public education and disqualifying Catholic teachers; only the vigorous reaction of the Catholic body, which proceeded to run its own schools at heavy financial sacrifice, saved the situation, and the law was modified when the Catholic parties were victorious in the elections of 1884. In Switzerland the religious orders were expelled in a Kulturkampf which followed a course closely parallel to that followed in Germany, but the attempt to secularise the whole of the educational system was defeated in a referendum on the subject held in 1882. In Austria, immemorially the centre of that bulwark of the Church, the empire of "His Catholic Majesty," the liberals had won power as a result of the Prussian victory in 1866. Civil marriage and state control of education were introduced, and the Concordat with Rome, signed as recently as 1855, was unilaterally revoked. Nor did the diets of the traditionally Catholic South German states of Bavaria and Würtemberg, or the traditionally mixed state of Baden, serve as buffers between the Protestants of Prussia and the Catholics of Austria, for those same states of the South proved to be so submerged by the wave of anti-clericalism, which characterised the 1870s, that their political leaders, backed by Bismarck, launched Kulturkampfs rivalling that of Prussia herself.

Across the South Atlantic the republics of Latin America, all now emancipated from Spain and Portugal, shared in varying degrees the secularist mood of the times. But, as against these disquieting signs of the almost universal secularisation of the old Catholic Order, Rome could set the more hopeful picture of progress in the Protestant countries and the immense expansion of missionary activity, especially in Africa and Asia. It is very tempting, on account of this progress in the Protestant countries, to conclude that the case for the separation of Church and State, which was still being argued by the Liberal Catholics, was being proved by the event. Very striking was the instance of Holland, where in 1889 the Catholic schools found themselves placed upon a footing of financial equality with the secularist state schools, or with the Protestant schools.

Yet although the Church suffered grave losses in the Catholic countries in this period, which make a striking contrast with her gains in Protestant lands, where the State was neutral, or where it favoured an Established Protestant Church, it would be rash to draw hard and fast conclusions from this phenomenon. Where Catholics were in a minority there was a natural incentive to zeal, not to say proselytising; an *esprit de corps* developed in the face of danger. But this zeal should not blind us to the fact that the religious gulf between Protestant countries, where Catholicism was gaining ground, and Catholic countries, where the Church was losing ground, still remained enormous. It could not be said that in England, despite the Irish immigration, the conversions arising from the Oxford movement, or the restoration of the hierarchy, Catholicism made any real impact upon the life of the country as a whole. Politics, literature, and the universities reflected either a secularist liberalism, or a nonconformist conscience, or a conventional conservatism associated with the Anglican Church of that day, all of which were un-Catholic; even the few spiritual and intellectual luminaries, such as Newman or Lord Acton, were regarded as "anti-Roman" Catholics, so untypical that they were treated as exceptions proving the popular rule that "real" "Roman" Catholics, such as Ward of the *Dublin Review*, or Cardinal Manning, were "un-English." By comparison Italy, where the anti-clerical storm raged as fiercely as anywhere, where religious congregations were suppressed and canonically invested bishops were prevented from occupying their sees, the country remained Catholic in a sense long since forgotten in England. Divorce might be legalised, but matrimonial suits were very seldom in fact filed; feast days might no longer be state holidays, but they were still observed. And if a Benedictine congregation might feel more secure in the English abbeys of Ampleforth or Downside than at Monte Cassino, in fact very many of the Italian monks soon returned again after each successive suppression. And, if they lost most of their lands and property, it has to be remembered that in England they had not acquired enough, since the suppression at the time of the Reformation, to merit any interest on the part of an acquisitive State.

These considerations had great importance in the eyes of Rome. Leo XIII was at one with his predecessors, Pius IX and Gregory XVI, in his belief that the encouraging developments in the Protestant countries furnished no argument at all in favour of the disestablishment of the Church in Catholic countries. The separation of Church and State in Catholic countries must lead, in his view, to a progressive secularisation of life, a secularisation which was held to have become very evident in those countries which had embraced the Reformation. Such a separation might, indeed, bring spiritual opportunities to the ardent few, but what of the indifferent? Would they not drift, with the current of life, right away from the Faith?

It has been so often the argument of this history that a close state control has been the chief evil from which the Church has suffered in modern times that it is right that these counter arguments should be clearly stated. And we have specially to bear them in mind as we come now to consider the struggle in France at the end of the nineteenth century, when this issue of the separation of Church and State was fought out in the country still regarded by Rome as "Eldest Daughter of the Church."

The French Third Republic was born in blood, sweat, and tears, of the defeat Napoleon III's France had suffered at the hands of Bismarck's new Germany in 1870. Not until the year 1875 did the French Provisional Assembly pronounce in favour of a republic, and then by only one vote. Until that date the majority in the Assembly, as well as in the country, were Monarchist, republicanism being strong only amongst the mob of the city of Paris where, in the dark days of the Communist Commune of 1871, two generals and one archbishop had been murdered, and the Tuileries and the Hôtel de Ville had been burned to the ground. In these circumstances, and thinking back to the dark days of the great French Revolution, it is hardly surprising that the clergy in France for the most part lent their support to the Monarchist cause, which it was generally assumed would prevail.

That it did not do so was due to the divisions within its own ranks. There were supporters of the Bourbon claim, represented by the Comte de Chambord, of the Orleanists (descending from King Louis Philippe), represented by the Comte de Paris, and of the Bonapartists, whose candidate was Napoleon III's son, the Prince Imperial. It was the refusal of the Comte de Chambord to adopt the tricolour flag (he insisted upon the white flag of the Bourbons) and the fact that the other two candidates were both children that prevented any effective initiative being taken by any of the Monarchist parties during the decisive years; in 1876 a popular vote established a republic *faute de mieux*.

It is certainly not surprising that the Church lent her support to the monarchical parties; but, once a republic had been voted, this fact did not help to endear her to the new republican political leaders. Probably a clear statement by Rome in 1876 or 1877, of the kind that Leo XIII frequently made later on, to the effect that the Church was not concerned to support one form of government against another so long as her rights were respected, would have gone far to propitiate French republican opinion. But Pius IX was eighty-five years old and Cardinal Antonelli was dead; it was a bad moment to expect an imaginative gesture from Rome. It is equally arguable that an assurance by the republican leaders that the Church's rights would be respected was what the situation demanded; but this too was not forthcoming. The result was that, from the start, a struggle set in between the Republic and the Church, a struggle whose key note was set by Gambetta in his famous phrase: *le cléricalisme, voilà l'ennemi!* It manifested itself, characteristically enough, in the expulsion of the Jesuits, and in the passage of Jules Ferry's education law, which created what amounted to a new and strictly secular educational system for France. But the government's hostility was shown in a number of smaller ways, such as a reduction of the stipends of the clergy, requirement of military service from those in the seminaries, prohibition of religious processions, and the like. There was also a new divorce law.

Leo XIII paid the closest attention to the problem presented by the new republican France. First, in the encyclical *Nobilissima Gallorum Gens*, of February 1884, he deplored the many hostile acts of the Third Republic and the scourge of irreligion in the country. But, realising how deeply the anti-clericalism of the politicians was rooted in a resentment against the anti-republicanism of the clergy, he saw that the time had come when a clear lead must be given to draw the French Church away from too close a preoccupation with politics, and towards a loyal acceptance of a régime which had gained the support of the majority of the people. To this end, first he prompted Cardinal Lavigerie to make, at Algiers in November 1890, an "inspired" speech in which he called upon Frenchmen and religious leaders to unite in support of the Republic, since "the will of the people has been clearly stated and the form of the government has nothing in itself which runs counter to the principles which alone can give life to Christian and civilised nations." In this speech was launched what was called Leo XIII's policy of the *Ralliement*; but it came as a shock to many members of the French hierarchy, and it was soon necessary for the Pope to make it clear that it was, indeed, papal policy Lavigerie had stated, a fact which Leo had concealed even from the papal nuncio in Paris. In February 1892 he gave an interview to a representative of the *Petit Journal* in which he declared: "Everybody is entitled to his own preferences, but in fact the government is that which France has chosen for herself. The Republic is as legitimate a form of government as any other . . . the United States is a

Republic and, in spite of the disadvantages which arise from an unbridled liberty, she grows greater day by day, and the Catholic Church there has developed without any conflict with the State. These two powers agree together very well, as they should agree everywhere, on condition that neither interferes with the rights of the other. Liberty is the true basis and foundation of the relations between the civil authority and the religious conscience . . . what suits the United States has still more reason to suit Republican France."

In the same month Leo XIII published the encyclical *Inter Numeras Sollicitudines* in which he amplified the same theme. But in a significant conclusion he guarded against giving the impression that he favoured the full separation of Church and State, a principle which he denounced as "tolerable in certain countries but not in France . . . a Catholic nation by her traditions and by the present faith of the great majority of her sons."

But the *Ralliement* came too late. Not all the French clergy could readily turn around and alter their attitude of a lifetime towards republicanism, which they regarded as an evil in itself rather than as a form of government which could be used well or ill like any other. Ardent patriots, they distrusted the new bourgeois politicians, whom they suspected of lining their own pockets whilst allowing the great cause of the recovery of France's lost provinces from Germany to be forgotten. Two major scandals fanned the flames; the Panama scandal over the construction of the canal, which proved that the critics of the politicians were right in supposing that there was plenty of bribery going on in high places, and the Dreyfus case, which proved that much of the Catholic press was gullible, and too ready to assume that military secrets were being betrayed for money, and that proofs to the contrary were forgeries. For Dreyfus, a Jewish officer in the Army, was sentenced to Devil's Island in 1894 for supposedly selling such secrets and, though pardoned in 1899, he was not fully vindicated until 1906. The events which had led to his arrest and sentence had been the work of a few officers, and they reflected upon the Army rather than upon the Church authorities, but the <u>Catholic press had</u> <u>made the error of assuming Dreyfus' guilt</u>, and it was an error that cost the Church dear.

In 1901 the government of Waldeck-Rousseau, beset by difficulties, decided to take advantage of the anti-clerical agi-

tation which had developed over the Dreyfus affair to proceed
to a wholesale suppression of the religious orders. By the Act
of 1901 these orders were forbidden to teach, and could only
continue in being if their superiors lived in France, if they
submitted their rules and other details of their life to examination by the Chamber, and if they came under the jurisdiction
of the bishops. The greater orders refused to comply with these
humiliating conditions of survival. The Benedictines emigrated, often to England; the Jesuits doffed their habits and
closed their schools, but often stayed and served the Church
in other ways. The Assumptionists were obliged to suspend
their powerful paper, *La Croix* (which had attacked Dreyfus),
and went into exile. Many orders of nuns were driven into
exile, forming schools which flourished in Belgium and Holland, in England and America, to the benefit of those countries, and as witness to the truth that the work of the Church
thrives on persecution.

The ruthless carrying out of Waldeck-Rousseau's law was
left to his successor, the sinister Émile Combes, under whom
it was executed with systematic severity. In many cases the
nuns were given only a few minutes in which to make their
departure. By September 1904 Combes was in a position to
boast, in a speech at Auxerre, that he had closed 13,904
schools. This is something which has to be remembered when
it is stated that popular education in France was virtually the
creation of Jules Ferry and his friends of the radical governments of the Third Republic.

The onslaught upon the orders was followed, in June 1904,
by the French Government's breaking off diplomatic relations
with the Vatican. This serious step was immediately occasioned by Pius X's protest against the visit of the French
President Loubet to King Victor Emmanuel III of Italy, at
the palace of the Quirinal—a palace which had been seized
from Pius IX. The Pope was happy enough that President and
King should meet, but not that they should meet in the city
to which he still laid claim. Behind this issue lay many others;
notably the Pope's refusal to institute to certain French bishoprics candidates proposed by Premier Combes' government
and who were evidently unsuitable.

These events led, in September 1905, to the step long urged
by the Radicals and Socialists, namely the separation of
Church and State in France, which finally became law in December 1905. Seen in its context, as the culmination of an

anti-clerical campaign as bitter and prolonged as any witnessed in Europe since the days of the great French Revolution, this seemed a sordid sundering of an intimate association which dated from the days of Clovis, the Frankish King, which had consecrated the empire of Charlemagne, which had been ennobled by Saint Louis, and which had been ornamented by the *Roi Soleil*. Contemporaries thought it must prove a shattering blow to the Church. What, indeed, could be the thoughts of a generation which had witnessed the fall of papal Rome and the collapse of Catholic Paris? And the separation was accompanied by every inconvenience and ignominy. At a blow the stipends of priests (save for pensions for those over sixty) were withdrawn; the Church was to "fend for herself." The injustice of this consisted in the fact that these stipends were the State's agreed compensation, in accordance with the Napoleonic Concordat (ratified by all subsequent régimes), for the confiscation and sale of Church property by the French revolutionaries. True, the Church in France had acquired a little property since the great French Revolution; it was assumed at least that this could be utilised to provide an income for her priests. But not at all. By the Combes law all Church property had to be handed over to local bodies, subject to state control, and called *Associations Cultuelles*. These bodies were to consist largely of laymen, who need not be Catholics, and who would administer the cathedrals, churches, presbyteries, charities, and other temporalities of the Church. So great was the outcry that it was conceded that, in respect of Catholic property, the associations should consist of Catholics, even of priests.

Even so, Pius X, with the support of the majority of the French bishops, refused any arrangement by which the Church would be deprived of every voluntary association's right to dispose of its own funds in its own way, subject only to its own authority. Seeking only, as he put it, the *good* of the Church in France and not her *goods*, by a gesture which astonished and edified public opinion in France and throughout the world, he renounced her buildings to the State so that she entered upon a new life untied by any secular contacts. Henceforth her priests would say Mass in the great cathedrals and churches only as tenants, on sufferance, in those edifices which are the glory of Western civilisation, but which soon fell into a shocking state of disrepair. Yet it could be counted for gain that, whereas in 1793 the doors of the churches were closed against the priests but opened to all sorts of pagan ceremonies, now, in 1906, no attempt was made to stop the saying of Mass.

From the ashes of this conflagration was reborn the Catholic Church in France. The internecine conflicts within the Church herself, between seculars and religious, between ultramontanes and liberals, between monarchists and republicans —conflicts which had gravely weakened the French clergy throughout the previous century—disappeared now in the face of the need for a common effort to maintain her mission. And, the link with the State being broken, the link with Rome was strengthened. The Pope was free now to institute such bishops as he wished in France; in February 1906 he consecrated no less than fourteen in St. Peter's, appointing them to sees which had become vacant during the quarrels. The *Oeuvre des Conférences populaires,* a largely lay organisation, undertook the social work and the organisation of the charities. Money was raised from the faithful to acquire new buildings for seminaries, for presbyteries, for hospitals, for schools. So great a sacrifice and so extensive an effort won a new popular admiration, an admiration mightily increased when the German invasion of 1914 ushered in the horrors of the First World War, horrors shared by the devotion of the priests in the trenches and the nuns in the hospitals, alongside their secularist opponents, so many of whom they were able to succour and sometimes to reconcile in their last agonies.

It would of course be wrong to attribute this beginning of the Catholic revival in France solely to the separation of Church and State in 1905, nor can the damage done by that great divorce be easily assessed. What, for example, can we know of the effect of the persistent anti-clerical teaching which for many years became a feature of some of the state schools, although they were supposed to be neutral in religious matters? All that can be said is that, cut adrift from the State, and freed from the necessity of propitiating public opinion, the Church in France, though more restricted in her sphere of action, was enabled to devote herself in a more single-minded manner to her mission.

If we wish to find the sources of her renewed strength and inspiration we should look further afield than in any political developments, we should look first of all to the rise of a great devotion to Our Lady. Encouraged by Pius IX's declaration of the dogma of the Immaculate Conception in 1854, and by the apparitions at Lourdes in 1858, this devotion gave rise to new pilgrimages to shrines such as Chartres, or Notre Dame des Victoires in Paris, where the Blessed Virgin had always been honoured. But Lourdes became the centre of the movement; in 1883 the foundation stone of the Church of the Rosary was laid there, and in 1901 the new church was consecrated. In Leo XIII's reign, alone, there were more than three million pilgrims to Lourdes. And in these years there developed, on a national and an international scale, the parallel devotion to the Sacred Heart of Jesus.

In France this devotion was provided with a home and a symbolic centre by the building of the great cathedral of the Sacré-Coeur, dominating Paris from the hill of Montmartre. The first stone was laid in 1875 and soon the crypt was the centre of pious devotions. The great dome was not completed until 1899, the campanile not until 1912. The whole was dedicated to the Sacred Heart in expiation of the crimes of anti-clerical France, and in order to appreciate all that it symbolised we may usefully turn to the words of the oratorian, Père Lecanuet: "One needs to remember all the obstacles with which the persecution hampered the builders, the threats of desecration made by the Radicals in the Chamber in 1882 and 1891, the insults of triumphant impiety and demagogy. One needs to describe with what pious enthusiasm, with what spirit of generosity, the great cathedral was raised. One needs to picture the whole of Catholic France sharing in this work, the dioceses, towns, associations, clergy, magistracy, army, navy, colleges, families, every condition of life, rivalling each other in their devotion, disputing with each other to adorn the chapels, the columns, the vaults, the arches, the stones of the building, one needs to recount the splendid gifts offered to Montmartre . . . and, by the side of these magnificent presents, the offering of the poor and the mite of the widow which so profoundly touch the heart of God."[1]

No modern cathedral, not even Westminster, raised during these same years in the heart of an astonished London, has held such large symbolic significance. For here, outlined in white high against the sky, was the outward assurance to Paris that the Faith was still alive.

[1] *La vie de l'Eglise sous Léon XIII* (Paris, 1930), p. 126.

Alive, and not only alive but vigorous in controversy, as is wont to be the way in France. We may step beyond the confines of this chapter to notice, in conclusion, how this new liveliness was to lead to a new quarrel between some of the French hierarchy and Rome. This new quarrel began when Pope Pius XI (1922–39), bent upon the pursuit of peace, affronted many French Catholic leaders by criticising (very gently) the continued French occupation, five years after the end of the war, of the Ruhr Valley of Germany, an occupation which many French patriots regarded as the only guarantee for the payment of German reparations. And many members of the French hierarchy, who were amongst those affronted by the Pope's attitude on this matter, were also amongst those who were giving support to the intransigent paper *L'Action Française*, edited by Charles Maurras, an authoritarian of great literary force.

Once more Rome had to choose between Right and Left in France, and once more she chose the Left. Maurras' paper was condemned in 1926, and in 1927 the leading French member of the Sacred College, Cardinal Billot, who had crowned the Pope, resigned, in consequence, his exalted office. French Catholic opinion was split on this issue, as it had so often been split in the nineteenth century, between ultramontane and liberal, or between monarchist and republican. But the future lay with the republicans and, on the whole, with the liberals. Though sometimes overstepping the bounds of what Rome could approve (as in the case of the worker-priest movement after the Second World War), the more radical elements in French Catholicism, amongst whom the Dominicans were prominent, were to inherit the twentieth century at the expense of the authoritarians of the school of the *Action Française*. The choice made by Leo XIII in the *Ralliement*, the decision that, France having voted for the Republic, the Church would not give support to monarchists or others who sought to seize power, held good throughout the subsequent decades, despite the persecutions of the Third Republic. And it was confirmed by Pius XI, the Pope whom some have chosen to call the "friend of Fascism," but whom many in France regarded as a "dangerous radical."

CHAPTER TWENTY

The British Empire, Europe, and the First World War

Concerned, as we are in this book, with the more critical issues of modern Catholic history, we need not delay over events in England after the age of Cardinal Manning (died 1892). After the great storm resulting from the restoration of the hierarchy in 1850 (see pp. 107–109) the progress of the Church in England, in Scotland, and in Wales, was steady if slow. It cannot be said that it fulfilled the hopes of those who expected a mass conversion movement as a result of what Newman called the "second spring" in the 1850s. The increase from about one to about two million Catholics, between the years 1860 and 1925, was only roughly proportional to the increase in the total population of the country. Conversions (impressive amongst intellectual groups, from the time of Newman to the time of Chesterton, and since), together with the large Irish immigration and the relatively large birth rate amongst Catholic families, were offset by the considerable numbers of those who lapsed. Manning's confidence that the definitions of the Vatican Council would rally converts to a Church which so clearly knew its own mind was shown to be misplaced; dogmatic definitions, as Newman suspected, may have tended at first to be a hindrance to conversion rather than a help.

Resistance to conversion arose much more from the secularism, materialism, and indifferentism which were so characteristic of the late nineteenth century than from continued hostility on the part of anti-Catholic religious groups, whether Anglican or nonconformist. In fact, during the discussions which were held concerning the important Education Act of 1902, in the parliamentary debates which preceded its passage, and in many issues which arose afterwards as a result of it, the Anglican bishops and the Catholic bishops found themselves struggling side by side to secure the essential point, which was that there should be state assistance for Church schools of all kinds, and not merely state maintenance for nonreligious schools. The agreement on this matter (which was followed in principle in subsequent legislation) represented a very important victory for the Church, and placed

Catholic schools in England upon a fairer financial footing than the one on which they found themselves in contemporary France, or in the United States, though not so favourable a one as came to be adopted in Scotland or in Holland. But it should be recognised that the Act of 1902 was really a victory won by the Church of England, and that the Catholics could never have obtained such favourable terms as they did if they had been fighting in isolation for the few schools they then possessed. After 1902 the conditions of the educational conflict gradually altered somewhat, on account of the rapid increase in the number of Catholic schools, an increase which eventually brought their numbers about level with those of the Established Church. Since the Catholics insisted upon a degree of independence for their schools which the Church of England did not always require, they came, in some measure, to occupy the front line in this conflict.

The educational conflict was the most important one in a scene of relative peace. The main battle had been won when the hierarchy stood its ground in the face of the storm in the 1850s. Discriminatory legislation passed by Parliament during that crisis was gradually removed from the statute book; in the year 1927 it became legal for Catholic priests to appear in public in their cassocks or vestments, to hold processions, and to ring their church bells; and, thanks to the firm line taken by King George V, the coronation oath was amended in 1911 so as to delete its offensive references to the "superstition and idolatry" of the sacrifice of the Mass and of devotion to Our Lady and the saints. British representation at the Vatican, begun during the First World War, was continued afterwards; the enormous Catholic population of the British Commonwealth (some parts of which—e.g. Malta—are almost wholly Catholic) made this representation eminently desirable and useful.

In Scotland the hierarchy was not re-established until the year 1879, when Leo XIII created the archdiocese of St. Andrews and Edinburgh. The Faith had never been extinguished in the Highlands of Scotland, but the chief factor which contributed to its progress in the second half of the nineteenth century was the Irish immigration into Glasgow. By the Education Act of 1918 a solution was found to the educational problem more favourable to the Catholic schools than had been found in England, for they were placed upon a footing of financial equality with those maintained by the State.

If the English and Scottish scenes were free from serious conflict after the 1850s, the same could certainly not be said of the scene across the Irish Sea.

We have had much occasion, in looking at the Catholic conflicts of the last two centuries, to notice the tremendous contribution of the Irish on both sides of the Atlantic, and we shall observe the same phenomenon in more distant parts of the British Commonwealth. From the bloodstained soil of Castelfidardo, where they strove to defend the Papal States against the Piedmontese, to the shanties around Boston or Philadelphia, where they gave the "Know-Nothings" as good as they got from them, the Irish sustained their reputation as mighty fighters in the cause of the Church. Yet what was really more remarkable was that, after two centuries of persecution in their own small island—centuries during which every ingenuity of political and economic pressure was employed against them—they emerged, in the nineteenth century, not only with their faith unimpaired, but with a loyalty to Rome as strong as any to be found in the world. In a worldly sense, that loyalty had brought to Ireland nothing but material disaster; it was therefore the more striking that she showed so keen an appreciation of what it meant in a spiritual sense.

By a series of laws in the nineteenth century, beginning with the Catholic Emancipation Act of 1829, successive British Governments sought, with some success, to make amends for the past; but the measure which might have brought a lasting solution, namely Gladstone's Home Rule Bill of 1886, suffered shipwreck upon the rock of British conservatism and the alarm of Ulster. It should be recognised that after the disestablishment by the British Government, in 1869, of the Anglican Church of Ireland, the primarily religious causes of conflict between Ireland and England had been removed. True, a settlement which left the historic Irish Catholic churches in Anglican hands, and which required a payment of ten million pounds from the poverty-stricken Catholics in computation of tithe, was not calculated to sweeten the relations between the Catholic inhabitants and the remnants of the Protestant ascendancy. Nevertheless, the great struggle in Irish affairs after 1886 was—superficially at least—political. Gladstone's 1886

Home Rule Bill had been defeated because neither the people of Ulster nor their British supporters were prepared to see Ulster merged in a union of all Ireland, in which power would pass to a Catholic majority at Dublin. And in 1914, when Asquith actually secured the passage of another Home Rule Bill through the British Parliament, the reaction in Ulster, and the desperate measures to which Lord Carson and others had resort, sufficed to prevent its being put into effect. So the outbreak of the First World War saw the situation unresolved. Catholic Ireland made a very large military contribution to that war, but she resisted the attempt of the British Government to introduce conscription in 1918. From that year until 1921 a savage war between the Irish Sinn Fein party and the British Black and Tans, a war involving horrors which the Irish hierarchy and the Pope did their best to mitigate, resulted finally in a peace, in December 1921, which set up the present Irish Free State (or Eire), enjoying legislative independence from Britain, and Northern Ireland (comprising Ulster, without two Catholic counties), which continued to send members to the Parliament at Westminster.

It cannot be said that this compromise, though it terminated a hideous conflict, and though it was warmly welcomed at the time, both by Pope Benedict XV and by the Irish hierarchy, has satisfied the country as a whole. The Catholics of the North—a very large minority, and in the rural areas often a majority—have felt that (for instance in education and in public employment) they have been severely discriminated against by the Belfast government; Protestants of the North, looking at some of the legislation of the Dublin government (for instance in relation to divorce, and to the censorship of immoral literature and films), have sensed a Catholic attitude which was certainly not their own, and in which they did not wish to share. This is a matter of historical fact. It is no part of the intention of this book to enter into the contemporary merits of a conflict which is very far from having been resolved at the time of writing; we are concerned with Catholic factors in history rather than with Catholic factors in current affairs. But of the struggle to date, it may be said that however strong the economic and political motives may have been upon both sides, however mixed the parties, however dignified and restrained the Church (all of them factors tending to obscure the underlying religious issue), it would be a strange diagnosis of the conflict which would not see its religious aspects as the most important ones.

Famines, particularly in the 1840s, were responsible, as we saw, for much of the Irish emigration to America. At an earlier date a still more distressful exodus had taken place when those Irishmen sentenced by the British Government for complicity in the uprising of 1798 were sent to Botany Bay in New South Wales. Amongst them were three priests, but they were not allowed to say Mass, and at the end of the Napoleonic wars the prison camps in Australia were without any pastors. Despite some heroic attempts on the part of individual priests, for months at a time, to run the gauntlet of governmental action, this position remained substantially unchanged until 1820, when the Colonial Office allowed one priest to be sent to Botany Bay and one to Van Diemen's Land (Tasmania). But neither of these was allowed to administer either to the convicts or to the orphaned children; it was only in 1830 that Father Therry secured the removal of these disabilities, and only after Dr. Ullathorne (a Benedictine of Downside Abbey in England, and future Bishop of Birmingham) had arrived as vicar-general in 1833, that religious freedom and religious equality for Catholics were won. An Australian hierarchy was established in 1842, with another Downside Benedictine, Dr. Polding, as Metropolitan Archbishop of Sydney. In New Zealand a parallel development was taking place, the lead being taken by Irish immigrants and French and Irish priests, and in 1848 the dioceses of Auckland and Wellington were established.

From the point of view of the kind of Catholic conflicts discussed in this book, what is most interesting about the life of the Church in Australia and New Zealand is the way in which her leaders threw themselves with energy into the social question, espousing the cause of labour in the spirit of the encyclicals *Rerum Novarum* and *Quadragesimo Anno*. At much the same time as Cardinal Manning was befriending the London dockers, Cardinal Moran, at Sydney, was giving his support to labour in the great industrial strike of 1890. The Church came indeed to play a more important part in the labour politics of Australia in the twentieth century than she has played in those of any other country, and her influence in helping to preserve the labour movement from communism has been a paramount one.

Any general survey of the life of the Church in Africa or India would be beyond our purposes here. But it is relevant to notice now that the British Government, which held a dominant position in India, and also in South Africa—until the Union of South Africa acquired dominion status in 1909—maintained, at least from the 1830s onwards, an attitude of impartiality in religious matters. This impartiality, however, might often be hard to distinguish from indifference; nor was it always the case that Catholic missions were so favourably placed as Protestant missions. Ceremonial occasions, with any official flavour, were naturally the province of the clergy and the services of the Established Church, whilst the habit of the Protestant missions of agreeing amongst themselves upon distinct "spheres of influence" meant that the Catholic missionaries, who could not adopt the view that they should be excluded from any territories, were often regarded as uncooperative.

Nevertheless, the British tradition of non-interference was not without advantage to the Church, and many were the British governors and residents who came to admire the Catholic missionary orders, and to help them in so far as it lay in their power to do so. Moreover, the close association of the Church with the State, which characterised particularly the Portuguese but also the French and Belgian colonies, was not always an unmixed blessing to the Catholic missionaries in those territories. In the Far East, in particular, it meant that the nascent native nationalism, already beginning to turn against the "Western oppressor," was liable to make no distinction between the officer of the State and the officer of religion.

But it is when we return again to the European mainland, at the dawn of the twentieth century, that we see most clearly the grave dangers to which too close an association with the State was liable to expose the Church. Nowhere were these dangers more evident than in Spain and Portugal. It would be tedious to recount the constant political disturbances which, in the nineteenth century, plagued both countries. But it is very relevant to notice that the close association between ruler and Church, in both countries, meant that, when the former was thrown out by a revolution, or was compelled to accept a "liberal" government which restricted his powers, the Church too had to suffer, in her religious congregations, in her schools, in her judicial courts, in her property. In Spain it so happened that the turn of the century was, in fact, a relatively quiet time. The very strong anti-clerical influence of the French Third Republic in the time of Waldeck-Rousseau, Combes, and Clemenceau, which so affected most of Europe, affected Spain at that date comparatively little, save on her northern seaboards—Bilbao on the Atlantic coast and Barcelona on the Mediterranean. King Alfonso XIII, who was crowned in 1902, was a religiously minded man; and, although the Cortes was subject to anti-clerical influences, he prevented any drastic attacks upon the Church; in 1919 he even felt strong enough to carry out the popular ceremony of consecrating the country to the Sacred Heart. But after 1923 he only ruled by sufferance, under the military dictatorship of General Primo de Rivera, which had established itself to combat socialist and anarchist influences. When the general fell from power in 1929 the King's own turn was soon to come (1931); and then the Republicans, with some strong Socialist, Communist, and Anarchist support, carried through anti-clerical policies of the traditional kind, which were not only directed towards establishing the whole programme of the secularist State, as it had been established in France, but were marked by a ruthlessness which was the prime cause of the reaction in many parts of the country in favour of General Franco in 1936, and of the bitterness with which the hideous civil war that followed was fought out. It may be true that the maintenance of Catholic beliefs, Catholic practices, and Catholic moral standards in Spain has owed much to the close association of Church and State; unfortunately this association has also meant that when the government has been overthrown the Church has had to suffer too. Strange as it seems in Anglo-Saxon eyes, the fall of a Spanish monarch or dictator has often meant the burning of convents and the rape of nuns.

In Portugal the crisis came sooner. By the year 1901 the religious orders had already been suppressed by law, though in practice their expulsion or liquidation had not always been carried out. French influence, like British, penetrated Portugal more easily than it penetrated Spain, and we find the very words of Waldeck-Rousseau used in the decrees of the Portuguese Government. By 1914 some of the furthest positions in anti-clerical legislation had been reached; all the religious orders had been proscribed, religious instruction had been banished from the schools, there were divorce laws, there was

compulsory military service for priests, there was separation of
Church and State, and diplomatic relations with the Vatican
had been broken off. That all this should have occurred in a
country in which 98 per cent of the population claimed to be
Catholic is certainly remarkable. It was after the revolution
of 1910, which expelled young King Manuel II and established
the Republic, that the execution of the laws against the orders
was seriously and severely undertaken; once again we are confronted by the phenomenon of an onslaught upon strictly
religious bodies following upon a successful onslaught upon
the centre of political power. With the emergence, after the
First World War, of the quasi-dictatorial régime of General
Carmona, and then of Dr. Salazar, the normal life of the
Church in Portugal was restored; but the danger implicit in
her association with the government remained.

The situation in France and Italy, during this dark night
of the Church, has already been discussed in the last chapter,
and her position in Germany in Chapter 18. But we need to
remind ourselves of the important effects which occurrences in
these major European countries would have upon their neighbours. Belgium, for example, found herself subject to two
pressures: first, that exercised by Bismarck at the time of the
Kulturkampf, which aimed at restricting the rights of Rome
and which we have already noted; second, that of the France
of the Third Republic. French influence in Belgium, on account of the common language and many common traditions,
has always been strong, and it was not to be expected that
the campaign conducted by Ferry, Combes, or Clemenceau
would be without effect across the frontier. But in fact the
Catholic party, before the First World War, maintained a
small though diminishing majority in the Belgian Chamber,
and the effect of that war, in which Belgium suffered all the
horrors both of fighting and of occupation, was to unite people
behind King Albert, and behind the heroic figure of Cardinal
Mercier. The liberal and socialist agitation for a complete
secularisation of the state schools, and cessation of the subsidy
to the free schools, though strengthened by the adoption of
universal suffrage after the First World War, made comparatively little headway until recent times and Belgium, in contrast
to France, maintained and still maintains that free schools
should not be at an undue economic disadvantage in relation
to those of the State.

Perhaps the most surprising anti-clerical campaign in Europe at the turn of the century was the *Los von Rom* (Freedom from Rome) movement in Austria. When it is remembered that, despite the policies of Joseph II in the eighteenth century, the Austrian Empire of the nineteenth century (the empire of Metternich, and of the Hapsburg revival after 1850) was always regarded as the chief mainstay, politically and religiously, of the papacy, it is rather surprising to find her causing such grave anxiety to Rome in the age of Bismarck. The fact was that, following her defeat in the Austro-Prussian War of 1866, her loss of the leadership of Germany, her expulsion from Italy, and the disappearance of the Papal States which depended upon her, the Austrian Empire was a changed power. She had become, through Bismarck's skilful diplomacy, the dependent ally of her conquerors, encouraged to look eastwards and southwards, and to assume new spheres of influence in the Balkans. Always a racially and religiously mixed empire, its Catholic elements had been weakened by the loss of Italy and by separation from South Germany, and it was now subjected to the pitiless pressure of the pan-Germanism of Prussia. The *Los von Rom* movement was organised partly by the "Old Catholics" (who refused to accept the decrees of the Vatican Council) and partly by Lutheran and other Protestant pastors, strongly backed by German evangelical societies. But the vital spirit of it was pan-Germanic, and the tragedy of it was that it represented the perversion of an older, universal, outlook at Vienna—imperialist and cosmopolitan in politics, and Catholic in religion—to narrower nationalist and racial notions. We should not overrate its success. Those who were estranged from Rome were to be numbered in tens of thousands only. But it strengthened the hands of the government which, though Catholic, jealously preserved the traditions of "Josephism." On the grounds that the Vatican Council had changed the constitution of the Church, the Emperor Francis Joseph denounced the Austrian concordat with Rome, and the succeeding decades saw marriage laws and education laws which introduced divorce and secularised the state schools. But these were the last days of that great empire which was heir to the Holy Roman Empire, and of that remarkable dynasty which had ruled at Vienna since the fourteenth century. By the Treaty of Versailles the great imperial city became the over-large capital of a tiny state of seven million inhabitants, and the victim of famine, while her historic provinces became small nation states which mostly fell in due course to the Communists.

And what of the First World War itself?

It lies, of course, outside our scope to discuss it save in some of its consequences for the Church. Rome was mostly a helpless spectator while Catholics, in a struggle she had striven to avert, destroyed each other. Even good Catholics, even the best of them, were often victims of the age, taught for too long by their governments and by the spirit of the times that the interests of State or of race were paramount, that religion was a "private affair." But at least enough has been said here already about what was happening at the turn of the century in Germany, in Austria, in France—everywhere— to give the lie to the pretence that "Catholic governments" or "Catholic peoples" armed themselves and flew at each others' throats. Responsibility for the First World War has been variously laid at the doors of the German, Austrian, Russian, French, and British governments; but just how far any of those governments could be called Catholic we have had occasion to observe.

The evils of conscription, that appalling modern legacy from Napoleon, had been denounced not merely by Leo XIII but by Pius IX before him. Leo, indeed, had emerged as an arbitrator in international disputes, being entrusted by Bismarck with the settlement of his dispute with Spain over the Caroline Islands in 1885; and, had the Italian Government not succeeded in preventing it, he would have been a participant in the Hague conference of 1899, which set up the Hague Tribunal, intended to settle international disputes. But the peculiarly anti-clerical atmosphere of the turn of the century was unfavourable to papal intervention, the deadly drift towards larger armaments and longer periods of conscription continued unchecked, and in August 1914 the First World War broke out. It is commonly considered that its outbreak killed Pius X, who issued his great appeal for peace on August 2 and on August 20 was dead. His successor Benedict XV (1914–22) devoted himself throughout the war years to the relief of distress, and to trying to persuade the belligerents to state their aims so that these might be reconciled. But, although he was careful to maintain a strict impartiality, both sides accused him of favouring the other, and no government paid serious attention to his initiative of August 1917 when he proposed, as a basis for agreement, that Germany should evacuate France and Belgium, that the Allies should restore the German colonies, and that the remaining territorial questions should be settled by arbitration. The war at that date seemed to have reached a stalemate. Had the Pope's proposals for peace been accepted, several million lives would have been saved, and it is hard to see what country would have been the loser; the United States would have been spared entry into the war, and the Bolshevik revolution in Russia would probably have been averted.

At the end of the war the festering sore of the continued conflict between Church and State in Italy once more exerted its influence when the Italian Government prevented the participation of the papacy in the peace conference at Versailles. The League of Nations thus came to be formed without including representation of that government whose policies had been most consistently directed towards peace, or that ruler whose sacred office made him the most natural arbitrator and peacemaker. The treaty settlement itself, so largely the work of Clemenceau, was vindictive in character, and thus carried within itself the seed of its own destruction. In no respect was the peace settlement more seriously lacking in true statesmanship than in its treatment of Austria, a country reduced, as we have already seen, to a head (Vienna) without a body, rendered economically unviable, and soon ridden with famine.

Benedict stigmatised the position to which Austria was reduced as "absolutely intolerable." He gave his blessing to the League of Nations—although it established itself without him, and at Geneva, the "Calvinist Rome"—and he continued to insist, as had his predecessors, that armaments and compulsory military service were the root of the evil, and just before he died he sent his blessing to the Washington disarmament conference of 1922.

As one surveys the period of the First World War and its aftermath one has the impression that even less than in the days of Napoleon did the governments of Europe pay any serious attention to Rome, that Benedict was even less likely to achieve anything to influence Clemenceau, or Lloyd George, or President Wilson, than Pius VII had been to influence Napoleon or Metternich. Napoleon had tried to bend the Church to his service, but at least he had recognised its power.

And at the Congress of Vienna, unlike the Conference of Versailles, a papal delegate had not only been present but had been offered the presidency.

In truth, the decades which preceded the First World War had been dark, as we have seen, for the Church, on most of the continent of Europe, and elsewhere too. The immense pressure of the new nationalism and the allure of a new socialism had turned men's eyes towards the State, whether to ask her for arms or for education. In a new sense the nation became the "norm," and the essentially secular ideal of being a good American, Englishman, Frenchman, German, or Italian, tended to supplant the Church's ideal of spirituality. And when the war broke out the passion for victory, or the passion for survival, obscured everything else; God was invoked, but He was the God of each warring nation.

But this was not the whole story, for in the flames of the war there was also being consumed much of the bitterness that had flavoured the feelings of Frenchmen, Italians, and the rest, when they contemplated the Church. They saw her now in the guise of priests by their side in the trenches, crawling through no man's land to give absolution to the dying, of nuns nursing in the hospitals, and of a faith in the eyes of men which helped them to face death. They saw, too, much more clearly, how the Mass and the sacraments were prized by their Catholic comrades; moreover the doubts which had been raised about the patriotism and loyalty of Catholics, with their "double allegiance," were silenced.

So, despite the disappointments of Benedict, the First World War did in fact mark the beginning of an extension of Catholic life in much of the West. The type of anti-clericalism which had disfigured the previous generation was very generally assuaged, and the new atmosphere made possible, for instance, the healing of the breach between Italy and the Vatican, achieved by Benedict's successor Pius XI, the renewal of French and Portuguese representation at the Holy See, the establishment of British representation there, the return of the Jesuits to Germany, and the restoration of religious orders generally to France.

CHAPTER TWENTY-ONE

The Americas in the Twentieth Century

It is something of a relief to turn once more from the bitter religious conflicts of Europe to the relatively freer air of North America. What was happening in the Germany of the Kulturkampf, in the Italy of Depretis, and in the France of M. Combes, amounted to no less than religious persecution. By the end of the century there was nothing of this sort left in North America.

In the New World, at the dawn of the new century, the fortunes of the Church were most hopeful in Canada, most doubtful in the United States, most disturbing in Central America.

In Canada, though language, history, and geography combined to keep the Catholics, mostly of French descent, apart from the Protestants, of British descent, yet the opening up of the West, and the penetration of the North, and the immigration of Irish Catholics were all helping to blur the sharp distinction. The North America Act of 1867, which conferred dominion status upon Canada, was political recognition of the fact that she was now one nation. The building of the Canadian Pacific railway, and the fur and whaling settlements on Hudson Bay, were pioneering adventures undertaken by Canadians of all faiths in common, the Irish or French Catholic alongside his Presbyterian or agnostic brother. And if state or city politics—Catholic at Quebec, anti-Catholic at Toronto—favoured the Church or put obstacles in her way, the growing economic development and expansion of the country, in which all alike were interested, militated against discriminatory religious policies, whether on the part of the federal government or in the new settlements. Furthermore, in a country whose population was increasing rapidly the Catholic element was increasing more than proportionately. Forty per cent of the population in 1911, Catholics were 43.8 per cent by 1941. In the decade preceding 1941 the total Canadian population rose by 10.5 per cent, but the Catholic population rose by 16 per cent. As the Catholics approached a numerical position from which it seemed likely they would become the absolute majority of the population, their status became safeguarded against all except isolated social and cultural groups, which preferred to maintain an ancient exclusiveness. After the Second World War the country was led for the first time by a Catholic Prime Minister of French-Canadian descent, Mr. St. Laurent; it is hardly necessary to add that the great federation which is Canada today is a country too deeply rooted, like the United States, in the concept of religious toleration, and of the separation of Church and State, for any group to feel fearful that a Catholic federal government might one day interfere with its liberties.

In the United States the progress of the Church after the turn of the century, though marked, was less certain than in Canada. Some superficial similarity may be seen between her position and prospects in the United States and in England. Just as in England, in the days of Cardinal Manning, there were many who confidently predicted that there would be a rapid increase in the number of conversions, that the logic of the Catholic position and the zeal of her protagonists would carry all before them, because the opposition was so divided, and often so unsure of itself, so in the United States the wide acceptance accorded to Gibbons or John Ireland, who were friends of Presidents, national and even international figures, led to a premature confidence that the strongholds of the opposition were crumbling. But in fact no landslide in the twentieth century occurred to carry with it the mass conversion of either the English or the Americans. In the higher ranks of American society, whether political, cultural, or financial, conversions were not very numerous, and opposition was tenacious.

Numerically speaking, certainly, the Church had made good progress in the United States. By 1950 there were twenty-five millions of Catholics, which was more than seven times as many as there had been in 1860; during the corresponding period the total population of the country had increased less than five times. Catholics had become at least one sixth of the total population, and incomparably larger than any other religious body in the country—almost as large as the rest of the actively churchgoing population as a whole. A number of factors had contributed to this growth: the continued immigration of the Irish, the very large Italian immigration in the decades leading up to the First World War (immigration into the United States was severely curtailed after that war), and the tendency of Catholics to have more children than non-

Catholics. Conversions, though important, were not a major factor; moreover the lapsing of Catholics was inevitably not inconsiderable where mixed marriages were frequent and where education in non-Catholic schools was the lot of at least half the Catholic children. There was also the natural "pull" of his new homeland upon the immigrant, anxious to become as soon as possible a "good" and "accepted" American, and discovering that the average American was not Catholic. This factor should not be overstated; the loyalty of the German, Irish, and Italian immigrant to Rome was usually very marked, and was sometimes strengthened by his initial sense of isolation, when the priest might well be his only friend. All the same, as a newcomer seeking acceptance and recognition, the immigrant was hardly in a position to be a proselyte for the Faith.

If the size and the devotion of the American Catholic body had become impressive by the middle of the twentieth century, there were yet some grounds for disappointment concerning the impact of the Church upon the country as a whole. In some states—for instance Massachusetts—there might be a majority of Catholics, and they might exercise an important influence upon political, cultural, and social affairs. In others—for instance the Carolinas—there might be a very small minority, with almost no influence at all. In national affairs, whether in federal politics, in big business, or in education and the arts, it could not be said that their impact upon the life of the country had become what the optimists at the turn of the century had hoped or expected. The American Protective Association, that successor of the "Know-Nothings," was no doubt only partially successful in its anti-Catholic objectives; it might succeed in keeping out a Catholic candidate here, in protecting an incendiary mob leader there; but the times of open violence or the cruder kinds of conspiracy were over. Opposition now took the form of a tighter-lipped chilliness. Gone were the days of Theodore Roosevelt, who was prepared to hobnob with Catholic archbishops; Woodrow Wilson was frigid, and scarcely even correct; neither Coolidge nor Hoover would run any risks. There was a traditional tendency for the Catholics to vote Democratic, supporting the party of the underdog; in New York and Boston there was a succession of Catholic and Democratic mayors. But when Al Smith, the popular Catholic governor of New York State, became the Democratic candidate for the presidency in 1928, the Republican campaign against him pulled out all the stops of anti-Catholic hostility, assuring the electorate that a vote for Al Smith meant "a private telephone wire from the White House to the Vatican," and that American freedom was at stake. Undoubtedly religion was a powerful factor in Al Smith's defeat.

After the election of Franklin Roosevelt in 1932 Catholic contacts at presidential level with political power became closer. There was much in the President's New Deal which was in harmony with the teaching of the social encyclicals, while his growing determination to break down American isolationism led him to make some effort—resisted by Congress —to provide for diplomatic representation of the United States at the Vatican. Soon after the outbreak of the Second World War the President circumvented the congressional opposition by sending Mr. Myron Taylor to the Vatican State as his personal representative with ambassadorial rank.

Various explanations have been offered for the relative failure of the American Church to obtain quite the influence which her growing numbers and religious zeal seemed to warrant. It has been said that her leaders were not of the calibre of Cardinal Gibbons or of Archbishop Ireland. It has been pointed out that there was complete decentralisation, no superior authority attaching to the premier see at Baltimore, each bishop remaining the supreme authority in his own diocese. We have been reminded how large a proportion of the Catholic population belonged to the poorest classes of the community, because they were the most recently arrived, and how great was the financial effort involved for Catholics in providing schools and colleges, with no help from the State, whilst contributing their share of the cost of the state schools.

It is not difficult to find reasons of this kind for a certain deficiency in worldly success on the part of American Catholics during this period. But worldly success is not the criterion of inner excellence, and the immense work of the American Church in providing religious education for her children, and social relief of all kinds for her unfortunates and sick, rightly ranks higher and has, indeed, met with something of the general recognition it deserves. And, if the numerous colleges and the great universities which the different orders have established have been distinguished more for their sound general education than for the higher flights of scholarship, it has first to be remembered that, as in other countries, the greatest scholarly achievements of individual Catholics have often been attained in non-Catholic colleges, whose faculties have shown an increasing infiltration of members of the Church, and secondly that the highest flights of scholarship and technical skill are only reached after a good general level of education has become established, whereas many of the Catholic colleges, even in 1950, were still young.

Though her progress had scarcely been alarming, opposition to the Catholic Church in most states of the Union continued to be marked, if intermittent, and some discerned something of a revival in this opposition after the Second World War. The principal line of attack was that the Church was "divisist," that it tended to divide the loyalties of Americans, and so to weaken their patriotism. It was not difficult for Catholic apologists to point out, as Manning had pointed out to Gladstone, Windthorst to Bismarck, or indeed Pius VII to Napoleon, that there was no antithesis between loyalty to the Church and loyalty to the State. The Catholic record in both world wars had proved as much; true religion and true patriotism, so far from being antithetical, nourish each other; moreover no theistic religion could possibly accept the view that all morality or all higher truth derives solely from the community or from the State, though this was the real belief of those who claimed that the one thing needful was to be a "good American."

Besides the fear of divisism there was the fear (as real in some quarters as the fears felt of old by the "Know-Nothings") that the Church constituted a secret society with a despotic head who wielded immense power behind the scenes, and who might one day overthrow the Constitution of the United States. It was very difficult to convince those outside the fold that, so far from having a secret directorate, the Church in America lacked even the elements of a centralised authority, or that, did they but know the truth, her opponents would be far more scandalised at the want of agreement between the bishops themselves on fundamental matters affecting the welfare of the Church than they would be afraid of her united action. In reality, though it has involved some outward weakness, this diversity has constituted one of the most promising features of the Church in America. A body which embraced such divergent but vital elements as the silent Trappists, whose religious purpose caught the popular imagination in the books of

Thomas Merton, the Jesuits (chief labourers in the vineyard of higher education), Dominicans, Franciscans, Benedictines, and Redemptorists; numerous orders of nuns; the charitable zeal of the Catholic Worker movement; or the practical endeavours of the Knights of Columbus—such a body drew its strength from the fact that it was truly a federation, a harmony of unlikes, united indeed on the supernatural plane by the wonder of the Faith, but only loosely linked on the earthly plane by the National Catholic Welfare Conference. And if the Church in America found herself at one time being condemned for being bolshevist (e.g. when the bishops' programme, after the First World War, gave support to the labour unions) and at another for being reactionary or fascist (e.g. when some Catholics supported the late Senator McCarthy's investigating committee) that was only as it should be in a body entirely free from political direction. And just as there had been no central religious or political direction, so there has been no central fund. The surprised householder in the residential quarters of the great cities, who has seen one spacious but outdated mansion after another falling into the hands of some religious community, has been tempted to suppose that a powerful financial corporation has been "buying up the district"; it has been hard for him to realise what self-denial and desperate shifts lie behind the new local venture.

Perhaps more central planning, more co-ordination, would have helped; but it could also be that the lessons to be learnt by the Church from the first half of the twentieth century in America are still the humble ones of patience and perseverance, which have necessarily played so large a part in her history in the past.

When we step across the southern borders of the United States and enter Latin America we are back again in a world of Established Churches, and so of strong governmental interest in the Church, an interest which has all too often become governmental persecution of the Church.

The twentieth century has been a time of acute anxiety concerning the Church in Latin America, but the seeds of the trouble had been sown in the previous century and earlier. We have seen already how closely identified were Church and State in the Latin-American republics and dictatorships, and how this was a legacy deriving from Spanish colonial days—it can indeed be traced as far back as fifteenth-century Spain, when Ferdinand and Isabella acquired royal control over the Spanish Inquisition, and when the Spanish Borgia Pope, Alexander VI, allowed to the Spanish Crown virtual independence in Church affairs in the Spanish colonies. We have also seen how, after independence from Spain or from Portugal had been won by the year 1824, the Church suffered from the reluctance of Rome to regard the Spanish Bourbon power as extinguished (causing her to support bishops appointed by that Crown), and then from the constant revolutions, many of them anticlerical in character, which undermined law and order, deprived the Church of her property, banished the religious orders, and introduced the secularist legislation which was characteristic of contemporary European liberal revolutions. During the whole of this century the general tendency in Latin America was for there to be few vocations for the priesthood, and for the general standard both of the zeal and of the education of priests to be low. Very closely associated with the civilisation of Spain and of Portugal, both of which countries had for long been in decline, and inheriting from the past too strong an identification with the traditional sources of power and wealth, the priests were too often ill fitted to understand, to civilise, or to lead the insurgent native populations released by the frequent revolutions, while difficulties of language and of race prevented missionary orders from other countries from entering Central or South America in any numbers.

But, while the health and vision of the Church in much of Latin America have often been in doubt amongst Catholic critics in recent decades, to outward appearance, at least, her hold upon the populations appeared to have been well maintained. Brazil, the most populous of the South American states, after becoming a republic in 1889, caused some anxiety when she separated Church from State and secularised education; but the new governments did not proceed to persecute the religious orders as such, and the country has enjoyed, in the twentieth century, cordial relations with Rome, and freedom for private Catholic schools to continue their work unhampered. Neither Peru nor Chile has been the scene of any sustained anti-clerical offensive, though both have had their disturbances. In 1920 President Leguía of Peru felt sure enough of popular support to go through the ceremony of consecrating his country to the Sacred Heart, thereby following the precedent set by García Moreno, the saintly dictator of Ecuador, whose constructive régime had been terminated by his assassination at the hands of the anti-clericals in 1875.

It is not easy to find in South American history any correlation between anti-clericalism and "democracy" or "liberalism," for governments have been very generally both anticlerical and dictatorial. The pattern has been rather one of instability, dictator succeeding to dictator, generally after a revolution, and with many of the dictators only too ready to launch an attack upon the Church, either as the "evil genius" of their predecessors or as the scapegoat for their own deficiencies. The Church has, indeed, often found herself upon the "democratic" side, being anxious to curb the dictator's "fascist" supporters, who have wanted to concentrate all power, educational, cultural, philanthropic, social, as well as administrative, in the hands of their political "boss." In recent times in the Argentine the quarrel between the dictator, General Juan Perón, and the Church, which began in October 1954 with an attack by Perón of the traditional kind concentrated upon education, feast days, marriage laws, and the like, led on to the wholesale arrest of priests; and the Church, though by no means the instigator of the revolt which expelled him, was not unnaturally sympathetic towards the aims of the anti-dictatorial movement which did so.

But in one Latin-American state, Mexico, a campaign against the Church of very different scope and intent developed just before the outbreak of the First World War and persisted for more than twenty years; indeed it would be rash to suppose that, despite some improvement, the situation there has yet been resolved. It was directly inspired by the extreme anticlericals of the French Third Republic, and its violent syndicalist elements were a part of something wider. The venom with which it was pursued is unique in the modern history of persecution in the New World and can only be compared with what has taken place in countries behind the Iron Curtain in Europe since the Second World War. It was a real "war to the death," which reduced the priesthood to a handful of less than two hundred hunted men, under sentence of death for the crime of being priests, whose pitiful position has been most vividly portrayed in Mr. Graham Greene's novel, *The Power and the Glory*. Essentially it was an ideological or religious war, inspired by the syndicalist-communist C.R.O.M. (*Confederación Regional Obrera Mexicana*), which was the effective power behind the successive governments of the Presidents

Carranza, Obregón, and Calles, although only the last named, who was President from 1924 to 1928 and exercised effective political power until 1934, was fully in sympathy with the more brutal side of its work. The philosophy behind it was not merely materialist, in the Marxian sense, it also embraced a worship of violence for its own sake, of the kind that was taught by the father of European syndicalism, Georges Sorel —who inspired the young Mussolini.

It might be supposed that so violent an assault must have been provoked by the wealth or privileges of the Church in Mexico. But this was not the case. It had been the achievement of the earlier Mexican revolutionary Benito Juárez (the leader who defeated Napoleon III's attempt to make Maximilian of Austria Emperor of Mexico) to nationalise the whole of the Church's property in the country, save only the ecclesiastical buildings themselves, and to close the monasteries in 1859; nor had the long presidency of his pupil Diaz (1876–1911) been a period when the Church had been enabled to recover anything of her position in the national life. The men who rose in revolt against the Calles persecution, in 1927, and were called the *Cristeros*, were simple peasants, fighting in a desperate endeavour to save the Faith, for the new persecution had seized the Church buildings themselves and proscribed the priests. They had much in common with the peasants of the Vendée, who had fought during the French Revolution in the same cause; but whereas the men of the Vendée had, in the end, succeeded, the *Cristeros* went down to a very bloody defeat. The temper of the Calles régime was the temper of Fouché or Hébert, an ideological determination to extinguish the Catholic Faith as such. But to do it justice one should recognize that, although a merely gangster element played a large part in the destruction and murder, the government was motivated rather by the missionary purpose of implanting its own religion of materialism.

Mexico did not occupy a sufficiently important position upon the world political stage for events there to have extensive international repercussions. But since the quasi-Communist government of 1938 seized and nationalised the foreign-owned oil fields, the United States Government began to become concerned, and the British Government broke off diplomatic relations. The religious side of the story remained however generally ignored, and indeed very little realised. In the view of Pius XI the ignoring by the world of this Mexican persecution was due to "the conspiracy of silence on the part of a large section of the non-Catholic press of the world. We say conspiracy because it is impossible otherwise to explain how a press, usually so eager to exploit even the little daily incidents of life, has been able to remain silent for so long about the horrors perpetrated in Russia, in Mexico, and even in a great part of Spain; and that it should have relatively so little to say concerning a world organisation as vast as Russian Communism . . ." Such were his words in *Divini Redemptoris*, his lengthy encyclical on communism, issued in March 1937. In the same month he issued *Firmissimam Constantiam*, giving detailed advice to the Church in Mexico, as to how, through the charitable and apostolic endeavours of Catholic Action, the country might be recovered for Christ, and reminding her that, since it was no longer possible for her priests to be trained in Mexico, the Latin-American college at Rome was available for those who could reach it.

CHAPTER TWENTY-TWO

Mussolini, Hitler, and Pius XI (1922–1939)

In each of the countries which participated in the First World War, the peace saw a tendency towards reconciliation with the Church. We have seen why this was so: the fellowship of the trenches, and respect for the way the Catholics practiced their faith; a religion which included pain and death within its central mystery could no longer be so easily ignored.

In no country were these influences stronger than in Italy, for no armies suffered greater hardships than did the Italian armies, ill clad as they were for the ice and snow of the Alps or for the festering heat of the plain of Lombardy, inadequately supplied with arms, and called upon to contend with the better-equipped Austrian and German armies possessed of a stronger military tradition. Innately Catholic, in spite of all that had happened since the days of Pio Nono, much of the young manhood of Italy now became outwardly as well as inwardly reconciled to the Church. Such men added greatly to the strength of the Christian Democrats and of Catholic Action. Some of them were now organised by that remarkable Sicilian priest, Don Luigi Sturzo, into a political party, the Popolare, a move made possible by the lifting of the papal ban upon Catholic participation in Italian politics. How strong was Catholic public opinion in Italy may be judged from the fact that, only founded in January 1919, the Popolare, in 1922, with 107 members, was only second in strength to the Socialists in the Italian Chamber. Their programme was partly religious and partly political. They wanted to see freedom for religious orders and for the schools, and a full return of Catholics into political life on every front; they also wanted decentralisation of the administrative system, with effective power for the different provinces of Italy, and proportional representation in the central Parliament.

But above all they were pacifists, their movement was a protest against the violence of all the different groups, from the extreme right to the extreme left, which were seeking to solve Italy's postwar problems by violent action of one kind or another. For the postwar years were a time of bitter discontent in Italy. To the fearful suffering of the war itself had been added the disillusionment of a peace that gave the country much less than she felt she was entitled to; there was mass unemployment; and the parliamentary régime, to which the country was indifferent, showed no sign of possessing the power to meet the situation. Apart from the Popolare, only the violent elements were possessed of any effective backing in the country; on the one hand the Syndicalists and Communists, with some of the more extreme Socialists; on the other, and opposed to them, the National-Syndicalists, organised by Edmondo Rossoni, and the Nationalists, or "Irredentists," whose pride was D'Annunzio—D'Annunzio, whose "mystique of blood" we have already met and who, after the war, became the hero of the hour because with his "legionaries," in Garibaldian fashion, he seized for Italy the port of Fiume denied to her by the diplomats at Versailles.

Whoever will look beneath the surface of the confused events of the postwar period in Italy will see not a straight fight between Communists (representing the workers) and Fascists (organised by the employers), which is an oversimplified picture drawn for purposes of propaganda; he will see rather a situation in which violent groups were striving for control, some of them looking to a nationalist or patriotic solution of the country's problems (as D'Annunzio did, or Rossoni's National-Syndicalists), others looking to an Anarchist or Communist solution, being opposed in principle to the Italian State as such. These latter, who should properly at this date still be called Syndicalists (though they were generally coming to be called Communists) belonged to the left wing of the Socialist party and were associated with the violent seizure of the factories in October 1920, the event which most impressed itself upon the Italian imagination.

Mussolini, son of a Socialist blacksmith, and embracing the violent syndicalism taught by Sorel, came to adopt, like Rossoni, a nationalist or patriotic solution to Italy's problems. But in 1920 he was still only the leader of a very small group of *Fasci di combattimento*. When, in January 1922, he allied himself with Rossoni's group, he greatly strengthened his movement and gave it effective working-class support. Moreover, by that year some of the other claimants to power had been weakened. The Communist seizure of the factories had alarmed the country and had failed in its purpose. D'Annunzio had been driven out of Fiume by the Italian Government (which had secured legal international recognition of Italy's right to the port) and had lost some "caste" to Mussolini,

who was becoming increasingly the favourite of the Nationalists and the Irredentists.

By October 1922 there were three effective groups in the
country, Mussolini's Fascists, the Communists who looked to
Moscow, and Don Sturzo's Popolare. All three were represented in Parliament, as were other parties. But a time had
been reached when Italians were not looking to parliamentary
political parties, as such, but to groups which had strong local
support in the country. Disillusionment with the parliamentary parties, with the administration, and with the police, was
so universal that it has been said, with some show of reason,
that the issue in 1922 was not whether the parliamentary
régime could withstand the outside groups, but which of the
outside groups would fill the evident vacancy.

This is an exaggeration. What however can be said with
confidence is that, when Mussolini's black shirts appeared outside Rome in October 1922 the King would not have been
interpreting the popular will if he had used government troops
to disperse them. The Fascists enjoyed the credit of having
defeated the Communist offensive over the seizure of the
factories, they enjoyed the credit of having lowered the red
flags from public buildings all over Italy, of having reversed a
situation in which the veterans of the World War were made
to feel ashamed of having fought for Italy. The government
of the premier, Facta, enjoyed no credit at all. If the troops
had been turned against the Fascists it would have been the
signal for civil war, and the most likely result would have been
a Communist victory.

Don Sturzo, leader of the Popolare, later blamed himself
for negotiating with the other political parties during the critical year 1922 and not boldly himself taking office. But it must
remain doubtful whether it was really possible for him to do
so. In southern Italy, certainly, the Popolare was supreme. But
a party which was avowedly pacifist, which "turned the other
cheek" when its buildings and property were attacked by the
Communists or the Fascists, could hardly have taken over the
government of the country at this juncture, when not only
the Communists and the Fascists, but the still strong anti-
clerical Liberals and Socialists, of different shades, were all
opposed to it. Moreover the Popolare only enjoyed the qualified approval of the hierarchy and of the papacy. We have
seen how anxious Leo XIII and Pius X had both been to ensure that Christian Democracy was properly under episcopal

control. We have seen how one of its leaders, Murri, had become an advanced Modernist. Sturzo had avoided that heresy; but he and his movement were widely regarded as "demagogic," and even as a "white bolshevism," to be compared with the "red bolshevism" of the Communists. These doubts on the part of the hierarchy may indeed have served to help the Popolare in the country, by placing it in the position of the German Centre party and demonstrating that it was free from "priestly control," that it was a non-clerical Catholic party. But they did not help to put Don Sturzo into power, because for that the support of the King (who regarded him as a dangerous radical) and in some measure of the hierarchy also would have been needed.

Rightly or wrongly—and we must allow at least that the decision was understandable—the King decided that the choice really lay between Mussolini and the Communists, and he chose the former. It was not a choice which could be palatable to the new Pope Pius XI, since Mussolini was an avowed atheist and boasted of it; moreover his Fascists, when not fighting the Communists, were often enough to be found attacking the houses of the Christian Democrats or breaking up the meetings of the Popolare. Yet the Pope, like Victor Emmanuel III, was confronted with a choice of evils, and no greater evil than a Communist victory could present itself. Mussolini was preferred as the lesser danger. When, in the following year (1923), having got the Communists under control, the Fascists turned their attention more seriously to crushing the Popolare, a dangerous situation arose in which an all-out Fascist assault upon the Church was threatened. To avert this danger Don Sturzo resigned the leadership of the party and the challenge of the Popolare was over. Christian Democracy, as a political force, gradually disappeared from the scene until after the Second World War.

In the sense described, but only in that sense, it may be said that Rome connived at the Fascist victory. It is hard to see what alternative she had, but easy to see how she suffered at the hands of the new dictator. Mussolini was not, as Napoleon had been, a Catholic by early upbringing. The piety of his mother had been overborne by the scorn of his Socialist father. But like Napoleon he was a realist; finding himself ruling over a country still predominantly Catholic, he would try to reach an accommodation with the Church.

What made that accommodation well-nigh impossible was a clear conflict of ideology, which involved a clear conflict over education. Mussolini's régime, like Napoleon's, depended upon his securing control over the minds and spirits of Italians and winning from them a devotion which can only rightly be called religious. Fascism, however pagan, was certainly religious in character, because it demanded devotion, self-sacrifice, and complete self-surrender to the nation, the party, and the Duce. Mussolini himself defined it, in the Italian Encyclopaedia, as a "conception of the State, its character, its duty, and its aim. Fascism conceives of the State as an absolute, in comparison with which all individuals or groups are relative, only to be conceived of in their relation to the State . . ."

How were Italian boys, very many of whom had been notably indifferent about the new State, to be made to feel in this way towards it? By "moral teaching" in the state schools; by "doctored" Italian history; by entry, at the age of six, into the *Figli della lupa* (children of the wolf, the wolf which suckled Romulus and Remus); by proceeding to the *Balilla*, the *Avanguardia*, and, at the age of eighteen, to the *Giovani Fascisti*; by becoming at twenty-one, if they were found worthy, full-fledged members of the Fascist party proper.

Against this scheme of indoctrination Pius XI waged a ceaseless warfare. The foundation of it, the notion that, in comparison with the State, all individuals or groups had only a relative significance, he castigated as a monstrous inversion, a denial of the primary rights of the individual, the family, the Church, all of which came before the State, whose business it was to protect them. As against the state monopoly of education, which allowed only a brief period of religious instruction to the Church, he claimed her right to run schools. As against the para-military youth clubs of Fascism he defended the cause of the Catholic clubs; especially dear to him were the Catholic boy scouts, whom he was compelled to dissolve in 1927. Even more important to the Church was Catholic Action, a world-wide movement launched by Pius XI and intended to enlist Catholic laymen effectively in societies for their mutual spiritual benefit, and that they might the better influence public life in a Catholic direction. Mussolini compelled the Pope in 1931 severely to curtail the scope of Catholic Action's activities in Italy, excluding it from politics and from the corporations and syndicates which had replaced the trade unions. We have seen in Chapter 17 how the economic structure of the Fascist Corporate State was criticised by the Pope for tending to "substitute itself in the place of private initiative instead of limiting itself to necessary and sufficient assistance." This was in Pius XI's encyclical *Quadragesimo Anno*, of 1931, which reiterated, in the face of the Fascists, the principles of *Rerum Novarum*. But much more striking was his encyclical *Non Abbiamo Bisogno*, of the following month (June 1931), which he had to smuggle out of Rome and publish in France. In it he denounced the "brutalities and beatings, blows and bloodshed," the monopoly of youth "from tenderest years up to manhood and womanhood, for the exclusive advantage of a party and of a régime based on an ideology which clearly amounts to a real pagan worship of the State—Statolatry—which is no less in conflict with the natural rights of the family than it is in contradiction with the supernatural rights of the Church." In this encyclical Pius XI specifically declared that the oath of blind obedience required by the régime from the members of its youth organisations was "unlawful."

In the face of so violent an antagonism the measure of support which Mussolini certainly did, from time to time, receive from Pius XI may seem surprising. The two rulers shared, however, certain common objectives and certain common qualities. First and most important was the antagonism they felt towards communism, and their determination that it should not capture Italy. The victory of Lenin in Russia, and after him of Stalin, had given an edge to the teachings of Marx and Bakunin, which the Russian dictators amplified and expounded in new treatises which only underlined the materialist basis of the Communist philosophy of life, and the "necessity of atheism," while the whole Western world was being shocked by the Russian anti-God campaign, with its ridicule of crucifixes and other holy symbols. When Pius XI and Mussolini both came to power in 1922 it was only a matter of months since not only Italy but Austria, Hungary, and even Germany had seemed likely to fall to communism; it was only natural that the Pope should have some sympathy, at first, for a régime which seemed likely to save Italy from such a fate.

The Pope and the dictator also shared a certain quality of political realism, which made it possible for them to do business together. Pius knew that the sixty years' quarrel with the Italian State was a grave source of weakness to the Church in

Italy; Mussolini knew that the same quarrel was a grave source of weakness to the State. Whereas previous Popes had been impressed by the brutality of the new State's anti-clerical policies, and had supposed that its extreme political instability meant that it was unlikely to survive, the outcome of the First World War had shown that the Italian State was a reality, however weak, and, from the Church's point of view, a reality preferable to either the anarchy or the communism which seemed to be the only alternatives in the peninsula. It was time to end an anomalous state of things and, after two years of secret and hard bargaining between Cardinal Gasparri (Pius' Secretary of State) and Mussolini's government, the Lateran Treaty of February 1929 created an independent and sovereign Vatican State and endowed it with some two billion lire—a smaller sum than the accumulated annual payments due to the papacy under the old Law of Guarantees of 1871 (and untouched by the Pope) but useful to meet the expenses of refitting the Vatican and building new administrative offices. To the Pope the important point was that he should be independent and sovereign; it did not matter how small his state was—indeed the smaller the better.

To the treaty was closely tied a concordat with Italy to govern the status of the Church in the country. Catholicism became once more the official religion to be taught in the schools. Catholic marriage became once more legal and sufficient; it was no longer necessary for there to be a civil ceremony as well. The status of the religious orders was safeguarded. Catholic processions were now protected, and the proselytising activities of Protestant bodies (but not of course their freedom of worship) were restricted. Nevertheless, as we have already seen, deep-seated causes of conflict remained, centering around Catholic Action and the Catholic schools. The Pope was not prepared to regard the doctrinal instruction given in the state schools as the limit of the Church's legitimate educational activities. Mussolini was not prepared to allow Catholic Action (protected by the Concordat) to have any political scope. And he required the liquidation of the Catholic boy scouts and girl guides in favour of his own militaristic organisations.

All the same, the treaty and Concordat were sensible measures which recognised the fact that Italy was Catholic, and if the spectacle, so widely published in the press, of the Duce kneeling in front of the Apostle's statue in St. Peter's was rightly received with more reserve than Napoleon's coronation in Notre Dame had enjoyed, it yet served a similar purpose.

Until his death in 1939 Pius XI continued to find Mussolini and his régime a dangerous ally, and one he was constantly driven to criticise and even to denounce; he is reported on one occasion to have likened dealing with Mussolini to dealing with the devil. Yet an ally on the whole he remained, because on the whole Mussolini's enemies were also the enemies of the Church. Such, for instance, were the Freemasons, who had been for a century and more the most implacable enemies of the Church in Italy, and who now found the activities of their lodges, their banks, and their press curtailed by the Fascist régime. Such, across the Mediterranean, were the claims of the Coptic Church in Northeast Africa, which Mussolini indirectly helped to expose to Catholic influences, as a result of his encouragement of emigration, and of his conquest of Ethiopia in 1935.

But it was in Spain that the interests of the Church and of the Italian State most nearly coincided.

We have seen already in Chapter 20 the pass to which matters had come for the Church in Spain by the year 1936. It was not so much a matter of anti-clerical legislation of the customary kind, intended to secularise the life of the country —though the Republic had gone further in this direction than any previous Spanish régime. It was rather the violence of Anarchist and Communist mobs, especially in Catalonia, which led to the burning of churches on a scale not previously seen save in Mexico. The winning of power by a left-wing government with Anarchist elements in 1936 aggravated the situation, because the power of the State no longer stood in defence of the Church. When the civil war started, in July 1936, it was inevitable that the Church, in self-defence, should side with the Nationalist movement in support of General Franco. In their collective letter of the following July the Spanish bishops explained to their brethren throughout the world why the Church "in spite of its spirit of peace, and in spite of not having wanted the war nor having collaborated in it, could not be indifferent to the struggle." As the struggle went on, the extremists on both sides necessarily grew stronger, and outrages were not confined to either. Neutrality, for Spaniards, became an impossibility. For the Church it was a simple issue of survival. By the year 1938, in Barcelona, which had become the republican capital, it had ceased to be a matter of isolated mob attacks upon convents or churches. It was the Paris of 1793 once again—only the bishop's chapel was tolerated, the churches were closed, priests had to disguise themselves, and Mass had to be said in secret. Already in March 1937, in *Divini Redemptoris*, Pius XI had recorded: "Not only this or that church or isolated monastery has been sacked, but as far as possible every church and every monastery has been destroyed. Every vestige of the Christian religion has been eradicated, even though intimately linked with the rarest monuments of art and science! The fury of Communism has not confined itself to the indiscriminate slaughter of bishops or of thousands of priests and religious of both sexes; it searches out above all those who have been devoting their lives to the working classes and the poor. But the majority of its victims have been laymen of all conditions and classes. Even up to the present moment masses of them are slain almost daily for no other offence than the fact that they are good Christians or at least opposed to atheistic Communism. And this fearful destruction has been carried out with a hatred and a savage barbarity one could not believe possible in our age."

Mussolini, on the other hand, was interested in the Spanish struggle for reasons of power politics as well as of ideology. The Popular Front Republican government in Madrid was unwelcome to him because it orientated Spain politically towards the Popular Front government in Paris, whereas previously the Spanish Government of Primo de Rivera had looked rather towards Rome. A friendly Spanish Government, which might provide him with submarine bases in the Balearic Islands, or on the east coast of Spain, was an important factor to him in his attempt to rival French and British naval power in the Mediterranean. But ideology probably mattered to him more. A left-wing government at Madrid, with Anarchist and Communist elements, at the same time as a Popular Front government in Paris, was a serious challenge to the ideology upon which his own régime rested, and it became more serious when Moscow interested herself in maintaining it there.

On the ideological side, then, the Pope's and Duce's views about Spain had much in common: both feared the Communists. But they did so for different reasons. Mussolini had little concern for the Church. Pius had little for Fascism—how little may be judged by his devastating encyclical, *Mit Brennender*

Sorge, of March 1937 (the same month as his *Divini Redemptoris* on Communism), in which he assailed the Hitler régime in Germany.

It is of course inaccurate to use the word fascism, which properly belongs to the Italian movement, for Hitler's Nazi régime. But by the year 1937, which we have now reached, the two movements had in fact grown closer together; for the Berlin-Rome Axis had become a working reality in Spain, and the two dictators were bringing their régimes into harmony—which meant that Mussolini was being compelled to adopt attitudes dictated by his more powerful partner. If a régime already brutal could properly be described as being brutalised, one would so describe the effect of nazism upon fascism. Amongst the early consequences of the new alliance was the persecution, for the first time, of the Jews in Italy. And another was a renewed hostility between Church and State—a hostility demanded by Hitler. For it was intolerable to the German dictator that his colleague across the Alps should be on friendly terms with the author of *Mit Brennender Sorge*.

Hitler had been brought to power in Germany in 1933 by circumstances analogous with those which had brought Mussolini to power eleven years earlier in Italy; but the analogy should not be pressed too far. At elections which were still free he had won, in 1932, 230 seats in the Reichstag, or more than a third of the total, which was a far larger parliamentary following than Mussolini won before he seized power at Rome. True, this figure dropped to 190 at the next election, in November of the same year but, by allying with von Papen and the Nationalists, Hitler manoeuvred himself constitutionally into power in January 1933, and only in the subsequent election (March 1933) was he in a position effectively to influence the outcome by terror tactics. The previous four years had been a period of growing crisis in Germany, caused by the great depression, the mounting unemployment, and the rioting of the "Reds," whose gains in the Reichstag had been only a little less spectacular than those of the Nazis. Dissatisfaction with parliamentary government, as it had been practised by the Weimar Republic (the postwar successor of Imperial Germany) was being felt both on the right and on the left; the call, as always on such occasions, was for a "strong hand." To obtain full emergency executive powers under the constitution it was necessary for Hitler to secure a two-thirds majority in the Reichstag; even after the elections of March 1933 he could only obtain such a majority with the support of the Catholic Centre party. The responsibility, then, of the Centre (representing a large proportion of German Catholicism) for the tragedy that was to follow was that, by voting these powers to Hitler, it enabled his dictatorship to begin.

In the light of what followed that is a very grave responsibility. But it did not seem so at the time. A Reichstag in which the strongest parties were the Nazis, on the one hand, and the Socialists and Communists on the other, was not a body which seemed likely to provide an executive capable of governing quietly in a parliamentary manner. As elsewhere in Europe the choice seemed to rest between the Right and the "Reds," and if President von Hindenburg, the Grand Old Man of Germany, was prepared to swallow his social prejudices and call Hitler to power, that seemed to many a sufficient guarantee that he was indispensable to the maintenance of law and order.

Such was the line of thought of respectable small men of the middle class, the "backbone of Germany," men who had always given their support to the Centre party, men who believed in the family, in order, in hard work, and who feared the Communists as the sworn foes both of Catholicism and of the whole social order. Hitler stood for Germany, for discipline, for effort—and against the "Reds." That was enough for them—and, it should be added, for most of the German hierarchy too. And some of the more thoughtful Catholics were reassured by von Papen. Here was a man who was a zealous Catholic, of good family, who was willing to work with Hitler; and Hitler had made him vice-chancellor. Von Papen, they believed, would "civilise" the new chancellor and keep him on the rails.

That he would need some civilising could not be denied because was he not, after all, the author of *Mein Kampf*, that notably un-Catholic book, and had not the bishops, earlier on, felt obliged to excommunicate the leading members of his party? But the general attitude in 1933 was that power (especially with Hindenburg above him and von Papen at his side) would make Hitler responsible, that *Mein Kampf* was a youthful indiscretion, to be taken no more seriously now than were the young Mussolini's atheistic diatribes as a revolutionary hothead in Switzerland. The excommunication was lifted in the same month as the full powers were voted, and von Papen proceeded forthwith to negotiate a concordat with Rome, which was completed with remarkable rapidity and signed in July of the same year. Cardinal Gasparri, who had negotiated the Lateran Treaty and concordat with Mussolini in 1929, had been succeeded as Pius XI's Secretary of State by Cardinal Eugenio Pacelli (the future Pope Pius XII) and to him belongs much of the credit for completing the new concordat. Ever since 1920, as nuncio first at Munich and then at Berlin, Pacelli had striven to secure a concordat with the Weimar Republic; but he had only succeeded in securing separate concordats with the governments of Bavaria and Prussia. The new concordat with Hitler's Germany, so rapidly concluded, seemed a happy augury. It secured freedom for the Church in Germany to administer its own affairs, the State retaining the right of veto over episcopal appointments and requiring an oath of loyalty to the Führer. There was to be freedom of communications with Rome, freedom for the religious orders, permission to establish Catholic theological faculties at the universities, and Catholic public primary education.

On paper it was a good concordat, and Rome is not in the habit of refusing the opportunity of negotiating such instruments for the protection and regulation of the life of the Church. And although the papal Secretary of State already knew only too much about Hitler, he had also to consider that the Catholic vice-chancellor, von Papen, was pressing the negotiations, that Hindenburg was still Head of the State, and that the Centre party had given its support to the new government. He had reason to hope that the concordat might serve to strengthen the sane and moderate men who stood around the new chancellor. And if Hitler had no intention of abiding by it, why had he asked for it?

For Hitler the concordat had a certain prestige value. In a matter of months he had brought to a successful conclusion negotiations which had eluded the Weimar Republic for more than ten years. Moreover a gesture of friendship towards the Centre party was opportune. He needed its support in those early months. Nor did he seriously assail the Church until after the vote of the Catholic people of the Saar, in the plebiscite of 1935, had safely landed that territory in the German net. But the Centre party proved to have been deluded when it supposed that the new régime might be civilised. It was not the only group which suffered from that delusion, which was shared by sober senators of the United States and by cautious conservatives in England. The fact was that nobody quite believed that any government, once in power, could really attempt to carry out the programme of *Mein Kampf*.

Within five days of the signature of the concordat Hitler showed how irreconcilable were his racial theories with Catholicism when he promulgated a law for the compulsory sterilisation of certain classes of the community. In the following year he called to power the fanatical philosopher of Aryanism, Alfred Rosenberg, whose *Myth of the Twentieth Century* Rome placed on the Index. The government replied by suppressing the pastoral letter in which the German bishops refuted Rosenberg's theories. Meanwhile the persecution of the Jews had begun, Cardinal Faulhaber, at Munich, was defending those "ancestors of all Christians according to the spirit," in his famous sermons, and soon brave bishops, such as the heroic Galen of Munster, or Preysing of Berlin, were condemning not only the laws which forbade intermarriage between Aryans and Jews, but the whole horrid heresy.

Although there were not lacking those who continued to suppose that, by its emphasis on work, order, discipline, obedience, sacrifice, and the like, nazism could provide a temporal habitude for Catholicism, the truth was that, as Hitler came to give more scope to Rosenberg and Goebbels, so his *mystique*, in its more revolting elements of race, blood, and conquest, became more apparent, and the more moderate men with whom he had surrounded himself at the start disappeared into the background or right off the stage. By the year 1937, although German arms, alongside Mussolini's, were helping to withstand the Communists in Spain, Pius XI issued *Mit Brennender Sorge* in condemnation of nazism. Printed secretly in Germany, it was read from the pulpits and it constituted, in the eyes of Germans and in the eyes of the world, the most serious public denunciation of Hitler's régime and its ideals to which the dictator was ever subjected in Germany. The Pope spoke of "the vain attempt to imprison God, Creator of the Universe . . . within the confines of a common blood or a single race," of "aggressive neo-paganism," of a "war of extermination" waged against the Church. Hitler replied, in November 1937, by saying that "recognition of the importance of blood and of race raises itself today above a humanist conception of the world . . . it is a victorious idea which is spreading like a wave across the entire world."[1]

So much for the conflict on the absolute plane of beliefs. On the practical plane of action it demonstrated itself in attacks upon Catholic Action, in all its branches, and especially in its youth clubs, which were not to be allowed to compete with the Hitler Youth; in violation of the concordat in respect of Catholic education and the freedom of the religious orders; in flagrant interference with liberty of speech, the press, and communications with Rome. Yet it was not until the Second World War had actually broken out that Hitler could be said to have waged a Kulturkampf. Wholesale imprisonment and execution of priests did not begin till then, and there still remained those who thought that an accommodation was possible. Such were von Papen, who had become ambassador at Vienna, and, amongst the Austrians with whom he was in contact, Cardinal Innitzer and the Chancellor Schuschnigg. The *Anschluss*, by which Hitler in March 1938 swallowed up Austria, was applauded by Cardinal Innitzer, whose indecent haste in recommending the new régime to the faithful earned him the rebuke of Rome. The anti-Catholic campaign which followed the *Anschluss* in Austria was directed primarily towards converting the Austrians from Catholicism to Nazi beliefs; for this reason it was directed against Catholic education, from the primary schools up to the universities.

A distinction may be noted here between the Nazi campaign and that of Bismarck. Whereas the latter had believed in the value of the Church and was concerned to gain control over it, so as to make sure that it gave support to his régime, Hitler's personal standpoint was fundamentally antithetical to Christianity as such. If he spared the churches and allowed the Mass to continue to be said, thereby deceiving many Catholics as to his real intentions, it was only because he felt he could not yet afford their outright opposition.

With the outbreak of the Second World War the pace of persecution quickened. The Catholic schools were closed and the Catholic press was suppressed. In the rapidly overrun territories of Poland (almost wholly Catholic) convents, monasteries, and seminaries were closed and their occupants, together with hundreds of the secular clergy, were sent to the

[1] Extracts from Hitler's speech are printed in J. Rovan, *Le Catholicisme politique en Allemagne* (Paris, 1956), p. 237.

notorious concentration camp at Dachau. By March 1945 there were 1493 priests, from all over the Reich, at Dachau alone.[2]

It is small wonder that when the one serious attempt to get rid of Hitler was organised, in July 1944, some of the leaders amongst the conspirators were Catholics and the chief amongst them, Colonel von Stauffenberg, fervent in the Faith. And with them stood Lutheran and other Protestant leaders. Informed Christian leaders knew by then what has since been brought to light by the Nuremberg trials, namely that the proscription of the Churches, required by Nazi ideology, was to be pursued after victory with the aid of "evidence" of the unpatriotic activity of priests, which the Gestapo was already collecting.

Potentially the Nazi threat to the Church was as serious as any it had encountered; but just as that had not been apparent in 1933 so, even during the Second World War, the full rigours of persecution were not released save in Poland, the Poles being treated as an inferior, subject people, and their religion as requiring no respect. In France, Belgium, and Holland, where the Nazi aim was to enlist co-operation, priests as such were not proscribed, while in Germany, although very many were sent to concentration camps, we do not find the archbishops and bishops generally imprisoned, as many were by Bismarck, though we need not doubt that their turn would have come at the end of a successful war.

The result of these tactics was that many good Catholics, believing the constantly reiterated warning that their country was in danger, and that Hitler was an instrument sent for her salvation, to safeguard her from communism, saw it as their duty to give to his government the obedience to which all legitimate authority is entitled; and many of them died, alongside their fellows in the Russian snows, or in Siberian prison camps, without ever having understood the destiny which their Führer held in store for their Faith.

2 Figures given by Rovan in *op. cit.*, p. 245.

CHAPTER TWENTY-THREE

Communism, Peace, and Pius XII (1939–1956)

The end of the Second World War brought with it major changes in the political balance of the world. The United States of America and the Soviet Union emerged as the two strongest powers, with Great Britain a rather uneasy third. Eastern Europe, as far as Berlin, Vienna, and the Balkan Mountains, fell under the control of Moscow, while the victory of the Communists in China brought the most populous country in Asia under a Communist government, and into friendly relations with the Soviet Union. Since the land forces of Russia were incomparably stronger than those of any other power, an ominous challenge in Europe and in Asia was set up at a time when the strongest traditional armies on the two continents, those of Germany and Japan, had gone down to total defeat.

From the point of view of Britain, France, and the other governments of western Europe, the situation was made much more serious by the fact that Communist parties emerged in the West, and notably in Italy and France, large enough to constitute the principal opposition parties in those countries, and even likely, in Italy at least, to win political power. It was a very much more serious situation than had arisen after the First World War. Moreover these parties were encouraged by the might of Russian arms, now thrust right into the centre of Europe.

The danger implicit in allowing such a situation to develop had been more evident to the British war leader, Winston Churchill, than to the American President, Franklin Roosevelt. It is no part of the purposes of this book to enter into the controversies, which will not for long be resolved, concerning the "bargain" struck between Roosevelt and Stalin at Yalta in 1945, or concerning Churchill's dislike of the plan to invade southern France, in preference to an invasion of the Balkans, though it is relevant to notice here that a successful Balkan invasion might well have had an important effect, after the war, upon the position of the Russians in eastern Europe. What we need to consider is the important fact that eastern Europe was "liberated" by the Russian armies, which made little use of local resistance movements. The heroic Polish up-rising, for example, at Warsaw, was left isolated to be crushed by the Nazis, although the Russian armies were on the door-step in overwhelming strength. The leadership in occupied eastern Europe was to be Russian leadership, a military con-trol responsible to Moscow. It goes without saying that this was not what the Western powers wanted but they were com-pelled, in 1945 at Potsdam, to accept it.

If Churchill had harboured few illusions about Soviet in-tentions, it was even more certain that Pope Pius XII had har-boured none at all. Although he had eschewed any criticism of Stalin or his régime whilst Russia had been fighting for her life, he knew much better than Roosevelt that the Communist aim was a Communist Europe, controlled from Moscow, and that the Soviet Government would not voluntarily stop the ad-vance. And he knew, too, what this would mean for religion.

As Secretary of State since 1930, the future Pope had been the right hand of Pius XI, a ruler who had understood where the greatest danger lay, and who had consistently denounced the persecution of religion in Russia, in Spain, or in Mexico, and had exposed the menace implicit in Communist and "fellow-travelling" teaching. Despite his robust attacks upon the Nazi ideology, and his indignation at Fascist statolatry, Pius XI, together with his Secretary of State, had never lost sight of the fact that, as Chief Shepherd of the Church, the Pope must keep his eyes upon the main menace to the flock, and already Pope and Secretary could see clearly enough where this was to be found.

But as the danger of war, in 1938 and 1939, had grown greater, they were also bound to strive, by all the means at their disposal, to preserve peace. This was Pius XII's first pre-occupation, in that fateful first year of his pontificate, which was the year 1939. Those who wanted to see him denounce the régimes of Hitler and Mussolini more openly and more im-mediately than his predecessor forgot that his overriding aim was, by avoiding openly taking sides between the Western powers, to reach a position from which he might hope to be able to help to negotiate a just settlement between them. It would have been useless, as well as wrong, for him to take sides, in advance, on the international issues at stake between the Western powers, although he had gone so far in the previous summer, when still Secretary of State, as to administer a stinging rebuff to the two dictators, when they met in Rome, by withdrawing with the Pope to Castel Gandolfo.

Now, as Pope, in pursuit of peace, he endeavoured in May 1939, through his nuncios in Paris, London, Berlin, Rome and Warsaw, to promote a five-power conference to settle outstanding disputes about the Polish Corridor, and about the various points at issue between Italy and France. It was the only kind of initiative which could hope to relieve the crisis. But already the Vatican was becoming aware that serious negotiations were on foot between Hitler and Stalin, and these it was that precipitated the war and settled the fate of Poland. A last-minute appeal by the Pope, on July 30, having failed, there remained for the moment no more that the Vatican could do save to denounce the treatment of Poland, together with the coercion by Russia of the Baltic states, and to strive to avert a conflagration in the West. He concentrated chiefly, now, upon striving to keep Mussolini from joining in; in this endeavour he undoubtedly had the support of most of the Italian people. It was also an endeavour in which he had the valuable assistance of Roosevelt's personal representative at the Vatican, Myron Taylor, who arrived at the end of the same year.

In his Christmas message the Pope placed before the world, while the conflict was still confined to the East, his five-point plan for a peace. Avoiding specific territorial proposals, such as had been included in Benedict XV's proposals of 1917, he enunciated what he considered should be the principles of a general settlement: assurance to all nations, great or small, of their right to life and independence; delivery of the nations from the slavery imposed upon them by the armaments race; international institutions for maintaining peace; revision of treaties by peaceful methods; an appeal to all Christians, whether within the Catholic fold or without, to accept as their common ground the principles of justice and charity, under the Law of God, proclaimed in the Sermon on the Mount. A year later, in the London *Times*, the leaders of all the Churches in England specifically endorsed the Pope's principles—an unprecedented event.

The fall of Denmark, Norway, Holland, Belgium, and France to Hitler in the summer of 1940, and the entry of Mussolini into the war, brought to nothing the Pope's endeavours, and there was even some talk of his having to remove to Canada, as Rome became surrounded by belligerent

orces; he determined, however, to remain. In June 1941 came
Hitler's invasion of Russia and for three years, at least, in the
overriding interests of peace, the Pope was silent about
the Communist persecution of Christianity, since the Russian
people very evidently were the victims of Hitler's aggression.
But his forbearance was ill requited, for Moscow, with an eye
upon the Catholics of eastern Europe, whom she intended to
incorporate within the Soviet system, was already, in 1943,
striving to depict the Roman Church as the friend of the
fascist aggressors and the foe of peace. It was a singular accusation; but in the excitement of war it gained some cre-
dence, and even official American opinion was concerned by
the Pope's refusal to agree with Roosevelt that the Soviet
tyranny was not so fundamentally inimical to religion as was
Hitler's. It was also surprised by his dislike of the war aim of
"unconditional surrender," agreed by the allies at the Casa-
blanca Conference of 1943, an aim which seemed to Pius to
be not only un-Christian but calculated to prolong the war by
causing the beleaguered European central powers to fight to
the last.

By the end of the European war the fate of the Poles, the
Hungarians, the Czechs, the Bulgarians, the Yugoslavs, and
the peoples of the Baltic states, oppressed by Communist
tyranny, cried aloud at Rome for pity, nor could the Pope
fail to heed. But the rulers of the Western powers (some of
which had gone to war for the defence of Poland) can scarcely
be blamed for their reluctance to turn from their costly defeat
of one tyrant to the still more difficult task of trying to drive
out another, and a stronger, from the lands he had occupied.
It was only possible to contain the colossus, and this the successors of Roosevelt and Churchill set themselves, with delayed determination, to do. While Molotov, the Soviet Foreign
Minister, and Vishinsky, the Soviet delegate at the United
Nations, obstructed every attempt to reach an international
agreement, Stalin retained powerful armies in eastern Germany and around Berlin. But every further encroachment was
resisted; the Western powers had at last begun to realise that
they were entering upon a period of "cold war" and Churchill,
though no longer in power, used his eloquence to arouse
Americans and Englishmen to a more vivid appreciation of
that sinister construction which he aptly named the "Iron
Curtain."

For Rome the Iron Curtain was no novelty. There had been

an iron curtain, spiritually speaking, screening Russia in the days of Gregory XVI and the Tsar Nicholas I. Nor had other powerful rulers hesitated, elsewhere, to impose prohibitions upon the Church's free communication with Rome. Such iron curtains had been erected by Napoleon, by Bismarck, and by some of the revolutionary governments in Latin America. But the iron curtain around eastern Europe after 1945 was more impenetrable, and behind it whole Catholic populations became, in the Pope's phrase, the "Church of Silence."

The persecution was naturally most rigorous in those territories which were incorporated within the Soviet Union proper, namely the eastern provinces of Poland (seized by Stalin in 1939) which became part of the Soviet republics of the Ukraine and of Byelorussia; the Carpatho-Ukraine, a territory seized from Czechoslovakia and incorporated in the Soviet Ukraine; and the three incorporated Baltic republics of Estonia, Latvia, and Lithuania. A large proportion of the Catholics in these territories were Uniates, using the Greek rite; by dint of imprisoning the Uniate bishops and finding pliant parish priests, the Soviet Government (following the precedent set by Nicholas I) secured the separation of these bodies of Catholics, once more, from Rome, and their union with the Orthodox Church; in this way nearly four million Catholics in Poland alone were lost. This was a technique less easily applied to those of the Latin rite, but the Latin priests, particularly in Lithuania (an almost wholly Catholic country), were expelled in hundreds on fabricated charges. Many were taken to Siberia; the more fortunate found their way to the West, and Pius XII founded the Lithuanian Ecclesiastical Institute to minister to their needs and to confirm them in their Faith.

The technique of separating the Uniates from the other Catholics and merging them with the Orthodox Church was also pursued in Rumania, which lay outside Soviet territory proper. It was facilitated by the Orthodox Patriarch of Rumania, who worked in close collaboration with the restored Patriarch of Moscow. By restoring the patriarchate of Moscow in 1943 the Soviet government had effectively provided itself with an instrument which, despite its own atheist principles, it could use to advantage in its endeavours to weaken the influence of Rome in eastern Europe. Not only would it facilitate the transfer of the Uniates, but it would tend to prevent the Orthodox from allying with the Catholics in a common defence of Christianity. Once again we may observe the Communist dictatorship at Moscow pursuing the traditional policies of the Tsars, for it was an ancient habit of Russian rulers to use their very compliant patriarchs in support of their own political purposes.

By 1950 the Pope, on account of what was happening in Rumania, was obliged to withdraw his acting nuncio from Bucharest. Meanwhile the persecution of the Church was proceeding in all the countries nominally independent but behind the Iron Curtain. In Yugoslavia, under Marshal Tito, and especially in the Catholic province of Croatia, priests were executed, imprisoned, or driven into exile or into hiding, and religious education ceased. The popular Archbishop Stepinac of Zagreb was accused, on account of his impartial assistance to all refugees, of collaboration with the Germans and was sentenced to sixteen years' imprisonment; the hope of better days for the Church when Tito subsequently quarrelled with Stalin was not realised. In Hungary, a Catholic country, the primate, Cardinal Mindszenty, was arrested in January 1949 and condemned in February to life imprisonment as a result of a trial which attracted the horror and amazement of the whole world. Aware that his Communist opponents would have resort to what we now call "brain-washing," the cardinal, protesting his innocence, warned the world in advance that human frailty might lead him into statements which would seem confessions of guilt. By the end of his trial he was a changed man and had, indeed, given utterance to a confession of the kind he had foreseen he might be induced to make. As a gesture of protest against this shocking affair the whole diplomatic corps accredited to the Vatican expressed its sympathy to the Pope.

It should not, however, be supposed that Catholic leaders could necessarily count upon the support of Rome in whatever course of action they chose to adopt. Where there had been reason for the Pope to doubt the propriety of their action, as in Austria at the time of the *Anschluss*, or later in Croatia, where it was alleged that some of the Orthodox had been coerced into becoming Catholics, or in Slovakia, where Monsignor Tiso was made President in Hitler's time, Rome made no attempt to defend those against whom it was felt that there might be a legitimate political or religious grievance. Cardinal Innitzer, at Vienna, was rebuked, the Croat régime was reminded that conversion was a matter of conscience, not of compulsion, and when Monsignor Tiso was executed, after the war, for collaboration with the Germans no protest was made by the Vatican, although many thought that the execution was mere political retribution. But where the hierarchy were simply doing their duty in fostering the Faith and insisting upon the rights of the Church, they could count securely upon Rome and upon the prayers of the faithful throughout the world. When the Communists acquired control over Czechoslovakia in 1948 the Archbishop of Prague, Joseph Beran, was put under house arrest, and the government tried to institute new bishops without reference to Rome. But Beran, like Mindszenty and Stepinac, could rely upon the Pope, who continued to recognise him as the lawful ruler of his see and refused to recognise any appointment, in substitution, by the government.

In Poland, the largest and most Catholic of the quasi-independent countries behind the Iron Curtain, the Communist government, set up by the Russians and recognised, perforce, by the allied powers (but not by the Vatican), concentrated its efforts upon trying to drive a wedge between the Vatican and the Church. In the delicate matter of the western territories awarded to Poland after the war, at the expense of East Germany, Rome was represented as supporting the Germans, although she remained neutral in the matter of the political boundaries, and the Pope's only offence was to express his sympathy with those who found themselves forcibly evacuated on account of the changes.

But it was hard for the Communist government at Warsaw to make headway so long as Cardinal Hlond, the Archbishop of Warsaw, remained alive, for he had been a prisoner of the Germans and nobody could doubt his Polish as well as his Roman loyalty. After his death in 1948 the government made more progress and, although it would be absurd to suppose that there was a danger that the papal authority would be denied by the Church in Poland, yet an agreement was reached, without consultation with Rome, between the Polish hierarchy and the government in April 1950, and the Vatican (which still recognised the Polish Government in exile) could only express its astonishment at the news. By this agreement the supreme authority of the Pope in matters of faith, morals, and jurisdiction was explicitly recognised, but in other matters the episcopate was stated to be subject to the direction of the Polish State. The heart of the agreement was the statement that allegiance to the new government was incumbent upon the faithful; resistance to it was stated to be "criminal." The traditional rights of the Church in education and the like were "guaranteed," but with reservations which left the government as free, in practice, to interfere in the interests of "security" as ever Napoleon's Organic Articles had left the French Government. Less than six months had passed before the Polish hierarchy found itself compelled to protest against numerous violations of the agreement. But the Communist masters at Moscow were well satisfied, and in August 1950 they procured a similar agreement in Hungary. Under the aegis of the "Orginform," established in the same year to undertake the training of those entrusted with the special task of dispelling the Faith (for which purpose they would pose as priests), an all-out effort was made by the Communists to sow religious confusion in eastern Europe generally, in particular by undermining allegiance to the Pope. It was a campaign which Pius endeavoured to meet by reaching the faithful directly, through the Vatican radio, there being no other reliable means of communication left.

Since 1950 the battle has continued. In that year the apostolic delegate was expelled from Moscow and his church (used by the embassy staffs) was entrusted by Stalin to a compliant nominee from Latvia. Archbishop Stepinac, released from prison by President Tito, but kept under house arrest, was not allowed to attend the Consistory of January 1953 to receive his cardinal's hat, and the Yugoslav Government made the dignity conferred upon him the opportunity to break off diplomatic relations with the Vatican. The primate of Poland, Archbishop Wyszynski, created a cardinal on the same occasion, was likewise prevented from attending, and a few months later he was arrested. Cardinal Mindszenty remained in prison. In Hungary there was a brief break in the clouds at the time of the revolution of October 1956, and Cardinal Mindszenty was released. A few words of peace, and of pardon for his enemies, and the clouds from the Carpathians descended once more, in the shape of Russian tanks, and the Church of Hungary became once again a part of the Church of Silence. Whether, in Poland, the Gomulka revolution, effected in the same year, was to bring any alleviation remained to be seen, though the release of Cardinal Wyszynski, who was allowed to visit Rome, seemed a hopeful sign.

It is against this sinister background of silence in eastern Europe, together with equally sinister news from Asia, where Catholic missionaries and religious orders (even the silent Trappists) were being expelled from Communist China, from Indo-China, and from Northern Korea, that we should set papal policy since the Second World War if we wish to understand it aright. This Communist-atheist crusade was the latest, and in some ways the most brutal of those which the Church had been called upon to face.

How was she to confront it?

Not, certainly, by a "Holy Crusade." But, equally certainly, not by unconditional surrender. Peace, assuredly, but not peace at any price, not peace at the price of the extinction of her spiritual liberty in Asia and Europe. By prayers for Russia; by appeals to what was common to Orthodox and Catholics alike, such as devotion to the Blessed Virgin, a mutual devotion of which the Pope reminded those Russians who could hear him, to whom he appealed in the name of Christ and of His Mother, without mention of Rome. But also by warning those whom the Communists sought to seduce in western Europe of the degree of their danger, of the utter incompatibility between communism and Christianity.

Clearly it was a prime duty for the Pope to warn Western Christendom of the danger in which it stood. And especially was this warning necessary for the Italians. Italian communism, forced underground by Mussolini, had burst into life with the anti-Fascist reaction of the liberation movement, in which Catholics and Communists found themselves fighting together to free northern Italy from the Nazis and from the puppet régime of a Mussolini kidnapped from Rome and installed on the shores of Lake Garda. In this "war of the partisans" men who called themselves Communists played a vigorous and a courageous part, but their final victory left a vacuum in authority. Mussolini had fallen, the King was discredited, and the country was under the control of allied military commanders. To whom should Italians turn?

Sometimes to Communist leaders, sometimes to the Pope— sometimes, oddly enough, to both.

The popularity of a Pope who had saved Rome from the fighting, who had befriended refugees of all sorts in the Vatican City, and who had worked tirelessly for the relief of suffering was not in question; more than anybody else he seemed to speak for Italy. And in the countryside a Communist mayor and a Catholic priest, in the early postwar period of reconstruction, might well find themselves labouring together, both good Italians and proud of the Pope, the only men who could get on with the job of rebuilding a shattered town. But this "little world of Don Camillo" soon became part of the big world of the Russian Army, the Cominform, and the Orginform, on the one side, and of the Catholic faith on the other, and the choice between the Cross and the Hammer-and-Sickle could no longer be avoided. In the face of the Communist offensive it became necessary for the Pope to make it clear that if the Italian Communist party were truly a part of international communism, whose headquarters were at Moscow (and its leader Palmiro Togliatti made no secret of this), then no Catholic could possibly belong to it, or assist it, on pain of excommunication. Such was the purport of his decree of July 1949, a decree intended to defend the West from the menace from the East. But this decree, which to some seemed harsh, was not designed to make life impossible for Catholics behind the Iron Curtain. That collaboration of Catholics with Communists in those territories was often inevitable, the Pope was well aware; he was therefore careful in his decree to state that what was condemned was "conscious and free" membership or collaboration. Those who lived under the shadow of Moscow, who were far from free, were left at liberty to receive the sacraments where they were fortunate enough to be able to do so.

The Italian Communist party was the largest Communist political party in the West and second only in size, in Italy, to the Christian Democratic party. But the Communist party in France was also very formidable, and in both countries there were times, in the late '40s and early '50s, when it seemed possible enough that a Communist government might emerge. The extent to which the Pope's resolution was responsible for preventing that from happening is incapable of being determined, but the influence of the Vatican in this matter must have been considerable.

There were, however, other powerful influences which helped to save freedom in the West. One was the resolution shown by President Truman, and also by the British Government, in organising that airlift which prevented the Russians from excluding the Western allies from Berlin. Another was the immense generosity of the United States in taking the lead in organising a vast system of relief and reconstruction in war-shattered Europe. There was also the North Atlantic Treaty, with its rapidly organised international forces. But perhaps the most important was the emergence in Italy, Western Germany, and France of political leaders, in the persons of De Gasperi, Adenauer, and Schuman, all of them Catholics and all of them possessed of courage and ability, who were determined to work for European reconstruction on the basis of liberty and mutual help through new international organisations. This joint endeavour on the part of the Christian Democratic parties was derided by the Communists, and by some of the Socialists, as a "bourgeois hypocrisy," intended to safeguard the propertied classes, and there was talk of an unholy alliance between American capitalism and the Vatican. In reality, however, these postwar governments, basing their policies on the maintenance of free institutions, both political and economic, did not prove unmindful, particularly in Italy, of the plight of the poor; and although it would be absurd to suppose that they were in any political sense inspired by the Vatican or "represented" it, or that Catholics were not perfectly free to support other parties and very often did so, it is yet true that these leading statesmen were genuinely Catholic, were nurtured in the concepts of *Rerum Novarum* and *Quadragesimo Anno*, and were inspired with a zeal to save Christendom by a closer Western unity.

The various associations formed to revivify the West and to defend her against Communist aggression, such as the Council of Europe, the Western European Union, the Schuman plan, and the Atlantic Treaty, naturally received the fullest support of the Vatican, since the Pope saw in them the best hope of peace and of the salvation of the Christian religion. Nor did he neglect any opportunity which presented itself for helping to foster a closer international unity. Upon all international conferences which met at Rome, whether those of the Parliamentary Union or of the postal workers, of the scientists or of the historians, he would impress, in the many addresses he gave, the paramount concern of the Church for international understanding and peace. And the same objectives inspired his association of the Church with the various cultural agencies of the United Nations, such as UNESCO. Yet his enthusiasm for the chief postwar international agency for peace, the United Nations, was necessarily qualified by the fact that it embraced such strong Communist elements, the sincerity of whose intentions could hardly convince him. From the start this was apparent, with the exclusion of the very name of God or of the divine order of being from the Charter, and with the exclusion not only of the Vatican State from membership (although she had unique experience of endeavours for international understanding) but also, for long, of many Catholic states, such as Austria, Italy, Portugal, or Ireland. And the permanent presence of the Soviet Union on the Security Council, with a veto which could paralyse action, seemed likely to frustrate the effective action of the new body. It was not quite the kind of organisation which the Pope had envisaged in his peace proposals of 1939. But that did not prevent his giving it, from the time of its foundation at San Francisco, such support as it permitted him to give—his messages of good will and his prayers.

It is, of course, impossible as yet to see in their true perspective these recent years since 1945; that will only be achieved with the passage of time. But it would have been unrealistic to ignore altogether in this book the contemporary scene, in which can so plainly be perceived problems and struggles the same in kind as those we have been tracing in earlier generations.

The same in kind, yet with an important difference.

The earlier struggles of the Church in modern history had been waged to keep her alive and united in the face of the omnicompetent State and the passions of a parochial nationalism. Napoleon and Bismarck had been concerned to bolster their régimes by trying to secure spiritual as well as temporal control. But they differed from Lenin and Stalin in that they were Christians, however loosely they sat to orthodoxy, and although they were preoccupied with limited, temporal empires of this world. Similarly the "Know-Nothings" in America, in so far as they were not merely selfish in their purposes, were concerned about what they believed to be the "national interests" of their country. But they, too, generally confessed Christianity of one kind or another, they did not despise the message of the Cross, as such, but, mistaking the nature of the Church, they resented her presence on their soil because she was "ruled by a foreigner," and because she claimed certain rights even against the State.

The reason why the Communist challenge is more radical

is that it not only persecutes the Church as "divisist" but denies the basic truths of Christianity altogether, regarding all supernatural religion as "superseded" and "degrading." And this is something new. One can, of course, find plenty of intellectual precursors of the Communists as far back as the age of the eighteenth-century Enlightenment and earlier; what one cannot find before the twentieth century is such beliefs exercising sovereign power for a generation and more over millions of people, through despotic governments.

The nearest parallel is to be found in the French Revolution. While Fouché and Hébert held power, and the provinces of France were imitating the Parisian Feast of Reason, and the Mass was forbidden, and sacrilege was encouraged, it is clear that an attempt on a great scale was being made to root out Christianity, as such, and not merely to persecute the Church for being divisist. But that persecution was not everywhere enforced, and in scarcely any parts of France did it last for more than six years. There was not time to indoctrinate a new generation in the schools with anti-Christian beliefs before Napoleon restored Christian education. But the new ideas have already determined the character of the teaching in the Soviet schools for forty years.

Had Lord Macaulay lived to see this fifth great challenge to the Church, the challenge of communism in the twentieth century, he might well have been inclined to rate it as even more dangerous than those previous four challenges which, following Ranke, he isolated so clearly and described so vividly in words which we quoted in the first chapter. But he would not have despaired of seeing the barque of Peter riding the tempest. Indeed he would have noted that, on this last occasion, the nature and reality of the danger, which concerned civilisation as well as the Church, had been widely and rapidly recognised and met in the West. Not so rapidly as at Rome, and not before much had been lost. But widely enough, it may be, to ensure that the free nations, together with that Church whose independence is a part of their own freedom, may survive the storm.

POPES	DATES	EVENTS IN EUROPE	EVENTS IN THE AMERICAS
PIUS VI (Since 1775)	1789	Estates General Summoned to Versailles	
	1790	Civil Constitution of the Clergy	John
	1791		
	1792		
	1793	The "Terror"	Carroll
	1794	Execution of Robespierre	
	1795		
	1796		Bishop
	1797		
	1798		
	1799	Napoleon First Consul	of
	1800		
PIUS VII	1801	The Napoleonic Concordat	
	1802		Baltimore
	1803		
	1804	Coronation of Napoleon	
	1805		(1790–1815)
	1806		
	1807		
	1808		
	1809	Pius VII abducted from Rome, taken to Savona	
	1810		

POPES	DATES	EVENTS IN EUROPE	EVENTS IN THE AMERICAS
	1811		
	1812	Pius VII taken from Savona to Fontainebleau	
	1813		
	1814	Pius VII returns to Rome. Congress of Vienna	
	1815	Battle of Waterloo	
	1816		
	1817		
	1818		
	1819		
	1820		
	1821		
	1822		
LEO XII	1823		
	1824		Independence of Latin American States completed
	1825		
	1826		
	1827		
	1828		
PIUS VIII	1829	Catholic Emancipation in Gt. Britain	
	1830	Revolutions in France, Belgium, Poland	
GREGORY XVI	1831	Lamennais at Rome. Revolution in Romagna	

POPES	DATES	EVENTS IN EUROPE	EVENTS IN THE AMERICAS
	1832	*Mirari Vos* condemns Lamennais' theories	
	1833		
	1834		
	1835		
	1836		
	1837		
	1838		
	1839		*In Supremo Apostolatus* on slavery
	1840		Act of Union in Canada
	1841		
	1842		John Hughes Bishop of New York.
	1843		Irish Immigration of the "Hungry Forties"
	1844		Period of "Nativist" Movement and of the "Know Nothings"
	1845		
	1846	Amnesty to political prisoners at Rome	
	1847		
	1848	Revolutions at Paris, Rome, Vienna and other capitals	
PIUS IX	1849	Mazzini's Republic at Rome	
	1850	Return of Pius IX to Rome. Hierarchy restored to England	
	1851		

POPES	DATES	EVENTS IN EUROPE	EVENTS IN THE AMERICAS
	1852	Hierarchy restored to Holland	
	1853	Dogma of Immaculate Conception defined	
	1854		
	1855	Turin government suppresses the Religious Orders	
	1856		
	1857		
	1858	The Apparitions at Lourdes	
	1859		
	1860	Cavour occupies most of Papal States	
	1861		
	1862		American Civil War
	1863	Montalembert at Malines	
	1864	Syllabus of Errors	
	1865		
	1866		
	1867		Dominion of Canada formed
	1868		
	1869	Vatican Council assembles	
	1870	Papal Infallibility defined. Napoleon III abdicates. Rome occupied by Victor Emmanuel	
	1871		
	1872		

POPES	DATES	EVENTS IN EUROPE	EVENTS IN THE AMERICAS
	1873		
	1874		McCloskey of New York
	1875	Bismarck's	created Cardinal
	1876	Kulturkampf	Gibbons Archbishop of
	1877		Baltimore
LEO XIII	1878	in	
	1879	Germany	
	1880		
	1881		
	1882		
	1883		
	1884		Third Plenary Council
	1885		at Baltimore
	1886		
	1887		
	1888		
	1889		
	1890		
	1891	*Rerum Novarum*	
	1892	The *Ralliement* to the French Republic	
	1893		Mgr. Satolli Apostolic
	1894	Dreyfus sentenced	Delegate at Washington
	1895		

POPES	DATES	EVENTS IN EUROPE	EVENTS IN THE AMERICAS
	1896		
	1897		
	1898		Testem Benevolentiae condemns "Americanism"
	1899		
	1900		
	1901	Suppression of Religious Orders in France	
	1902	Loisy's L'Evangile et L'Eglise	
PIUS X	1903		
	1904		
	1905	Separation of Church and State in France	
	1906		
	1907	Pascendi Gregis condemns Modernism	
	1908		
	1909		
	1910		
	1911		
	1912		
	1913		
BENEDICT XV	1914	First World War	Beginning of Mexican persecution
	1915		
	1916		
	1917	Russian Revolution	America enters First World War
	1918		

POPES	DATES	EVENTS IN EUROPE	EVENTS IN THE AMERICAS
	1919	Treaty of Versailles. League of Nations	
	1920		
	1921	Irish Partition Treaty	
PIUS XI	1922	Mussolini wins power in Italy	
	1923		President Calles in Mexico
	1924	Stalin succeeds Lenin at Moscow	
	1925		Revolt of the *Cristeros* in Mexico
	1926		Al Smith ran for the presidency
	1927		
	1928	Salazar in power in Portugal	
	1929	Lateran Treaty creates Vatican State	
	1930		
	1931	*Quadragesimo Anno*	
	1932		President Franklin D. Roosevelt
	1933	Hitler becomes German Chancellor	
	1934		
	1935		
	1936	Franco's revolt in Spain	
	1937	*Mit Brennender Sorge* and *Divini Redemptoris*	
	1938	Austrian Anschluss	
PIUS XII	1939	Second World War	
	1940		

POPES	DATES	EVENTS IN EUROPE	EVENTS IN THE AMERICAS
	1941		America enters Second World War
	1942		
	1943		
	1944		
	1945	End of Second World War in Europe	End of Second World War in Japan
	1946	Arrest of Archbishop Stepinac	
	1947		
	1948	Arrest of Archbishop Beran of Prague	
	1949	Imprisonment of Cardinal Mindszenty	
	1950	Holy Year. Dogma of Assumption defined	
	1951		
	1952		
	1953	Abduction of Cardinal Wyszynski. Tito breaks off relations with Rome	
	1954		Revolt against Perón in Argentine
	1955		
	1956	Hungarian Revolt	

Bibliographical Guide

The aim of this guide is to assist the reader who may wish to pursue further the study of particular phases of the modern history of the Catholic Church. Clearly it can only be introductory; what is attempted is to mention, in particular, the major works (especially those in English and French) in which more detailed bibliographies are to be found.

GENERAL

The standard *History of the Popes*, by L. Pastor (Routledge and Kegan Paul, London) concludes with Pius VI, who died in 1799. But it was continued, in German, for the period 1799 to 1922, by J. Schmidlin, *Papstgeschicte der Neusten Zeit* (Munich, 3 vols., 1933–36), Vol. 1 of which (Pius VII, Leo XII, Pius VIII, and Gregory XVI) has been translated by L. Marchal into French (2 vols., Paris, 1938–40).

The whole period has been covered in outline in Vol. 2 of C. Poulet's *History of the Catholic Church* (translated by S. A. Raemers, Herder, 1948). Theological problems are best tackled in E. Hoçedez, *Histoire de la Théologie au XIXᵉ Siècle* (Paris, Desclée de Brouwer, 3 vols., 1947–48). The articles in the Catholic Encyclopedia and, still more, those in the *Dictionnaire de Théologie Catholique*, are always useful. For the influence of the Jesuits we have M. P. Harney, S.J., *The Jesuits in History* (America Press, 1941).

THE ANCIEN RÉGIME

In English: A general account of the condition of the Church, and of her public relations, in the eighteenth century, is to be found in Vol. 7 of the Mourret-Thompson *History of the Catholic Church* (Herder, 1947). For the Church in France the books of W. H. Jervis (*History of the Church of France from the Concordat of Bologna to the Revolution* and *The Gallican Church and the Revolution*, London, Kegan Paul, 1870–82) are still very useful, being excellently documented.

In French: A useful recent survey, with detailed bibliography, will be found in the first chapter of the Fliche et Martin *Histoire de l'Eglise*, Vol. 20 (*La Crise Révolutionnaire*, by Jean Leflon, Paris, 1951). For the special problem of the relation of Jansenism to the French Revolution see E.

Préclin *Les Jansenistes du XVIII*ᵉ *Siècle et la Constitution Civile du Clergé* (Paris, 1929).

THE FRENCH REVOLUTION AND NAPOLEON

In English: Recent secular scholarship in this field has tended to emphasise much more strongly the importance of the religious factor; cf., in particular, J. M. Thompson's *The French Revolution* (Blackwell, Oxford, 1943) and his *Napoleon Bonaparte* (Blackwell, 1953) both of which have good bibliographies.

In French: See, again, Vol. 20 of the Fliche et Martin *Histoire de l'Eglise* (bibliography), also A. Latreille, *L'Eglise Catholique et la Révolution Française* (2 vols., Hachette, 1946 and 1950), M. Artaud *Histoire du Pape Pie VII* (2 vols., Paris, 1837), and V. Bindel, *Histoire Réligieuse de Napoléon* (2 vols., Paris, 1940).

THE PERIOD 1815–46 IN EUROPE

In English: Wilfrid Ward's *Life and Times of Cardinal Wiseman* (Longmans, London, Vol. I, 1897) is still a standard work, also his *William George Ward and the Catholic Revival* (Longmans, 1912). See also Dom. Cuthbert Butler's *Life and Times of Bishop Ullathorne* (Vol. I, Burns Oates, 1926). But in this period it is especially necessary to consult the continental authorities, and in particular:

In French: G. Weill, *Histoire du Catholicisme Libéral en France, 1828–1908* (Paris, 1909) and Vol. 20 of the Fliche et Martin *Histoire de l'Eglise*, already quoted. The writings of Lamennais, especially his *Paroles d'un Croyant* and *Affaire de Rome* are contemporary documents of importance; so are the sermons of Lacordaire. For Germany, see G. Goyau, *L'Allemagne Réligieuse, Le Catholicisme* (Paris, 1905–9), and the first chapter of a brilliant recent book *Le Catholicisme Politique en Allemagne*, by J. Rovan (Paris, Seuil, 1956).

In Italian: U. Padovani, *Vincenzo Gioberti e il cattolicismo* (Milan, 1927) is valuable.

THE PERIOD OF PIUS IX (1846–78) AND THE VATICAN COUNCIL

In English: *Pio Nono* (with bibliography) by E. E. Y. Hales (Kenedy, 1954), *Italy in the Making* by G. F. H. and Mrs. Berkeley (Vols. 2 and 3, Cambridge University Press, 1932

-40), *The Vatican Council*, by F. Hayward (translated by Wicklow, Dublin, Clonmore and Reynolds, 1951), *Italy and the Vatican at War*, by S. W. Halperin (Chicago, 1939), books quoted by W. Ward, and also his *Life of John Henry Newman* (Longmans, 1912), Vol. 2 of Butler's *Life of Bishop Ullathorne* (quoted) and also his *Vatican Council* (Longmans, 2 vols., 1930), which is the best book in English on the subject. On the great protagonists at the Vatican Council see F. Lagrange, *Life of Mgr. Dupanloup* (translated by Herbert, London, 1885), and Shane Leslie, *Cardinal Manning* (Clonmore and Reynolds, 1953). Lord Acton's essay, "The Munich Congress" (in Acton *Essays on Church and State*, London, Hollis and Carter, 1952), is a contemporary document of importance. Two recent histories of France in this period, *Louis Napoleon*, by J. M. Thompson (Blackwell, Oxford, 1955, bibliography), and *The French Nation*, by D. W. Brogan (London, Hamish Hamilton, 1957) may usefully be consulted.

In French: R. Aubert, *Pontificat de Pie Neuf* (Fliche et Martin, *Histoire de l'Eglise*, Vol. 21, 1951); this is a fundamental volume, containing a full bibliography. See also R. P. Lecanuet, *Montalembert* (3 vols., Paris, 1909), and J. Maurain, *La Politique Ecclésiastique du Second Empire de 1852 à 1869* (Paris, 1930). The latter is critical of Rome but fundamental to an understanding of French Catholic and anti-Catholic opinion, and their effects on policy. Amongst contemporary writings of particular interest are C. de Montalembert, *L'Eglise libre dans l'Etat libre* (Paris, 1863), and L. Veuillot, *L'Illusion Libérale* (Paris, 1866).

In Latin: The speeches in the General Congregations of the Vatican Council are printed, with other documents concerning the Council, in Mansi, *Amplissima Collectio Conciliorum*, Vols. 49–53.

In German: The attitude of Döllinger and the Old Catholics can best be appreciated from J. Friedrich, *Tagebuch wahrend des Vatikanischen Concils* (Nordlingen, 1873).

THE CHURCH IN NORTH AMERICA

The most useful general history is that by Theodore Maynard, *The Story of American Catholicism* (Macmillan, 1941), which provides a full bibliography. The classic account of the early nineteenth century in the United States is still J. G. Shea's *History of the Catholic Church in the United States*

(4 vols., New York, 1886–92). Amongst the many writings of
P. Guilday, his *Life and Times of John Carroll* (2 vols., New
York, 1922) and his *Life and Times of John England* (2 vols.,
New York, 1927) remain especially valuable. F. J. Zwierlein,
The Life and Letters of Bishop McQuaid (3 vols., Louvain,
1925–27), J. T. Ellis' *Cardinal Gibbons* (2 vols., Bruce Pub-
lishing Co., 1952), H. J. Browne *The Catholic Church and
the Knights of Labor* (Washington, Catholic University of
America Press, 1949), and R. D. Cross *The Emergence of
Liberal Catholicism in America* (Harvard University Press,
1957) throw light on the end of the nineteenth century.

In recent years the attacks of Paul Blanshard upon the
Catholic Church in America, and particularly his *American
Freedom and Catholic Power* (Beacon Press, 1949), have
helped to throw into prominence discussion about the Church-
State relationship. They have been effectively answered in
many books, e.g. J. M. O'Neill's *Catholicism and American
Freedom* (Harper, 1952), or J. J. Kane's *Catholic-Protestant
Conflicts in America* (Regnery, Chicago, 1955). See also
Curvin V. Shields *Democracy and Catholicism in America*
(McGraw-Hill, 1958). Meanwhile the writings of J. C. Mur-
ray, S.J., in *Thought* (e.g. No. 113, Summer, 1954) have
thrown much light on the historical and theological issues in-
volved in the separation of Church and State.

THE AGE OF LEO XIII IN EUROPE

In English: The standard biography of the Pope by E.
Soderini was translated by Barbara Carter (Burns Oates, Lon-
don, 2 vols., 1934). Translations of the social encyclical
Rerum Novarum are readily available: e.g. in *The Papal
Encyclicals in Their Historical Context*, by Anne Fremantle
(Mentor book, New American Library, 1956). But the most
authentic source for all Roman documents, in the original
Latin, is the volumes of the *Acta* of the various Popes, pub-
lished in Rome.

In French: For the Church in France under the Third Republic see R. P. Lecanuet, *La vie de l'Eglise sous Léon XIII*
(Paris, 1930).

In Italian: The recent book by G. Spadolini, *L'Opposizione
Cattolica da Porta Pia al '98* (Florence, Vallechi, 1954) is of
fundamental importance.

In German: The standard traditional German history of the

Kulturkampf is J. B. Kissling, *Geschichte der Kulturkampf im Deutschen Reiche* (Fribourg, 1911–16), but see also the chapter on this subject in J. Rovan's French book, already quoted, *Le Catholicisme politique en Allemagne*.

THE TWENTIETH CENTURY

The most exhaustive and balanced study of Modernism, and of its condemnation by St. Pius X, is given in Jean Rivière's *Le Modernisme dans l'Eglise* (Paris, 1929). An idea of what Modernism was about can best be obtained in English from G. Tyrrell's expression of it in *Christianity at the Cross-Roads* (Longmans, 1910); the Pope's encyclical *Pascendi Gregis* of 1907 is available, in part, in Anne Fremantle's collection, *op. cit.*

The most useful life, in English, of *Pope Pius XI*, though published before his death, is that of Philip Hughes (London, Sheed and Ward, 1937). For a complete life, see *His Holiness Pope Pius XI* by Mgr. R. Fontenelle (translated by M. E. Fowler, London, Catholic Book Club, 1939). The best life to date in English of *Pope Pius XII* is that by Oscar Halecki (Weidenfeld and Nicolson, 1954), which gives a good account of the Church behind the Iron Curtain and also in Italy.

For the life of the Church in Hitler's Germany, see *The Persecution of the Catholic Church in the Third Reich. Facts and Documents.* (London, Burns Oates, 1940), which is a valuable collection of translated documentary material, with illustrations. For an able appraisal of German Catholicism both under Hitler and under Adenauer see J. Rovan, *op. cit.*

On twentieth-century problems generally, and especially on the efforts of Popes Benedict XV and Pius XII for world peace, on the Spanish Civil War and dictatorship, on South America, and on the United States, see W. Gurian and M. A. Fitzsimons (editors) *The Catholic Church in World Affairs* (Notre Dame, 1954).

Index

Image Books

... MAKING THE WORLD'S FINEST
CATHOLIC LITERATURE AVAILABLE TO ALL

Image Books

... MAKING THE WORLD'S FINEST
CATHOLIC LITERATURE AVAILABLE TO ALL

ON THE TRUTH OF THE
CATHOLIC FAITH
*Summa Contra Gentiles Book II:
Creation. Newly translated, with
an Introduction and notes by
James F. Anderson*   D27—95¢

ON THE TRUTH OF THE
CATHOLIC FAITH
*Summa Contra Gentiles Book
III: Providence. Newly trans-
lated, with an Introduction and
notes by Vernon J. Bourke*
          D28a Book III, Part 1—95¢
          D28b Book III, Part 2—95¢

ON THE TRUTH OF THE
CATHOLIC FAITH
*Summa Contra Gentiles Book
IV: Salvation. Newly translated,
with an Introduction and notes,
By Charles J. O'Neil*   D29—95¢

THE WORLD'S FIRST LOVE
By Fulton J. Sheen   D30—85¢

THE SIGN OF JONAS
By Thomas Merton   D31—95¢

PARENTS, CHILDREN AND THE
FACTS OF LIFE   *By Henry V.
Sattler, C.SS.R.*   D32—75¢

LIGHT ON THE MOUNTAIN : *The
Story of La Salette
By John S. Kennedy*   D33—65¢

EDMUND CAMPION
By Evelyn Waugh   D34—75¢

HUMBLE POWERS
By Paul Horgan   D35—75¢

SAINT THOMAS AQUINAS
By G. K. Chesterton D36—75¢

APOLOGIA PRO VITA SUA
*By John Henry Cardinal New-
man   Introduction by Philip
Hughes*   D37—95¢

A HANDBOOK OF THE CATHOLIC
FAITH
*By Dr. N. G. M. Van Doornik,
Rev. S. Jelsma, Rev. A. Van De
Lisdonk. Ed. Rev. John Green-
wood*   D38—$1.45

THE NEW TESTAMENT
Official Catholic edition
                      D39—95¢

MARIA CHAPDELAINE
By Louis Hémon   D40—65¢

SAINT AMONG THE HURONS
By Francis X. Talbot, S.J.
                      D41—95¢

THE PATH TO ROME
By Hilaire Belloc   D42—85¢

SORROW BUILT A BRIDGE
By Katherine Burton D43—85¢

THE WISE MAN FROM THE WEST
By Vincent Cronin   D44—85¢

EXISTENCE AND THE EXISTENT
By Jacques Maritain D45—75¢

THE STORY OF THE TRAPP
FAMILY SINGERS
By Maria Augusta Trapp
                      D46—95¢

THE WORLD, THE FLESH AND
FATHER SMITH
By Bruce Marshall   D47—75¢

THE CHRIST OF CATHOLICISM
By Dom Aelred Graham
                      D48—95¢

SAINT FRANCIS XAVIER
By James Brodrick, S.J.
                      D49—95¢

SAINT FRANCIS OF ASSISI
By G. K. Chesterton D50—65¢

11

Image Books

*...making the world's finest
Catholic literature available to all*

VIPERS' TANGLE
by François Mauriac **D51—75¢**

THE MANNER IS ORDINARY
by John LaFarge, S.J. **D52—95¢**

MY LIFE FOR MY SHEEP
by Alfred Duggan **D53—90¢**

**THE CHURCH AND THE RECON-
STRUCTION OF THE MODERN
WORLD:** *The Social Encyclicals
of Pius XI.* Edited by T. P. Mc-
Laughlin, C.S.B. **D54—$1.25**

A GILSON READER: *Selections from
the Writings of Etienne Gilson.*
Edited by Anton C. Pegis.
D55—95¢

**THE AUTOBIOGRAPHY OF
ST. THERESE OF LISIEUX:** *The Story
of a Soul. A new translation by*
John Beevers. **D56—65¢**

HELENA
by Evelyn Waugh **D57—65¢**

THE GREATEST BIBLE STORIES
A Catholic Anthology from
World Literature. Edited by Anne
Fremantle. **D58—75¢**

THE CITY OF GOD—St. Augustine.
Edited with Intro. by Vernon J.
Bourke. Foreword by Etienne
Gilson. **D59—$1.45**

SUPERSTITION CORNER
by Sheila Kaye-Smith **D60—65¢**

SAINTS AND OURSELVES
Ed. by Philip Caraman, S.J.
D61—95¢

CANA IS FOREVER
by Charles Hugo Doyle
D62—75¢

**ASCENT OF MOUNT CARMEL—
St. John of the Cross.** Translated
and Edited by E. Allison Peers.
D63—$1.25

**RELIGION AND THE RISE OF
WESTERN CULTURE**
by Christopher Dawson
D64—85¢

**PRINCE OF DARKNESS AND OTHER
STORIES**
by J. F. Powers **D65—85¢**

ST. THOMAS MORE
by E. E. Reynolds **D66—95¢**

JESUS AND HIS TIMES
2 Volumes **D67A—95¢**
by Daniel-Rops **D67B—95¢**

ST. BENEDICT
by Justin McCann, O.S.B.
D68—85¢

THE LITTLE FLOWERS OF ST. FRANCIS
Edited and Translated by
Raphael Brown. **D69—95¢**

THE QUIET LIGHT
by Louis de Wohl **D70—95¢**

CHARACTERS OF THE REFORMATION
by Hilaire Belloc **D71—85¢**

THE BELIEF OF CATHOLICS
by Ronald Knox **D72—75¢**

FAITH AND FREEDOM
by Barbara Ward **D73—95¢**

**GOD AND INTELLIGENCE IN
MODERN PHILOSOPHY**
by Fulton J. Sheen **D74—$1.25**

If your bookseller is unable to supply certain titles, write to Image
Books, Department MIB, Garden City, New York, stating the
titles you desire and enclosing the price of each book (plus 5¢
per book to cover cost of postage and handling). Prices are subject to change without notice.

Image Books

. . . MAKING THE WORLD'S FINEST CATHOLIC LITERATURE AVAILABLE TO ALL

THE IDEA OF A UNIVERSITY
By John Henry Cardinal Newman. Introduction by George N. Shuster   D75—$1.35

PLAYED BY EAR: *The Autobiography of Father Daniel A. Lord, S.J.*   D76—95¢

MY BELOVED: *The Story of a Carmelite Nun.* By Mother Catherine Thomas   D77—75¢

DARK NIGHT OF THE SOUL
By St. John of the Cross. Edited and translated by E. Allison Peers   D78—75¢

TERESA OF AVILA
By Marcelle Auclair. Translated by Kathleen Pond   D79—$1.35

SAINT PETER THE APOSTLE
By William Thomas Walsh   D80—95¢

THE LOVE OF GOD
By Dom Aelred Graham, O.S.B.   D81—85¢

WOMAN OF THE PHARISEES
By François Mauriac. Translated by Gerard Hopkins   D82—75¢

THE PILLAR OF FIRE
By Karl Stern   D83—85¢

ORTHODOXY
By G. K. Chesterton   D84—75¢

THIS IS CATHOLICISM
By John J. Walsh   D85—$1.25

MEDIEVAL ESSAYS
By Christopher Dawson   D86—95¢

VESSEL OF CLAY
By Leo Trese   D87—65¢

SAINTS FOR SINNERS
By Alban Goodier, S.J.   D88—65¢

THE LONG LONELINESS
By Dorothy Day   D89—85¢

THIS IS THE MASS
By Henri Daniel-Rops. Photographs of Bishop Fulton J. Sheen by Karsh   D90—95¢

THE ORIGIN OF THE JESUITS
By James Brodrick, S.J.   D91—85¢

A POPULAR HISTORY OF THE REFORMATION
By Philip Hughes   D92—95¢

THE RESTLESS FLAME
By Louis de Wohl   D93—85¢

PROGRESS AND RELIGION
By Christopher Dawson   D94—85¢

THE CATHOLIC CHURCH IN THE MODERN WORLD
By E. E. Y. Hales   D95—95¢

THE LIFE OF TERESA OF JESUS: *The Autobiography of St. Teresa of Avila.* Translated and with an introduction by E. Allison Peers   D96—$1.25

GIANTS OF THE FAITH
By John A. O'Brien   D97—95¢

SCHOLASTICISM AND POLITICS
By Jacques Maritain   D98—95¢

THE SON OF GOD
By Karl Adam   D99—85¢

THE MAN WHO WAS CHESTERTON
Edited by Raymond T. Bond   D100—$1.45

25

Image Books

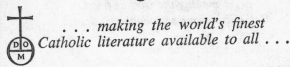

*. . . making the world's finest
Catholic literature available to all . . .*

Image Books

. . . making the world's finest
Catholic literature available to all . . .

THE DIVINE PITY
by Gerald Vann, O.P.

Meditations on the social implications of the beatitudes. "Absorbing, haunting, unforgettable." *Book Week*   D109—75¢

SPIRITUAL CANTICLE
by St. John of the Cross. Translated, with an introduction and notes, by E. Allison Peers

The most sublime canticle in the literature of mysticism by the greatest of all mystical theologians.   D110—$1.45

THE WHITE FATHERS
by Glenn D. Kittler

A true story of the White Fathers' missions in Africa since their founding in 1868 to the present. "An exciting adventure tale and a narrative of profound religious devotion." *The Sign*
D111—95¢

SAINT AMONG SAVAGES: The Life of Isaac Jogues
by Francis X. Talbot, S.J.

An outstanding biography of the intrepid pioneer, adventurer, missioner among the North American Indians and saint. "The greatest book so far written about our American saints and savages." *Extension*
D112—$1.45

THE THIRD REVOLUTION: A Study of Psychiatry and Religion
by Dr. Karl Stern

An authoritative and timely exposition on the need for integrating psychiatry and religion.
D113—75¢

WE HAVE BEEN FRIENDS TOGETHER and ADVENTURES IN GRACE
by Raissa Maritain

The celebrated memoirs of a gifted woman's journey toward, and adventures in, grace and of her friendships with many illustrious French artists, poets and writers.   D114—$1.25

WE DIE STANDING UP
by Dom Hubert van Zeller, O.S.B.

Vigorous and inspiring meditations on the spiritual life written expressly for the modern reader.
D115—65¢

STAGE OF FOOLS
by Charles A. Brady

A rich and poetic, thoroughly authentic re-creation of the magnificent character of Sir Thomas More and the Tudor England in which he lived. "An extraordinary book!" The *New York Times*   D116—95¢

If your bookseller is unable to supply certain titles, write to Image Books, Department MIB, Garden City, New York, stating the titles you desire and enclosing the price of each book (plus 5¢ per book to cover cost of postage and handling). Prices are subject to change without notice.